THE

PROOF PALPABLE

OF

IMMORTALITY.

SARGENT.

It shall assuredly come, that day of a new, an immortal evangel.—*Lessing.*

The advent of Spiritualism is through facts and not theories. Its purpose is positive knowledge.—*Hudson Tuttle.*

Spiritualism is an experimental science, and affords the only sure foundation for a true philosophy and a pure religion.—*Alfred R. Wallace.*

Even in the most cloudless skies of Skepticism I see a rain-cloud if it be no bigger than a man's hand: it is Modern Spiritualism.—*Lord Brougham.*

In the whole universe all is contingent, nothing is necessary, nothing a cause of itself. To explain the cause of all, therefore, we must admit a cause which may be necessarily a cause of itself and of all things. This cause being, since it is necessary, it follows that God is, for it is God.—*Leibnitz.*

The soul of man can know the Divine only so far as it knows itself.—*Marcus Antoninus.*

PORTRAIT OF THE SPIRIT "KATIE KING."

Copied from a Photograph taken by the Magnesium Light.

THE

PROOF PALPABLE

OF

IMMORTALITY;

BEING

AN ACCOUNT OF THE MATERIALIZATION PHENOMENA
OF MODERN SPIRITUALISM.

WITH

REMARKS ON THE RELATIONS OF THE FACTS
TO THEOLOGY, MORALS, AND RELIGION.

BY

EPES SARGENT,

AUTHOR OF "PLANCHETTE, OR THE DESPAIR OF SCIENCE; A HISTORY OF THE
FACTS AND THEORIES OF MODERN SPIRITUALISM."

"*Nullus in microcosmo spiritus, nullus in macrocosmo Deus.*"

BOSTON:
COLBY AND RICH,
9 MONTGOMERY PLACE.
1876.

PREFACE TO THE SECOND EDITION.

To the uninformed many the narrative portions of this volume will seem like the fantasies of a mediæval superstition. But the faithful observer of what is going on in the world must be well aware that the accumulation of facts corresponding with those here presented is getting to be irresistible. For their refutation something more than a word or gesture of contempt is now required. Those critics who hope to dispose of them thus easily will soon be counted in the long procession of infatuated opponents of dawning truths. The phenomena are fast spreading and becoming better known; they attract new converts daily, and are beginning to be admitted by respectable scientific authorities, such as Wallace and Crookes in England, Perty in Berne, and Wagner and Butlerof in Russia. All the frauds of real or pretended mediums are powerless to neutralize the effect of what has been proved, and has now taken its place among the certainties of science. Moreover, the question is beginning to be raised whether much that we have set down as the conscious imposture of certain known mediums may not be the work of foreign forces, the eccentric operation of which we do not yet understand.

But in the revision of this work I have been careful to note all those instances in which testimony has been weakened or withdrawn since the first edition was printed. Thus I have stricken out the accounts which Mr. R. D. Owen gave of phenomena through Mr. and Mrs. Holmes, though he has since admitted that in this case genuine manifestations were probably mixed up with those he suspected as questionable. I have also made such qualifications as seemed pertinent in other cases. Spiritualism needs no invalidated supports.

The fact that the present volume grew out of a series of familiar communications respecting the materialization phenomena, will explain, if it will not excuse, the somewhat free and desultory manner in which the many-sided subject has been treated. If my transitions from fact to theory should seem irregular, the fault lies in the original unambitious form of the publication.

I have brought down the record of phenomena to the beginning of the year 1876; and it will be interesting to the student of them to remark how what seemed incredible at one time, even to advanced Spiritualists, has been confirmed as the manifestations have gone on and multiplied; and how every new "exposure" has resulted in a reaction favorable to the confirmation of the fact involved. The course of truth, Goethe tells us, is spiral, and progress cannot be had without occasional retrogression.

That Spiritualism now offers the grounds for a science founded on observed facts is the belief of all persistent investigators. It has made its way in spite of the most vehement opposition that ever a great truth encountered. The large majority of the cultivated classes, the religious and the scientific, have all combined to hoot it down, almost blind to the consideration whether it is a thing of facts or chimeras; for there is much in it that to a superficial observer is repulsive. But it still lives and grows. If true, it is God's truth, and we must not fear it, however portentous to our short-sightedness it may appear. It is time for people of common sense to accommodate their opinions to the facts, since it is evident that the facts will not accommodate themselves to the preconceptions and dislikes of any majority, however wise and worthy.

E. S.

No. 68 *Moreland street*, *Boston*, *Feb.* 1*st*, 1876.

TABLE OF CONTENTS.

CHAPTER I.

CHAPTER II.

CHAPTER III.

CHAPTER IV.

CHAPTER V.

CHAPTER VI.

CHAPTER VII.

CHAPTER VIII.

CHAPTER IX.

CHAPTER X.

CHAPTER XI.

CHAPTER XII.

CHAPTER XIII.

THE

PROOF PALPABLE OF IMMORTALITY.

CHAPTER I.

The surprising character of the developments which the phenomena of Modern Spiritualism have recently attained to seems to call for a clear, succinct review of the whole subject of similar contemporary manifestations. The concurrent testimony of well-known scientists and of unprofessional investigators, so numerous that to attempt to set aside their attestations as inadmissible is simply irrational, is now in the keeping of science. It is of a nature so astonishing, so truly wonderful, that I can hardly blame the incredulity that still assails the reported facts with ridicule and denial in the face even of all the confirmations by which they are established.

As introductory to an account of the extraordinary manifestations through Miss Florence Eliza Cook, now Mrs. Corner, of London, in which manifestations, as proved by Professor Crookes, Dr. J. M. Gully, Mr. C. F. Varley, Mr. Benjamin Coleman, and many others, a spirit form, temporarily materialized, and undistinguishable from a human being in the flesh, has come forth in the light, conversed, and submitted to the most convincing tests, and then disappeared, leaving no visible trace, I will give a brief account of the manifestations that have preceded or accompanied this crowning wonder.

In all ages of the world and among all nations, it has been claimed that there have been men and women with certain supersensual faculties; faculties exceptionally or abnormally developed, and by the exercise of which they have become clairvoyant, clairaudient, and able to receive impressions not known to the generality of mankind. All times and all tribes have had their prophets, seers, sensitives, psychics, or mediums. The inference is that these same powers are possessed in different degrees by all human beings, but that it is only under certain conditions of organization, temperament, or influence, that they are developed as we find them to be in particular instances.

The ready objection of skepticism is: "I will not believe that another man possesses such extraordinary powers while I can discover no sign of them in myself. I am the measure of all other human beings; and when you tell me that such persons as Abraham, Balaam, Hagar, Paul, Peter, Swedenborg, Home, Foster, Mrs. Fox-Jencken, Mrs. Andrews, Miss Cook, Miss Showers and others, can see spirits, manifest clairvoyance, and fall into trances, I will not believe it."

But consider to what inconsistencies assumptions like this would lead us! One man is utterly destitute of the musical faculty; he cannot tell one tune from another; and yet here is a little child, Wolfgang Mozart, who at five years of age shows a musical genius, power of execution, originality and taste, which can be characterized only as inexplicable and amazing. And again: Here is a man of average intelligence who is slow at figures, and finds it hard to perform an ordinary sum in addition or multiplication; and here is a boy or an idiot, who will in a few seconds, by a mental computation, solve a sum in arithmetic which a skillful accountant, with the aid of his slate, could hardly verify in half an hour. The cases of Zerah Colburn, Professor Safford, and others, proving this statement, are known to all inquirers into the abnormal powers of the human mind. These instances would seem to show by analogy that there may be also a faculty of spiritual vision and clairvoyance, which may be undeveloped in one person and manifested in another.

Mr. Alfred R. Wallace, in his recent "Defence of Spiritualism," has accurately stated the fact, of which ample proofs may be given, that different individuals possess the power of seeing spirit forms and figures in very variable degrees.

"Thus it often happens at a séance," he says, "that some will see distinct lights of which they will describe the form, appearance and position, while others see nothing at all. If only one or two persons see the lights, the rest will naturally impute it to their imagination; but there are cases in which only one or two of those present are unable to see them. There are also cases in which all see them, but in very different degrees of distinctness; yet that they see the same objects is proved by their all agreeing as to the position and movement of the lights. Again, what some see as merely luminous clouds, others will see as distinct human forms, either partial or entire. In other cases all present see the form—whether hand, face, or entire figure—with equal distinctness. Again, the objective reality of these appearances is sometimes proved by their being touched, or by their being seen to move objects—in some cases heard to speak, in others seen to write, by several persons at one and the same time; the figure seen or the writing produced being sometimes unmistakably recognizable as that of some deceased friend."

The question is often asked, "What are the sensations of the medium himself when under spiritual impression?" As, where the impression is very strong, the medium is generally thrown into a state of unconsciousness, or trance, this inquiry is not often satisfactorily answered. As a contribution to the philosophy of the subject, the following remarks, read by Mr. T. Herbert Noyes, B. A., (himself a partially-developed medium) at a meeting of the London Dialectical Society, are of interest:

"I have learnt by practical experience the difficulty of inducing prejudiced men to listen even to one's premises—let alone one's conclusions. The extent of that difficulty may be estimated from the consideration of the absolute impossibility of conveying to the apprehension of a man, born without any one of our five senses, the exact sensation experienced by those who possess them.

"The gifts of mediumship seem to me to involve the development of a latent sixth sense; indeed, I am inclined to think that they may, perhaps, involve the development of several latent senses not yet acknowledged by science—latent senses or spiritual faculties, which are probably inherent in all spiritual natures, prematurely developed in a few only, but destined to be developed in all when they emerge from the prison-house of the body, just as are the wings of the butterfly or the limbs of the frog, which are latent in the caterpillar and the tadpole.

"I know that I should excite the derision of the skeptics if I were to say that I have conversed with spirits after a fashion which was asserted to be that in which spirits communicate with each other—by an 'inner voice,' which I could only compare to the sensation which would be caused by a telegraphic apparatus being hooked on to one of the nerve-ganglia—a distinctly audible click accompanying every syllable of the communication, which one could not say one heard, but of which one was made conscious by a new sense, and which was clearly distinguishable from thoughts originated in one's own mind; but it is nevertheless a fact, which I know to be as true as that I am now in full possession of my five normal senses, and in no way qualified for Hanwell.

"This enabled me, for the first time in my life, to understand the rational *inspirational* speaking, as writing mediumship, which has also been given to me, enables me to understand inspirational writing. But this latter gift involves an expenditure of vitality and nervous force which is excessively debilitating if too long continued; and I am now paying the penalty of excess by enforced abstinence from the exercise of the new faculty.

"If it be only the unconscious action of one's own mind, how will our scientific infallibles account for this anomalous result of automatic writing? But I have already trespassed too long on your patience; suffice it to say, that I can affirm, with the certainty of absolute knowledge, that Modern Spiritualism is true; that it affords the most satisfactory evidence that the soul of man survives the death of the body, retains its individuality and its personal identity and its fallibility, and the power of communicating, under certain delicate conditions, with those with whom it is still in sympathy in earth-life."

The fact of palpable and tangible apparitions from the spirit-world is asserted in all the records of psychological phenomena that have come down to us from remotest antiquity. The angel who met Jacob at Peniel, and wrestled with him, must have been a materialized spirit, if a legitimate inference may be made from parallel phenomena, repeatedly certified to as occurring within the last year. The hand that appeared on Belshazzar's palace-wall was a materialized hand, such as I myself have felt and seen, while in company with other witnesses who confirmed my experience by their own.

With the first irruption of the modern spiritual phenomena at Hydesville, N. Y., on which occasion little Kate Fox, then nine years old, may be said to have initiated the modern spiritual movement by interrogating the raps, and finding an intelligence in them, there were instances of the appearance of phantom forms and partial materializations. At the rooms of J. Koons, in Athens County, Ohio, in 1854, spirit-hands and voices were among the common manifestations. Before this, in 1850, the Davenport Brothers began to be developed as mediums; and among the phenomena at their séances was that of the appearance of entire spirit-forms, so far materialized as to be visible not only to sensitives, but to all the parties present.

Mr. Home, the well-known medium, has, on several occasions, had spirit-forms appear to parties in his presence. One in particular is mentioned, in which a sister of Mr. S. C. Hall was recognized by her brother and seen clearly by Lord Lindsay and the entire party.

The first carefully-prepared account that we have, in modern times, of the repeated appearance of a materialized spirit-form, is that furnished by my friend, Mr. C. F. Livermore, of New York, formerly of the well-known firm of Livermore & Clewes, bankers. Another friend, one I have known and honored for thirty years, Dr. John F. Gray, of New York, writes (Jan., 1869): "Mr. Livermore's recitals of the séances in which I participated are faithfully and most accurately stated, leaving not a shade of doubt in my mind as to the truth and accuracy of his accounts of those at which I was not a witness. I saw with him the philosopher Franklin, in a living, tangible, physical form, several times; and, on as many different occasions, I also witnessed the production of lights, odors, and sounds; and also the formation of flowers, cloth-textures, &c., and their disintegration and dispersion. . . . Mr. Livermore is a good observer of spirit-phenomena; brave, clear, and quick-sighted. I have known him from very early manhood, and am his medical adviser." He was an entire skeptic before he witnessed these phenomena.

Of Miss Kate Fox, Dr. Gray writes: "She has been intimately known to my wife and me from the time she was a very young girl; that is to say, from 1850 to this date (1867). At that early day in the history of the manifestations she was frequently a visitor in my family; and then, through that child alone, without the possibility of trick from collusion with others, or, I may add, of imposture of any kind, all the various phenomena recorded by Mr. Livermore, except the reproduction of visible, human forms, were witnessed by Mrs. Gray and myself, and many other relatives and friends of our family."

That Modern Spiritualism was initiated by the action of the child, Kate Fox, seems to admit of no doubt. The family of David Fox, at Hydesville, N. Y., were disturbed by certain inexplicable knockings. His little girl, Kate, aroused from her evening slumber by the noise and the alarm of the family, asked the unknown cause of the sounds to give a certain number of raps. It did so; and "Oh, mother," the little girl exclaimed, "it hears what I say! it knows what I tell it, for it has rapped the number of times I asked it!"

Here was a discovery: the phenomena had an intelligent cause! A similar intelligence had been manifested by the phenomena investigated by the Rev. Joseph Glanvil, at Tedworth, England, in 1661, and by those which attracted the attention of the Wesley Family, in Lincolnshire, in 1716; but the hint was not acted on, and the manifestations ended in the families where they originated. The discovery, when made by Kate Fox, however, was productive of consequences that can be only estimated by the growth and future influence of Modern Spiritualism.

There is an interesting prediction connected with the subsequent career of Kate Fox. It was communicated to Mr. R. D. Owen by Mr. and Mrs. H. P. Townsend, living on Madison Avenue, New York City. In the winter of 1869 Miss Fox was the guest of Mrs. Townsend, who slept with her one night in the hope of getting some manifestations of spirit power. Waking before day the two entered into conversation. Mrs. Townsend said, "Kate, you are a strange creature. You will never get married. You will be sure to die an old maid." There came a loud rap on the head-board, and there was spelled out through the raps: "Kate will be married, and will bear a child who will be the wonder of the world. Kate herself will be a cypher in comparison. She will only be remembered as his mother." "*His* mother!" said Mrs. Townsend: "it is to be a boy!"

This was related to several of Mrs. Townsend's friends long before Kate went to Europe. In December, 1872, Kate was married in England to Mr. H. D. Jencken, barrister-at-law, London, whose acquaintance I had the pleasure of making in Paris in 1869. He is the son of a well-known man of science, and himself an earnest and intelligent investigator of psychological phenomena, and one well able to give reasons for his belief in Spiritualism, as his paper read before the London Dialectical Society (April, 1869) abundantly shows.

In September, 1873, there was born to these parents an infant son who, before he was three months old, began to develop powers as a medium. On one occasion his nurse, Mrs. McCarthy, saw four spirit hands making passes over his little form. Rappings on his pillow and on the iron rail of the bedstead would occur almost every day. A few weeks later a still more marked evidence of the wonderful power of spirits to use this infant's organization was given. A legible communication was written through his hand, of a part of which the following words, a fair specimen of the chirography of the whole, are a *fac simile:*

God bless him

The entire communication was as follows:

"*I love this little child God bless him advise his father to go back to London Monday by all means Susan.*"

The following testimonial is appended to the *fac simile*, as published in the London Medium and Daybreak of May 8th, 1874:

"The above sentence was written through the hand of the infant boy of Mrs. and Mr. Jencken, aged five months and fifteen days, on the 6th day of March, 1874, at Lansdowne Terrace East, Western Road, Brighton, by an invisible agency, in our presence, the pencil used having been placed in the right hand of the infant by invisible means. Witness the hands of the parties present, March 6th, 1874, J. Wason, K. F. Jencken, the X mark of Mrs. McCarthy, the nurse who held the child."

The communication was supposed to come from the departed wife of Mr. Wason, a respectable solicitor of Liverpool, and one of the witnesses. The advice given was acted upon and found to be good.

In a letter, published June, 1874, Mr. Jencken writes of this little infant: "Some few days ago, late in the evening, his eyes sparkled, and the restlessness of his hands warned Mrs. Jencken that he wanted to write. A large sheet of paper, the only one at hand, was then placed before him. He wrote a long sentence, covering the sheet." That he does not get his power from the presence of his mother is proved by the fact that, on a recent occasion, when she was absent from home, on Mr. Jencken's taking him up to play with him, while the infant was trying to catch his gold chain, soft raps came by which intelligible messages were spelt out.

Mr. Livermore's sittings for manifestations through Miss Kate Fox commenced in February, 1861, extended over a period of five years, and were more than three hundred in number. The chief phenomenon was the appearance of a tangible, visible female figure, which was sometimes accompanied by a male figure purporting to be Dr. Franklin, and strongly resembling the portraits of that well-known philosopher.

In the female figure Mr. Livermore recognized unmistakably the face, form and voice of Estelle, his wife. "The recognition," he says, "was complete, derived alike from the features and her natural expression. The figure displayed long flowing hair, which, even in its shade of color, appeared like the natural tresses of my wife, and, like hers, was unusually luxuriant. . . . I asked her to kiss me if she could; and, to my great astonishment and delight, an arm was placed around my neck, and a real palpable kiss was implanted on my lips, through something like fine muslin. A head was laid upon mine, the hair falling luxuriantly down my face. The kiss was frequently repeated, and was audible in every part of the room."

The tresses that dropped over his face Mr. L. describes as "having the scent of delicate, freshly-gathered violets." He says: "I laid hold of the hair, which seemed to the touch, at first, identical with human hair; but, after a brief space, it melted away, leaving nothing in my grasp.

During the manifestations, cards, provided by Mr. Livermore, were placed on the floor with a pencil; and long messages in his wife's chirography were found written on them. "These manifestations," says Dr. Gray, "could not have been produced by human means; and if you admit the competency of the witness, of which, from my knowledge of him, I have no doubt, they are, in my opinion, conclusive evidence of spirit identity."

The following passages I quote, somewhat at random, from Mr. Livermore's diary:

"The spirits of my wife and Dr. Franklin came to me in form at the same time—he slapping me heavily upon the back, while she gently patted me upon the head and shoulder."

"The spirit-robe was shown in a variety of ways, and the texture was exquisitely beautiful. Whenever it approached closely, we discovered a peculiar scent of purity, like a very delicious perfume of newly-gathered grass or violets."

"I asked to be touched; when she advanced, laid her arm across my forehead, and permitted me to kiss it. I found it as large and as real in weight as a living arm. At first it felt cold, then grew gradually warm."

"My wife came in full form, placing her arms completely around my neck. Something resembling a veil in its contact, was thrown over my head; and while it was resting there,

2

spirit-flowers were placed at my nose, exhaling the most exquisite perfume I have ever smelt. I asked what this was, and was told, 'My wreath of spirit-flowers.'"

"Dr. Franklin was apparently dressed in a white cravat and a brown coat of the olden style; his head was very large, with gray hair behind his ears; his face was radiant with benignity, intelligence, and spirituality. . . . The light becoming very vivid discovered to us Dr. Franklin seated, his whole figure and dress complete."

"Something like a handkerchief of transparent gossamer was brought; and we were told to look at the hand which now appeared under the gossamer, as perfect a female hand as was ever created. I advanced my own hand, when the spirit-hand was placed in it, grasping mine; and we again grasped hands with all the fervor of long-parted friends, my wife in the spirit-land and myself here."

"It was a reality which lasted through nearly half an hour. I examined carefully that spirit-hand, squeezed it, felt the knuckles, joints, and nails, and kissed it, while it was constantly visible to my sight. I took each finger separately in my hand, and could discern no difference between it and a human hand, except in temperature; the spirit-hand being cold at first, and growing warm."

"The flowers in her hair and on her person were real in appearance. Over her forehead was a crown of flowers. The light shone vividly upon her face and figure; and while we stood looking intently, she instantly, as quick as thought, disappeared, with a rushing sound. Then, by raps was communicated, 'The electricity is very strong; and we did this to show you how quickly we can disappear.' Very soon she returned, as real as before."

"The figure of Dr. Franklin appeared perfectly delineated, seated in the window, and permitted me to examine his hair with my hand. The hair was to sight and touch as real as human hair."

"Estelle and Dr. Franklin appeared alternately. Dr. Franklin's shirt-bosom and collar were as real to appearance as though made of linen. We handled them, and examined in the same manner his tunic, which was black, and felt like cloth."

"My wife appeared leaning upon the bureau, with white lace hanging in front of and around her head. This lace or open work (like embroidery) was so real, that the figures were plainly discernible and could have been sketched. The body of her dress or robe was of spotted white gossamer, while the lace-work was in diamonds and flowers."

"Flowers again appeared. A bright light rose to the surface of the table, of the usual cylindrical form, covered with gossamer. Held directly over this was a sprig of roses, about six inches in length, containing two half-blown white roses and a bud with leaves. The flowers, leaves, and stem were perfect, and smelled as though freshly gathered. We took them in our fingers, and I carefully examined the stem and flowers."

"By raps we were told to 'Notice, and see them dissolve.' The sprig was placed over the light, the flowers drooped, and, in less than one minute, melted as though made of wax, their substance seeming to spread as they disappeared. By raps : 'See them come again.' A faint line immediately shot across the cylinder, grew into a stem, and, in about the same time required for their dissolution, the stem, bud and roses had grown into created perfection. This was several times repeated, and was truly wonderful."

"The flowers were reproduced in the same manner as last evening. I felt them carefully, and a rose was placed in my mouth, so that I took its leaves between my lips. They were delicate as natural rose-leaves, and cold; and there was a peculiar freshness about them, but very little fragrance."

On one occasion a bunch of flowers, consisting of a red rose, with green leaves and forget-me-nots, was shown. "I inspected them," says Mr. L., "for several minutes, at intervals; turning off the gas and relighting five or six times. The flowers still remained. Above them was written: '*Flowers from our home in Heaven.*' Finally the flowers began to fade, and we were requested to extinguish the gas. When we did so, it was replaced by a spirit-light, under which the flowers were again distinctly visible. Then, by the raps: 'Do not take your eyes off the flowers; watch them closely.' We did so. They gradually diminished in size, as we gazed, till they became mere specks; and then they disappeared before our eyes. When I lighted the gas I found no trace of them on the card. Then I carefully examined the seals on the doors and windows, and found them intact."

These phenomena took place in four different houses (Mr. Livermore's and the medium's being both changed during the period over which the séances extended), and were accompanied with the most rigid tests. The figure of Estelle not only moved freely about the room, but it displaced objects and wrote messages. It allowed a portion of its dress to be cut off, which, though at first of strong and apparently material, gauzy texture, in a short time melted away and became invisible.

At ten of these remarkable séances Dr. Gray was present with Mr. Livermore, and at eight of them the latter's brother-in-law, Mr. Groute. On one occasion Dr. Gray and Mr. Livermore were allowed to cut off with scissors a piece of the garment of the spirit, coming under the appearance of Franklin. The cloth seemed of so firm a texture that for a time it could be pulled without coming apart. It was examined closely until it melted away. During one sitting (No. 355, of May 1st, 1863) both Dr. Gray and Mr. Groute were present with Mr. Livermore, when the form of Dr. Franklin appeared; it was perfect, and fully recognized by all the parties. The last time the figure of Estelle appeared was the 2d of April, 1866. The number of séances had been three hundred and eighty-eight.

Having had the opportunity of questioning Mr. Livermore closely in regard to these occurrences, and of comparing them with the equally remarkable experiences of other friends, well known to me, both in England and in the United States, I am satisfied that he has used the most scrupulous care in describing the phenomena and recording his investigations. Every conceivable precaution was taken to guard against imposture. The medium's hands were held during the most important manifestations. Doors and windows were carefully secured; and the phenomena took place often in Mr. Livermore's own house, under circumstances which render the theories of fraud or illusion wholly inadmissible. And to crown the testimony we have the corroborative experience of Dr. Gray and Mr. Groute. These gentlemen are all still (1874) fully convinced of the objective reality of the phenomena and of the absence of any attempt at exaggeration or imposition on the part of any human being.

Of the mediumship of Miss Kate Fox (now Mrs. Jencken) through whom these remarkable phenomena occurred, Mr. Wallace justly remarks: "We have here a career of twenty-six years of mediumship of the most varied and remarkable character; mediumship which has been scrutinized and tested from the first hour of its manifestation down to this day, and with one invariable result—that no imposture or attempt at imposture has ever been discovered, and no cause ever been suggested that will account for the phenomena except that advanced by Spiritualists."

CHAPTER II.

The inference from the phenomena of spirit-forms is not that these forms represent the spirit as it appears in its own world. By an effort of the will, or by some ethereal chemistry hardly conceivable to man in his present state, the returning spirit is supposed to reproduce certain *fac-similes* of its appearance while in the earth-life; doing this mainly for the purpose of identifying itself to surviving relatives and friends. A feminine spirit, who manifested herself at Moravia, was on one occasion known to produce, in rapid succession, *fac-similes* of her personal appearance at six different periods of her earth-life, ranging from childhood to old age.

According to Prof. Daumer, author of "Das Geisterreich," (Dresden, 1867), these apparitions are neither bodies nor souls, but a third entity, which he calls *eidolon* (a shape), by which he understands the direct self-manifestation of the *psyche* (soul). The soul, according to his theory, is restricted to the corporeal exhibition only so long as it animates the body. Once released by the death of the latter, it can manifest its immanent reality in any way it pleases; it can even reproduce whole episodes from its former life, including any number of figures of itself or of other persons; it can also produce sounds and other material acts.

That spirits have these powers is proved by the recent phenomena; but if the theory would imply that the soul manifests itself without an organism in the spirit-world, this is contrary to nearly all the teachings we have from spirits and seers. How can it be said that the apparition is not a body, when the body in which it appears is tangible and undistinguishable from the human form? Mrs. Florence Marryatt Ross-Church (1874) was allowed to put her hand on the nude person of the spirit Katie, and felt her heart beat. A spirit has been known to cut its finger with a knife, then to borrow a handkerchief to wind around the wound, and, at the end of the sitting, to return the handkerchief marked with blood.

In a lecture delivered May 12th, 1858, Chavée, an eminent French chemist and scientist, put the following questions:

1st. Is it possible for an individual being to exist without an organism?

2d. Ought the admission of the existence in man of an ethereal, invisible organism, of which the component elements are not patent to the senses, to be considered as contrary to the ordinary laws of chemistry, physics, or science in general?

3d. Are there cases in this life in positive pathology which teach us that the organism which succeeds the one we are using now, occasionally acts by itself, or nearly so, in such a manner as to give us glimpses, as it were, of an organism superior to our present one?

To the first question Chavée replies in the negative; in his opinion there is no individual being without an organism, for he thinks the soul never exists alone as simple spirit, entirely separated from all organism; in his present state man has two organisms: the terrestrial, which falls under the cognizance of the senses, and the ethereal, which is invisible; at the dissolution of the first the soul continues to retain the second.

The celebrated lecturer replies to the second question by affirming that *we contravene no known law of science, chemistry, physics, mechanics, etc., in admitting the existence of an ethereal or electro-luminous organism.*

The third question he answers in the affirmative: Yes, there *are* cases of positive pathology where we can grasp the superior organism, and observe its action, while the inferior one—that which is perceptible to the senses—is no longer in exercise. These cases are natural and magnetic somnambulism and the trance. Thus observation leads us to conclude that there *is* a future life.

And thus neither reason, observation nor science is opposed to the belief that man survives the death of the body, and that, provided with organs analogous to our present ones, he may be able to manifest himself to us by means appropriate to his new sphere, and subject to the laws which regulate the intercommunication.

My attention was first called to Chavée's lecture by M. Léon Favre, a name honored by Spiritualists. Since Chavée delivered it, the progress of the spiritual phenomena has supplied wonderful confirmation of the truth of his opinions. Spirits have manifested their power, not only of re-materializing, for the purpose of temporary use or exhibition, parts and members not distinguishable from those of the human body, but they have presented entire human figures, appropriately clad, conversing and moving about in the light in the midst of a circle of inquirers, walking arm-in-arm with mortals, writing letters, performing, with high powers of execution, on the piano, and giving other proofs of faculties not differing from those of ordinary mortals.

The unceasing atomic changes of the material body, and the preservation of the human identity through them all, present the sufficient and logical reason why there should be a superior and permanent organism; in short, *a spiritual body.* The wings of the butterfly lie folded in the worm. If man is destined to a future state, all the analogies of Nature conspire to suggest that the future body ought to exist wrapt in the present.

The resurrection of the natural body of Jesus is neither a pledge nor a type of our own. There is much in the Bible narrative of this event that is incongruous and inconsistent. I cannot deny the power of spirits to work a seeming miracle. But what we want for the proof of our own immortality is a fact that shall show us that, after the destruction and disappearance of the natural body, the spirit can still manifest itself to the human senses. Immortality must be inferred from a resurrection of life quite independent of the corruptible body that is laid in the tomb to mingle, like other corporeal exuviæ which we are all the time casting off, with the elements.

If, as clairvoyance proves, the mind can see without the aid of light or of the optic nerve, and hear without the agency of the apparatus of the ear, there must be spiritual organs of sight and hearing distinct from the physical; and if there are spiritual organs of sight and hearing, it is legitimate to conclude that there is a complete spiritual organization or body.

The phenomenal facts of Spiritualism all concur in establishing this hypothesis. All apparitions of departed men and women are in the human form.

"In apparitions," says Locke, "there is something that appears; *that which appears is not immaterial.*"

With more force than he was aware of (for he wrote in ignorance of the recent phenomena), Caro, an eloquent French writer, whom I here translate, demands: "Does the whole question of our future life reduce itself for us to the inquiry *whether the soul's metaphysical principle shall subsist?* Assuredly not! What Spiritualism, in accordance with the instinctive faith of the human race, calls immortality, is the immortality of the *person;* of that particular soul which has thought, loved, acted, struggled, suffered during a life of more or less extent. It is the persistence of this individual existence, *keeping, if I may so say, after death, the physiognomy which it created for itself here,* the sign of its distinct and separate reality. This immortality alone interests us; every other kind of immortality leaves us absolutely unaffected and insensible. It is only by an effort of abstraction that I can separate my substance from my person."

There are those who, in order to magnify the moral element in our nature, would have us rest apathetic in regard to all physical evidences of a future life. According to these writers it is only a coarse realism that seeks for palpable proofs. Kant tells us that the disinterested nature of our morality is impaired if we give to our actions for end the perspective of immortality.

Mr. Emerson adopts this idea; he objects to our severing duration from the moral elements; to our teaching the immortality of the soul as a *doctrine,* and maintaining it by evidences. "*No inspired mind,*" he tells us, "*ever asks this question, or condescends to these evidences.*"

This is high talk, but is it true talk? These echoes of Kant (who, in his turn, gets his sentiment from the ancient Stoics and Sadducees), were finely satirized by Schiller who, I think, will pass for an "inspired mind." He says: "I find pleasure in my friends; it is agreeable to me to do my duty; *all this distresses me, for thus I am not virtuous.*"

Was Paul, then, not "inspired" when he said to his disciples, "If Christ be not raised, your faith is vain?" Did he not here "condescend" to phenomenal evidences as the basis of faith? Does our Concord sage claim an inspiration superior to that of Paul?

Was Socrates not "inspired" when he drew his confident belief in immortality from the fact that he was in communication with a spirit?

"No inspired man condescends to these evidences," says Mr. Emerson; which I would supplement with the remark, No inspired man *condescends* to any thing or to any person. Condescension is for the vulgar and self-seeking. If Mr. Emerson means that the inspired man overlooks or disdains any facts of Nature, however lowly, then I say, Nay; on the contrary, his inspiration will be just in proportion to his recognition of what is true, and he will see in the physical *evidences* of a hereafter none other than the Divine imprint.

The Rev. Joseph May repeats a common but fallacious remark when he says: "The doctrine of immortality cannot be demonstrated scientifically and to the intellect. It rests altogether on faith."

Nay, it may rest on knowledge. Why is it that the belief in immortality is stronger among savages, Hindoos, and Chinese than among cultivated Christians? It is because the former have encountered hard, objective facts which have forced on them the belief. They have seen, have felt, have heard the spirits.

It is related of a Hindoo woman that she allowed her son to cut off her head, so that she might, as a ghost, pursue and punish an enemy who had wronged the family. Parallel cases are numerous. They do not spring from faith; they are not the chimeras of mere superstition; they rest on the conviction inspired by familiar objective facts.

Arguments for the immortality of the soul have been drawn from the universality of the belief among all tribes and at all periods of time. I have heard of a pious Frenchman who used to peruse every new book of travels with fear lest he should learn of some tribe who did not have this belief. He dreaded the loss of a staple argument for a future state.

But an argument that is thus contingent is of little value. Still the fact remains; but Spiritualism traces it to its true source, and puts on it the only construction that makes it of any importance.

If any one doubts that the belief in a future state is common to all races of men, let him read Mr. E. B. Tylor's "Primitive Culture," in which work the fact of this belief being thus universal is made to take its place among the admissions of a careful and comprehensive critical science.

The researches of geologists show that even the men of the pre-historic period believed fully in a hereafter for man. In the tenth chapter of Lyell's "Antiquity of Man," there is an account of the discoveries in the cave of Aurignac, in France, from which it appears that men even in the far-off times, that only geology can reckon, had their funeral feasts and preparations, showing that, like the North American Indians, they fitted out the departing spirit with food and implements for his journey. They believed in immortality.

But what is the genesis of the belief? "It comes," says one, "from the poetical fancy." "Nay, it is born of the moral element in man," says another. "My affections demand it," say Buckle, Hortense Bonaparte, and every loving soul. "It is the mere craving of egoism and morbid desire," says Büchner. "It exists only in the subjective imagination," says Feuerbach. "It originates," says Strauss, "in the survivor's retention of the conception of the deceased, which meets him with delusive reality in dreams." "It is a sentiment, a day-dream, a morbid and presumptuous conceit, the offspring of a diseased state of the pulmonary organs," say Messrs. Vogt, Moleschott, Taine, and others.

All these theories are scattered like mist, by Spiritualism, which declares to us that the proofs which have made the belief in immortality so universal and effective do not come in the large sense from anything so capricious as human fancy and desire, so questionable and evanescent as human tradition, or so transient and fickle as human sentiment and opinion. They do not spring from any arbitrary systems, rituals, theologies, philosophies, religions, whatsoever. On the contrary, the abiding proofs spring from certain constantly recurring facts of human nature, such as Modern Spiritualism adduces, and which, though they may have their limitations, and may not be open to the immediate experience and command of all persons at will, are yet so general, so surprising in their character, and so widely credited by those who have experienced them, that they have kept alive through the ages, among the cultivated as well as the uncivilized races, that belief in a future state for which merely speculative reasoners assign so many false origins.

The author of "Oriental Religions," Mr. Samuel Johnson, does not dissent from Kant and Emerson. He thinks that the evidences of immortality which do not meet certain conditions of assurance are "crude and imperfect." These conditions, as far as I can glean them from his text, are: "To live in the whole; to know God by discernment of the soul as real being; to know one's self as one with necessary being. For," asks Mr. Johnson, "how can we possibly know ourselves immortal otherwise than by experience of what is imperishable, and by knowing that we are in and of and inseparable from it?"

Among the evidences to which Mr. Johnson objects, as lacking "spiritual vitality and relation," are those which rest "on testimonies to *the reappearance of many persons after their bodily death, as through some natural law;* and those which proceed on the ground that we can be spiritually fed by the reflection of our curiosity or desire, *or even by the echoes of our gossip, from behind the veil.*" A blow would seem to be here aimed at Modern Spiritualism.

When the question is, *What is the destiny of man?* to reply by telling the interrogator to "live in the whole," to "discern the soul as real being," may be, for all that I know to the contrary, to address a certain class of minds profitably and intelligibly; but surely there must be a large class of thoughtful persons whose wants are not at all met by "conditions of assurance" like these. As well might you point them to a fog-bank, and say, "See there a proof of the eternal world!"

To assume that these unsatisfied persons are an inferior order of minds will hardly answer. Alexander Humboldt was a stubborn realist and disbeliever, but a great man nevertheless. The notion that the belief in immortality, which one gets from the phenomenal proofs of it, is "crude and imperfect" as compared with that which another gets from discerning "the soul as real being," is certainly not established by any evidences of superior insight, faith, or refinement on the part of those who would undervalue the process by which the Spiritualist arrives at his convictions.

Nothing can be trivial which impresses me with a belief in my immortality. Whether it be a "testimony to the reappearance of a person after his bodily death," or an "echo of gossip from behind the veil"—whether it be the waving of a long-vanished hand or the simple movement of a table independent of human touch—if it serve the purpose of convincing me that I shall survive the dissolution of the mortal body, then is the evidence to me good and sufficient, and I will "condescend to it" with a grateful heart.

Is the *proof palpable* not wanted? Consider the deadness of all belief in a future for man among some of the foremost minds of the age. Listen to the almost contemptuous denials that come from such men as Haeckel, Vogt, Feuerbach, Büchner, Moleschott, and many of the leading scientists of Germany. See the indisposition of their brother scientists in England and America to gainsay what they so persistently and boldly assert. Hear the shouts of approval from a crowded scientific assemblage in Germany when Vogt proclaimed atheism and annihilation as the creed of science.

If facts like these will not satisfy you that the "condescension" which stoops to palpable evidences of immortality is not superfluous or untimely, listen to the words that come from the lips of so devout a Christian as the late Albert Barnes, of Philadelphia, well known to the religious public at home and abroad. Hear his cry of doubt and despair: "It is all dark, dark, dark to my soul, and I cannot disguise it. In the distress and anguish of my own spirit I confess that I see no light whatever."

Hardly less desponding than this in tone was the recent

utterance of President McCosh, of Princeton College, while officiating at a funeral.

Turn from wailings of anguish like these to the last words, almost playful in their serenity, of the Spiritualist, Socrates. Crito asks him, "How and where shall we bury you?" Socrates rebukes the phrase. "Bury me," he replies, "in any way you please, *if you can catch me, and I do not escape from you!*" And, at the same time smiling and looking around on his hearers, he said, "I cannot persuade Crito, my friends, that I am this Socrates who is now conversing with you and arranging each part of this discourse; but he obstinately thinks I am that which he shall shortly behold dead, and he wants to know how he shall bury me. But that which I have been arguing with you so long, that when I have drunk this poison I shall be with you no longer, but shall depart straightway to some happy state of the blessed, I seem to have argued in vain, and I cannot convince him. . . . Say not, at the interment, that Socrates is laid out, or is carried out, or is buried. Say that you bury my *body*. Bury it, then, in such a manner as is pleasing to you, and as you think is most agreeable to our laws."

The sequel of the familiar narrative, the introduction of the hemlock, the drinking of it amid the tears and lamentations of friends, the solemn silence enjoined by himself, the pacing to and fro, the perfect equanimity and the unquenchable faith manifested in all his last words and acts, show that Socrates fulfilled in his death all the professions of his life.

As no unworthy pendant to this picture of the death of Socrates, learn how another Spiritualist, Mrs. Rosanna C. Ward, of Cincinnati, met her end. For several years she had said to her husband that she should pass away in the autumn of 1873, in the twilight of a beautiful day. The fact verified her prediction. She, too, like Socrates, was a sensitive or medium, in her relations to spiritual influences.

A few days before her departure she sent for a Unitarian clergyman, the Rev. Mr. Vickers, and requested him to conduct the services at her funeral, and to say, "This woman did not die in the *faith* of Spiritualism, but *in an absolute knowledge* of the reality of the after-life and the fact of spirit-intercourse."

She arranged all her affairs, and gave minute directions. "After the spirit leaves the body," she said, "lay the body out for cooling in this room; lower the windows about six inches, and allow nobody to come in," &c. . . . "There must be no sitting up. Go, all, and take your needed rest, *as I shall be doing.*"

The day preceding her death she lapsed into a deep trance, and was absent three hours. During this time her arm was pulseless and her breathing was imperceptible. When she re-took possession of her body, she said, "There is so much life in the back brain that I could not pass away. The back brain must die a little more before I can leave." She then said to Mr. Ward, who had just handed her a flower, "The flowers are a thousand times more beautiful in the spirit-world than these! But all God's works are beautiful, if we are only in sympathy with them. My dear, it is all right."

She then spoke of the interviews she had been having with departed relatives and friends, and said, "I will go to-morrow." On the morrow, a few moments before she passed away, she gave some instructions for her husband's comfort, and then, with a smile, looking him in the face, said, "My work is now done; the curtain falls." And so the well-prepared spirit passed on to the better clime, "the purer ether, the diviner air."

What truly "inspired" mind can depreciate evidences that could lend such a lustre to death as they did in these cases of Socrates and Mrs. Ward? Who shall disparage the proof palpable of immortality when it can thus give us joy for mourning, beauty for ashes, and make the dissolution of the mortal body the opened pathway to a nobler and more beautiful life?

It is by no means contended that the mere knowledge of immortality, any more than of anatomy, inspires all the virtues. We have seen that it may be accompanied with extreme vindictiveness and malignity. Belief in anything must be vitalized by right thinking before it can be productive of good.

But to say that the reflective mind is not lifted to a higher plane of thought and aspiration by an assured sense of continuous life, is an absurdity. As well might it be said that the man who expected to live only a week would make the same provisions for his life that he would if he expected to live a century. As well might it be said that the Ptolemaic view of the universe is as fruitful in sublime conceptions as the Copernican.

Spiritualism regards man, not only from the side of his limitations, but of his possibilities. "Why dost thou wonder, oh, man," says Isidore, "at the height of the stars or the depth of the sea? Enter into thine own soul, and wonder there!"

CHAPTER III.

In the year 1871 the materializations of spirit-forms at the house of Mr. Keeler, in Moravia, N. Y., began to attract public attention. The medium, Mrs. Mary Andrews, was of Irish parentage, and lived for some time as a domestic in Mr. Keeler's family. She was described (Dec., 1871) as "a well-formed, comely married woman between twenty-five and thirty years old, and the mother of three little girls."

Mr. Thomas R. Hazard, of Rhode Island, has given, in his "Eleven Days in Moravia," a clear account of the character of the phenomena. Mr. Hazard—who must now have numbered his three-score and ten years—is well known to me personally as one of the most diligent and careful investigators of the facts of Spiritualism. A man of culture and of leisure, a wholly independent witness, his testimony is entitled to the greatest respect. He is a brother of Rowland G. Hazard, distinguished among metaphysical writers for his volume entitled "Freedom of Mind in Willing."

The manifestations at Moravia used to commence with a "dark circle," at which questions would be answered by spirit-lights, three appearing as an affirmative. Then the keys of the piano would be struck, water would be sprinkled in the faces of the sitters, and stars, or lights, would appear in various parts of the room, and sometimes engage in playful exhibitions, as if mingling in a dance. Spirit-voices would join in the singing. The heads and persons of sitters would be patted by spirit-hands, and often spirits would manifest themselves to the sitters by speaking audibly, or in distinct whispers, and sometimes at considerable length. A spirit-voice would at last call for a light, and the dark séance would close.

The medium would then take her seat in a cabinet some ten feet by four or five in size, and having an aperture of about twelve by thirteen inches, screened by a piece of black broadcloth some fourteen inches square. The cloth was fastened at the top only, on the inside of the aperture, so as to admit or exclude the light, and the spirits in attendance would raise or drop it at their pleasure. The room where the spectators sat would be partially lighted by a kerosene lamp, so adjusted as to reflect on the aperture.

After singing, in which spirit-voices would sometimes join, faces, busts, arms and hands would appear, the faces being visible, and even the motion of the lips in speaking being plainly discernible. Frequently these faces would be readily recognized by some one or more of the spectators as representations of departed friends; and the voices would be sometimes so characteristic as to afford a sufficient test of identity.

Mr. Hazard describes the apparent efforts made by his deceased wife to manifest her presence at Moravia. For several years previous he had been promised, through various mediums, that, before he joined her in spirit-life, she would be able not only to show herself, but to converse with him as plainly as she ever did whilst on earth. Through two mediums she had expressed her intention of manifesting herself at Moravia.

On the 14th and 21st of December, 1871, a message, purporting to be from Theodore Parker, in regard to these manifestations, came through Mrs. Staats, of New York, in which the following extraordinary passage occurs: "As these manifestations increase, they will spread everywhere, and the result will be *spirits talking face to face with man.* I see great advancement and earnest investigation everywhere. One thing is certain: nothing else can make man a law to himself and a light to others, and there is but one thing to look for progress in, namely, individual reform—learning to think and act for one's self."

The prediction, italicized above, was soon singularly verified, in the case of the spirit "Katie King" in London.

On one occasion an accompanying spirit described Mr. Hazard's wife as "standing back, partly because she could not attain the proper conditions and partly to give place to other spirits who were anxious to manifest themselves to their friends." Several times she would throw her arms at full length, with hands clasped, out of the aperture. The exhibition was perfectly life-like and natural.

Another day, when Mr. Hazard asked if she still meant to make another effort to show her face, in reply an arm was thrown upward some twelve or fifteen inches above the top of the aperture, in the full light, while she made lively raps on the partition with her fingers.

At length, on one of the last days of his stay at Moravia, he saw a face gradually developing, or approaching the aperture, that he soon recognized "unmistakably" as that of his wife. She seemed highly gratified, and so expressed herself. At first she wore spectacles. Then the face disappeared, but quickly returned without the spectacles, and "looking as natural as in earth-life."

Upon this Mr. Hazard said: "It is enough, Fanny. I want no more; I am now fully satisfied;" at which she thrust her face partly out of the aperture, and said, in a clear, loud whisper, "We have tried hard, Thomas, to make myself plain to you, and I thank God that we have succeeded."

The figure was within six feet of where Mr. Hazard sat, and he saw her lips move as distinctly and naturally whilst she was speaking as he ever saw them in earth-life. Overcome with joyful emotion he said, "Kiss me, darling!" whereupon her hand was twice raised to her lips as she threw him two kisses.

"It may be imagined," says Mr. Hazard, "what my emotions were, just as the last moment of my last seance was about to expire, to see my wife's face suddenly presented before me, as plain and distinct as I ever saw it in our own house—not as it looked in the last weary hours of life, nor even yet as it was in less mature years, when the color had partially faded from her cheeks, but in the full bloom of health, and all the glorious beauty that so pre-eminently distinguished her early womanhood. Before this crowning proof, my experiences had banished all doubts from my mind as regards a future state of existence; but now, even belief that had passed into *knowledge*, was doubly confirmed. I had at last obtained all I sought for. I had looked upon the re-incarnated spirit-face of a loved one, the identity of whose features I am not only willing to affirm to, under the pains and penalties of perjury, before any assemblage of mortals or tribunal on earth, but, if need be, swear to it, on peril of my salvation, before the assembled hosts of heaven and the judgment seat of God."

In a letter, dated 1873, Mr. Hazard writes:

"For the last seventeen years I have been an investigator of the alleged spirit phenomena; during which time my leisure, as well as my inclination, has prompted me to hold converse, through the agency of many scores of those sensitive and peculiarly organized persons called 'spirit mediums,' with what I deem to be spirits of the so-called dead; and of the many hundreds or thousands with whom I have in this way communicated, all that have referred to the subject alike testify that there is a spiritual form involved in every human body, and that this form not only retains its natural life and identity on passing to the higher life, but is clothed in vesture more or less resplendent and beautiful, or otherwise, in accordance with its moral attainments or degrees of innocence or guilt, that attached to it at the period it passed from earth, or which it has since acquired in spirit-life.

"With like unanimity returning spirits allege that under

mediumistic conditions they have, with the aid of some occult alchemy unexplainable to material senses, the power to extract elements from their surroundings, wherewith they are enabled to present themselves in an exact resemblance to their earth body, together with its clothing and peculiarities, and thus enable their earth friends to identify them, and, in many instances, respond to their loving advances more readily than they otherwise would. Absurd as this seems to some, and once seemed to me, of the fact I have now no doubt; nor, with the many and varied experiences I have had, can I believe that anything will ever shake my belief and acceptance of it."

Mr. L. A. Bigelow, of Boston, an investigator who shrinks from no trouble in verifying a fact, and whose candor is beyond a question, was at Moravia, October 20th, 1871; and he relates the following as a part of his experiences there:

"As the circle was small, we were within eight feet of the opening, so that everything was visible. Very soon two delicate female hands, closed and then opened, as if in benediction, appeared at the window before us; a face was next seen, but indistinctly. When asked whose friend it was, a finger seemed to point to a lady at my left, and then move toward me. I inquired if I were the one indicated, whereupon the whole hand was shown and shaken, as if for joy. I then requested the face to come more into the light. It did so, but not far enough to enable me to distinguish it clearly. I then said, 'Please present yourself fully in the aperture,' when I most plainly saw a man's face, with gray whiskers, gold spectacles and *bald head.* I recognized it beyond question as that of my father-in-law, the late Otis Tufts, of this city, and so remarked aloud. It bowed as if to give assent, and disappeared. I endeavored to recall it, that it might speak to me, but without avail. . . . No one present knew my name or address till after the close of the séance."

Mr. Isaac Kelso, of Alton, Ill., writes to the St. Louis Democrat, (January, 1873,) as follows:

"I saw many strange faces at the aperture—some days from ten to fifteen or twenty—the most of whom were recognized by some one or more present in the circle. At length two of my sisters succeeded in materializing themselves, and appeared side by side at the aperture. The recognition was undoubted, my sister at my side recognizing them at the same moment I did; and strangers present remarking upon the family resemblance. But the certainty was made doubly certain when the apparitions mentioned incidents in their earth-life and ours which we readily and vividly remembered.

"A few days subsequent, our mother appeared, threw open the door of the cabinet, and showed herself to us from head to foot.

"Six times during the three weeks an old acquaintance,

who died a materialist, appeared to me, looked and talked naturally; referred repeatedly to his materialistic notions, and how unhappy they made him; said much about his present condition, and its advantages over the former; tried to give me an idea of spirit-life, the pursuits, pleasures and amusements of spirits, as well as their institutions for doing good, educating the ignorant, and lifting higher the low and debased.

"A few days before I left the place a gentleman came there, bringing with him two little girls—his own daughters—the elder perhaps eight years old, the younger about six. Before going into the séance room he said to me: 'When about leaving home my wife observed, "I would go too if I thought mother would show herself there; but as she was always opposed to Spiritualism, I'm sure she'll have no desire to make any manifestation!" But lo! after the light séance began, who should appear first at the aperture but this same old grandmother! She bent her eyes affectionately upon the children. The little girls gazed a moment in mute astonishment, then both at once, clapping their hands in ecstacy, exclaimed: 'Grandma! Grandma!'

"'Keep still,' said the father, in a low tone of voice, and evidently much moved; then to the apparition he said, 'You did n't believe in this a few weeks ago?'

"'No,' replied the spirit; 'but, thank God, it is true!' These words were uttered very distinctly and with a peculiar stress of voice, indicating earnestness and deep feeling. The old lady had been dead but three weeks."

Messrs. Daniel D. Bonnett and John Hayward, under date of New York, Sept. 25th, 1872, testify that in the light circle they saw several faces, arms and hands, and that the faces so closely resembled those whom they represented, that in nearly all cases they were readily recognized; that the late Rev. John Pierpont came and was simultaneously recognized by many, and that he made a short address, concluding with the words, "Thank God, we live after death."

The following is a specimen of the addresses made by the spirits at Moravia:

"Friends, it is much better to say nothing, unless you can say something good. You will all be sorry if you have injured any one, but never for the good you have done. Be not ashamed, friends, to proclaim the truth of Spiritualism to the world. The time is approaching when you will be proud of it. Oh, how I long to speak to the hearts that are crushed when their loved ones are taken from them, and they think they have laid them in the ground! I long to say, 'Rejoice! they are all free. Be glad! they are all happy in the spirit-land.' And, friends, it is but a short time before you will meet them. God bless you all!"

All very simple this—very common place, you will say—language which a child might have uttered! And yet may it not be that the highest truths are ever the commonest, like the common sunshine and the common air? What more, after all, than this substantially, could the highest seraph have said in the way of saving truth?

Occasionally, in the dark circles at Moravia, the spirits would speak through a trumpet; and in one instance, a skeptic having blackened the small end of it with printers' ink, the ink was found, as soon as a light was struck, on the mouth of the medium. Suspicions of fraud were raised, as usual, but there was no fraud in the case. The fact has been repeatedly proved that when an adhesive or coloring matter is taken on the hand or lips of the spirit, it may reappear on the corresponding part of the medium's person. The "nerve aura," "Psychic or electric force," or what ever it may be that is abstracted from the medium to form the materialization, carries back with it the foreign substance it has contracted. Innocent mediums have sometimes been unjustly condemned by persons ignorant of this curious fact.

At a sitting described by Mrs. Chester Packard, No. 83 Lancaster street, Albany, N. Y., as occurring Nov. 21st, 1871, at Moravia, a spirit with a white beard and long white hair came to the aperture, and said, "Friends, I am glad to see you here. You have come to Moravia to see strange things, but they will be seen in other places within a few years at furthest; you will meet your spirit-friends on the highway, and they will come into your houses, and you will recognize them without fear or doubt."

The first part of the prediction has been verified in a striking manner as we have already seen. This spirit, when about to leave, having been asked for his name, laughed and said: "You have been singing 'John Brown's body lies mouldering in the grave,' and you did not know John Brown when he was talking to you."

Mrs. Packard gives the following account of her recognition of the presence of three of her departed relatives:

"Among the floating lights was one, star-like in appearance, that seemed to work by itself, or for a purpose of its own. Finally it became detached from the rest of the lights, and floated away to the extreme corner of the room, when it began to cross and recross the room, coming a little nearer to me each time it crossed. It was nearly as high up as the ceiling. My whole attention was attracted to it. Soon it gained a position immediately over my head, and, while I was straining my eyes to look upward, I was aware of a presence around me, and in a moment the sweet voice of my spirit-son said, 'Mother! mother!'

"He took hold of my left hand and patted it so lovingly; he seemed to have my hand between both of his, as I could feel a hand on each side of mine. He then raised his hand to my head, and smoothed my forehead. He drummed on the glasses of my spectacles, and then seemed to take hold with both hands and remove the spectacles entirely from my head, and then place them back again—this operation being repeated three times. Just then the spirits called for a light, my son's manifestations at once ceased, and the star became invisible. The spectacles my son removed from my head were a pair that he placed there himself for the first time, some seven or eight years ago."

After the lamp was lighted, the spirits began to show themselves at the aperture. Soon, in a full glare of light, she saw her deceased husband. She writes:

"He stood before me smiling; his lips were moving, as if holding an earnest conversation, although I heard no sound. As he seemed about to move away I called him back, saying, 'Do not leave; I want to see you again.' In a moment he was back again, and my mother stood beside him, looking so happy and smiling at me! She stood long enough for all in the room to observe that she wore a cap with a full border on each side, and plain across the top, with loops of narrow white satin ribbon in the border on each, and tied under the chin with white satin ribbon. She wore (as in life) a band of brown hair across the forehead. The band seemed pushed back a little too high, and showed some of her gray hair below the band—which was very natural. She looked precisely as she did when in the form.

"As she was moving away, I asked her to come back again that I might see her more. She nodded, smiled, and was gone, but did not return. My husband went out of sight, and returned five or six times at my request. Each time he came I looked at him closely; I saw a dimple on his cheek and a peculiar wrinkle in the out-corner of his eye—the same he used to have in earth-life when much pleased. All was so life-like! My husband looked as he used to in health, and very much better than he did for months before he passed away; his lips moved as if talking, but I did not see my mother's lips move at all. I looked after them until they were gone; I felt the great question answered—that the soul lived on, and, under proper condition, could return and look at, and be looked upon by, those left behind!"

Dr. A. S. Hayward, writing from Moravia, under date of Aug. 31st, 1872, after describing the phenomena, remarks: "In conclusion, I would say, that what occurs in the presence of Mrs. Andrews I believe to be done by disembodied spirits that have once lived on this earth. I could find hardly a person who has attended the séances who did not hold to the same opinion."

Testimonials similar to these could be multiplied to fill large volumes; but the time has gone by when they were needed. They are now corroborated by the larger and more conclusive phenomena to which I have yet to call attention.

The phenomena of materialization have attended the mediumship of so many in the United States that I can only attempt to narrate a few well-attested cases.

In the presence of Dr. Henry Slade, of New York, remarkable physical proofs of spirit power have been repeatedly witnessed. Mrs. A. A. Andrews, of Springfield, Mass., (1873) testifies in regard to some of these as follows: —

"I have had a spirit-hand write a letter on paper placed upon my lap, when the room was sufficiently lighted by gas for me to see distinctly the long lead pencil held in the white fingers, and remaining in sight, directly under my eyes, until the writing was finished, when both hand and pencil disappeared; in a moment afterwards the latter was thrown upon the table, close to our hands, from a point opposite to where the medium sat.

"I have seen the faces of spirits within three feet of me, about whose identity I could no more mistake than I could fail to recognize members of my own family who are still in the material body. I have watched these faces condense and form from what seemed a luminous mist. I have seen them smile brightly and naturally upon me.

"I have had one among them, in compliance with a suggestion made from the impulse of the moment, turn away, showing me the back of the head, that I might recognize the naturally curling hair, falling upon the neck, as worn in life. I have watched the moving lips, and heard whispered messages of love and warning sent to absent friends."

Communications purporting to come from Mrs. Andrews's spirit-son were written upon a slate which was laid in full view, with a fragment of pencil beneath it; and sometimes this took place while the slate was held by herself. The mental proofs of identity were so strong, that after many repetitions and ever-recurring tests, doubt became more difficult to her than belief. A hand, in shape and size like her son's, came forth in broad daylight. She saw and felt it; it patted and caressed her, and played with her dress; it took out her watch by a guard which used to belong to him, and then the following words were written :—"Dear mother, always wear my guard; I love to see you have it."

The phenomenon of slate-writing in the light, independent of human touch, has been witnessed by hundreds at Dr. Slade's séances. Mr. Clarke Irvine, of Oregon, Holt County, testified that he received a message which was written on a slate, placed on his own head, while Dr. Slade sat some yards from him, and the message was correctly signed, "Thomas Irvine, your grandfather;" Mr. Irvine never having seen the medium before, or communicated with him in any way.

Mr. H. Barnard, of Minneapolis, Minn., a stranger to Dr. Slade, brought a folding slate of his own; a grain of pencil was put inside of it, and while no one touched the slate, and it lay before him in plain sight on the table, a message, purporting to be from Mr. Barnard's mother, was written, which was so characteristic and apt, that he says of it: "I now have as good evidence of my mother's existence as I have of that of my brothers and sisters whose letters I receive by mail."

Many of the manifestations known to Modern Spiritualism have occurred in the presence of Mrs. E. J. Hollis, of Louisville, Kentucky. These include levitations of the medium, slate-writing independent of the human touch, the exhibition of spirit hands, transmission of messages through a common telegraph by spirit power, singing and talking by spirit voices, and, finally, the materialization of spirit forms.

For a period of thirty weeks, Dr. N. B. Wolfe, of Cincinnati, investigated the phenomena through Mrs. Hollis, sparing no expenditure of time, money or personal ease, in order to satisfy himself of their character, and engaging other persons of well-known intelligence to coöperate with him. He gives the result in a volume of 543 pages (1874). On the

27th of May, 1872, he received a test which could not fail to make a deep impression; he saw and heard his deceased mother under circumstances which he describes as follows:

"The table on which the music-box was placed, stood not more than two feet from the cabinet. I proceeded to wind it up, and was just turning to resume my seat in the circle, in doing which I had to face the aperture. *As I did this, I beheld my mother's face in the opening of the cabinet door.* 'Why, mother,' I exclaimed, 'is it possible?' I riveted my gaze upon her for twenty seconds, during which time she smiled, bowed, and pronounced my name. The curtain then swung between her face and me. All in the room saw and heard as I did. I was not more than two feet from the cabinet and aperture.

"I am not given to illusions, and rarely dream when asleep, much less when awake. I am a very cool, quiet man in emergencies, and was never more so than upon this occasion. Every person in the circle saw this face, but only I recognized it. *It was my mother's face.* She recognized me, and called me by my given name. To make assurance doubly sure, I said, 'Mother, please materialize your *left hand*, and present it at the aperture.'

"In a very brief space of time a left hand appeared at the opening, *with the forefinger shut at the middle joint.* My mother had just such a finger on her left hand. When a child she received a burn which contracted the tendon, and fixed the forefinger of her left hand permanently in that position."

Instances innumerable could be named where peculiarities similar to that here described have been reproduced, in these extemporized representations of the mundane body. Quick as thought the communicating spirit seems to be able to show the bodily scars or malformations which are needed for identification.

On another occasion the spirit-representation of Dr. Wolfe's mother remained at the aperture two minutes, and was recognized not only by himself but by his nephew, a lad fifteen years old, who had never been at a séance before.

It is unnecessary to record the many explicit testimonials to the recognition of departed friends in the materializations through Mrs. Hollis. Mr. D. H. Hale and his son, Clinton B. Hale, from Indiana, being present, both recognized simultaneously, the one a daughter, the other a sister. A young lady appeared and wrote: "Dear Mr. Hale, how kind you were to me!" Mr. Hale wept as he recognized the features of one whom he had assisted in her destitution.

Mr. F. B. Plimpton, associate editor of the Cincinnati Commercial, gives, under date of May 8th, 1873, an account of his investigations. In the autumn of 1872 he had studied the phenomena that take place in the presence of Mrs. Hollis, and, though thoroughly satisfied of their genuineness, was not quite sure that they could not be explained upon some other than the spiritual solution. But to this he was driven after prosecuting his inquiries further; and such has been the fate of nearly all the *persevering* investigators with whom I am acquainted. He concludes his Report as follows:

"Beginning these investigations as a skeptic, with a feeling almost of contempt for believers in Spiritualism, but at the same time determined to testify to the truth, regardless of the consequences to myself, to what other conclusion can I come, as one after another of my doubts have been vanquished, and my unbelief overcome, than that these manifestations are *precisely what they profess to be?* The conviction is forced upon me, that intelligences, invisible to us, save as they manifest themselves through the medium of persons peculiarly endowed, can and do communicate with the living, and that they have as absolutely a personal existence and identity as ourselves.

"They not only assert this, but assure us that they live in a world as rationally constructed for the development of their finite capacities and for their progression to still higher conditions of being. In manifesting their presence to our grosser sense, they assure us they employ natural agencies; and as the world becomes more receptive of the truth, they anticipate still greater power to reveal themselves, and convince us that we are indeed compassed about by an innumerable cloud of witnesses, testifying to the immortality of man."

The 12th of May, 1874, a spirit calling herself "Katie King" appeared in a materialized form at a séance in Philadelphia, Mr. and Mrs. Holmes being the mediums. Dr. Henry T. Child, himself a "sensitive," and at the same time an experienced and studious investigator, was present. He writes that on the 5th of June, while he and Robert Dale Owen were among the witnesses, Katie King appeared in "a very beautiful shape, clothed in white robes." June 7th, they had a long conversation with Katie at the cabinet window. She allowed Dr. Child to count her pulse; it was about seventy-two per minute, and perfectly natural. She also permitted him to see her tongue, and asked if he thought she was "right well."

Mr. Owen was of the opinion that the "Katie King," or "Annie Morgan," who thus appeared, was identical with the spirit who for three years communicated through Miss Cook in London. There were many circumstances, however, that threw doubt on the identity. The features were unlike those of the London Katie. In London the Holmeses, one or both, had been proved to possess remarkable medial powers; but it was also charged that they would sometimes eke out their manifestations with imposture. It will be seen further on in my narrative (page 114) that both Mr. Owen and Dr. Child, having encountered what seemed to them doubtful features in the phenomena, withdrew their confidence and publicly expressed their dissatisfaction. When we consider that they had been forewarned by English investigators that frauds might be anticipated, the wonder is that they should have been so over-sanguine in their expressions of confidence under the circumstances. That genuine phenomena were given, however, there is now every reason to believe. The whole subject of spirit materialization was thrown under a cloud for a time by the conflicting statements growing out of the Holmes affair. But as the phenomena through other mediums were multiplied, and test conditions were adopted, and the number of witnesses greatly increased, the affair gradually dwindled into insignificance.

In weighing charges of imposture, it should be borne in mind by investigators, that however the ignorant may scout and ridicule the idea, it is nevertheless probable that under certain inharmonious conditions such mischievous spirits may be attracted as will force an unconscious medium to do things automatically which, to the inexperienced, look like deliberate frauds on his part. The more we study the phenomena the larger becomes our charity for the sensitives through whose peculiar receptiveness to influences good or bad the wonders are wrought.

The power of spirits to reproduce *simulacra* of persons who have passed from the earth-life suggests the question, How far can we be assured of the identity of any spirit, let the tests be what they may? We have not yet arrived at that stage of enlightenment that would enable us to reply confidently to this inquiry. The John Kings and the Katie Kings who have come in the full form, and conversed with mortals, have not yet given proofs of their identity, that can be substantiated by documentary evidence. In claiming to have been Sir Henry Morgan and a contemporary of Raleigh, John King does not give us such minute corroborative proofs as must be had before his declaration can be accepted.

There is much that is yet a puzzle in the language and action of this class of materialized spirits. How far they are limited in their mental operations and in their recollections by the act of materialization, or how far by the intellectual horizon of the medium, is still a question. In other cases, proofs of identity, both mental and physical, satisfactory to the recipients, have been given, as Mr. Hazard, Mrs. A. A. Andrews, and others from whom I have quoted, testify.

It is satisfactory to discover that the further we proceed in investigation the more apparent does it become, that if there are deceptive, frivolous, immature spirits, there are also those who are sincere, intelligent, affectionate and earnest in their efforts to do good. The great majority, as in this world, are of the unintellectual sort. Perhaps the development of a spiritual sense in ourselves is needed before we can have a confirmation, that can be conclusive, of identity. Perhaps, under mortal and spiritual limitations as they now are, we can have only an approximate assurance. The science of Spiritualism being still in its infancy, we may hope for more light on this question.

As for the Orthodox notion that "the devil is the only spirit authorized to communicate with the laity," and that all spiritual communications that do not come through certain prescribed channels are Satanic, this will hardly weigh with people of common sense engaged in a strictly scientific investigation.

"Nothing is so brutally conclusive as a *fact*," says Broussais; and, therefore, facts must win in the long run. The truth itself, and not our mere conceptions of what ought to be true, must ultimately prevail.

Meanwhile we see the significance of the caution to us to "*try* the spirits;" to try them not by conjuration through this or that name, however sacred, but by our reason, the purification of our motives, and the singleness of our aspirations for the truth.

Plainly it is not the proved law of our being, that we should surrender to any one, mortal or immortal, the custody of our individuality, our reason, and our self respect. Every earnest and rational spirit, whether in the flesh or out of it, at the same time that he has relations to the universe, and the universe to him, would seem to be impelled by the environments, the restrictions, and the varied experiences to which he is subjected, and by the fallacies with which he soon finds that all human teachings and interpretations are mixed, to exercise his own reason, to discipline his own powers, and to develope his own individuality; and, while courting all good influences, to resist the dictation of those who would constrain him, by aught else than appeals to his sense of right, to adopt their opinions or walk in their ways.

"Think as I do, or drink the hemlock," embodies in words the monster sin that is not confined to mortals or to ancient Athens. As there were spirits of old who would try to force a way for their authority by a "Thus saith the Lord," so there are spirits now who claim a divine infallibility when they can find dupes to heed them.

Spiritualism enforces upon us the fact that in being loosened by death from this exterior husk we call a body, the veritable man is not greatly changed. With a corresponding organism of subtler elements, he starts on his new career from the vantage-ground, low or high, which he has attained to here. Condition follows character; and the spiritual environments which our prevailing thoughts and affections, our noblenesses or our meannesses, have created for us in this life, will impart their beauty or their deformity to our objective surroundings on our entrance into what is now to us the unseen world.

CHAPTER IV.

The news of the manifestations through Mrs. Andrews, at Moravia, N. Y., was received by Spiritualists in England with some incredulity, accompanied by a wish to ascertain if similar phenomena could be had through their own mediums. Accordingly, several of these began to sit for spirit forms. The faces appeared at the séances of Mrs. Guppy, and subsequently Messrs. Herne and Williams succeeded in obtaining these manifestations at dark circles, the spirits manufacturing a light of their own, which they held in their hands to show themselves by.

Certain phenomena in the presence of Miss Florence Eliza Cook, a young lady of fifteen, daughter of a member of the Dalston Association of Inquirers into Spiritualism, began to attract attention in England the latter part of the year 1871. The spirits producing these manifestations claimed to be John and Katie King, and their daughter Katie; but *Morgan*, they said, was their true earth-name; and Katie, on several occasions, would sign herself, Katie King, *properly* Annie Morgan.

At numerous séances in America, and at those of Herne and Williams, in England, spirits calling themselves John and Katie King have frequently manifested themselves. The name *King* would seem, for some reason, to be a favorite one among the class of spirits giving physical manifestations.

"John King" used to make himself audible, at an early period, at the sittings of the Davenport Brothers; and, subsequently, at those of Jonathan Koons, in Dover, Athens Co., Ohio, where he once made a long address, written by a spirit hand supposed to be his own, in which he calls himself, a "servant and scholar of God," and says: "We know that our work will be rejected by many, and condemned as the production of their King Devil, whom they profess to repudiate, but do so constantly serve by crucifying truth and rejecting all that is contrary to their own narrow pride and vain imaginings."

In manifesting himself through the English mediums, John King claimed to be identical with this spirit, and it cannot be denied that a certain unity of speech and character has distinguished him on these occasions. He asserted that his name on earth was Sir Henry Morgan, and that he was a contemporary of Sir Walter Raleigh.

The 20th of March, 1873, at a sitting in London, of which full particulars are given by the well-known publisher, Mr. James Burns, in "Human Nature," for April, 1873, the spirit claiming to be John King manifested himself in a materialized form so successfully that a sketch was made of him by a skillful artist. The séance took place in the daylight, Charles E. Williams being the medium. This sitting was followed by another the next week (March 27th), when John King appeared visibly, as before, as solid and material as an ordinary human being, while the medium's hands were held by Mrs. Burns, and he sat entranced in his seat.

On this last occasion the spirit spoke aloud, saying: "You won't doubt any more, will you? It is God's truth, is it not? It is a glorious truth. God bless you! It is. God bless you!" Having more than satisfied the sitters, he withdrew inside the cabinet, but returned to the aperture to renew the colloquy. While Mrs. Burns dragged the medium's hands through the door of the cabinet into full view, John King also showed his at the window: the test was complete.

Of the sincerity and intelligence of Mrs. Burns, no one who has made her acquaintance, as I have, can doubt.

The genuineness of the mediumship of Mr. Williams has been tested by Prince Wittgenstein and others, who have satisfied themselves of the objective appearance of "John King" and his wonderful lamp. Even Serjeant Cox admits that he has found Mr. Williams "most trustworthy." On the 14th of May, 1874, at a séance held at the house of Mr. Chinnery, in Paris, 52 Rue de Rome, when John King with his lamp was seen, a young man rushed forward to seize the spirit. The latter eluded his grasp, leaving behind only a small portion of the drapery which covered the form. A light was struck, and the medium was found entranced in his chair. He was searched, but nothing in the slightest degree suspicious was discovered. What had become of the *drapery?* The integrity of Mr. Williams was fully vindicated.

At some experiments at Mr. Cook's house, April 21st, 1872, of which Mr. W. H. Harrison, editor of the London Spiritualist, has given an account, a dark séance for the voices was held, Miss Cook and Mr. Herne being the mediums. The following remarkable incident occurred: A tapping was heard upon one of the window panes; the bar of the shutter was unlocked and taken down, and the shutter opened, and John King's voice said: "Cook, you must take that plug out of the gutter, if you do n't want the foundations of your house sapped. The gutter is stopped up." On examination this proved to be true. It had been raining, and the area was full of water. Nobody inside the house knew of this until told in this remarkable way.

"Strangely human all this!" you will say; "so strangely human, that we think there must have been a human personator of the spirit!" But, as I shall have stranger things than this to relate by and by, I will only pause to remark that the incident is in full harmony with occurrences the confirmation of which, under test conditions, is ample.

We now approach the early manifestations through Miss Cook, in whose presence the phenomena eventually became so marked. On the 22d of April, 1872, a séance was held at which Mrs. Cook, the children, and the servant were witnesses. In the endeavor to abolish dark séances, Mr. Harrison had made experiments with different kinds of light. He had tried, at Mr. Cook's house, a phosphorescent light, made by coating the inside of a warm bottle with phosphorus dissolved in oil of cloves, and then letting in the air.

The oil was left at Mr. Cook's, as will be learnt by the following passage from a letter from Miss Cook herself to Mr.

Harrison, under date of April 23d, 1872. I quote the passage because it is interesting as giving us some notion of the intellectual calibre of the writer, Miss Cook, who was soon to become so famous as a medium :

"Yesterday afternoon Katie told us that if we liked to put up a cabinet of curtains for her, she would try to show us something, but as I was not developed enough for her to take enough phosphorus from me to show her face by, we were to give her some of your phosphoric oil. I was delighted, and at half-past eight yesterday evening all was ready. Mamma, auntie, the children, and the servant stood on the stairs. I was left alone (not in my glory, for I was very frightened) inside the breakfast-room. Katie began by giving mamma some fresh ivy leaves; none were in our house or garden of the size she brought. A hand and arm with a white sleeve came to the opening holding the bottle of oil; then, at the lower opening in the curtain, came a face, unveiled, the head covered with a quantity of pure white drapery. Katie held the bottle to her face so that all outside could see her plainly. She remained for quite two minutes. It was an oval face, straight nose, bright eyes, and a very pretty mouth. She again came to the opening, her lips moved, and at last she spoke. All outside could see her lips moving; she talked with mamma some few minutes. I could not see her face plainly, so asked her to turn and show me. She said, 'Of course I will,' came to my chair and bent over me. She was materialized only to the bust. From there she went into a cloud, slightly luminous. She told mamma to look at her carefully, and made the observation that 'she knew she looked most unearthly.' It was indeed very startling. I was too frightened to move or call out when she came near me. She used no tubes for speaking. The last time she appeared she stayed quite five minutes, and directed mamma to send to you, asking you if you could come here one day this week.... Katie King finished her sèance with 'God bless you all. I am so pleased to show myself.'"

On the occasion here referred to by Miss Cook, the face of Katie King was described by Mrs. Cook, as "looking white and deathlike, while her eyes were fixed and staring, as if made of glass."

At a séance at Mr. Cook's, April 25th, 1872, Katie made several efforts to materialize a form. Mr. W. H. Harrison was present. He has given a curious description of some of the performances. The medium, Miss Cook, sat in a dark room. A scraping noise was heard; Katie had some spirit drapery in her hand, which she rubbed down over the medium to collect some of the "influence" used by spirits in materialization. A conversation, in low tones, varied with an occasional scraping noise, then took place between Florence Cook and the spirit:

Miss Cook—Go away, Katie; I do n't like to be scraped.

Katie—Do n't be stupid. Take that thing off your head and look at me. (*Scrape, scrape.*)

Miss Cook—I won't. Go away, Katie; I do n't like you. You frighten me.

Katie—Do n't be silly. (*Scrape, scrape, scrape.*)

Miss Cook—I won't sit for these manifestations. I do n't like them. Go away.

Katie—You are only my medium, and a medium is nothing but a machine. (*Scrape, scrape.*)

Miss Cook—Well, if I am only a machine, I do n't like to be frightened. Go away.

Katie—Do n't be stupid.

Miss Cook, who as yet had not been entranced by the spirit, said that the spirit's head and shoulders were materialized; but below, her form melted into thin air. Katie would be sometimes high up and sometimes low down, so that the bust nearly touched the floor, in which position she looked "most unearthly." It sometimes appeared as if a head were "wandering about with no legs or body, visible or invisible."

At the next sitting Miss Cook was entranced by the spirit, and a little benzoline lamp was used for seeing the materialization. The spirit would cry out "higher," or "lower," as she wanted the light adjusted. Mr. Harrison gives the following interesting account of what occurred:

"Katie's face came out, all the rest of the head being bandaged round with white, 'in order,' she said, 'to keep the power by which she materialized herself from passing away too quickly.' She said that only her face and not all her head was materialized. This time all present had a good look at her, and saw her features. It was remarked that her eyes were closed. Each time the face came out for, perhaps, half a minute. Afterwards she said, 'Willie, see me smile,' and, again, 'see me talk,' suiting the action to the word. Then she said, 'Now, Cook, turn on the light.'

"The light was turned fully up, sending a bright glare upon the face for an instant, and for the first time Katie King was clearly seen. She had a young, pretty, happy face, and sparkling eyes, with some little mischief in them. It was not ghastly, as when Mrs. Cook and family saw it, on April 22d, 'because,' said Katie, 'I know now how to do it better.'

"When her face in its natural colors was seen in full light, nearly all the observers said, 'We can see you all right now, Katie.' 'Well, then,' said she, 'clap!' Accordingly, there was a shower of applause, in which Katie joined by thrusting out her arm and hand, holding a fan taken from the mantelpiece; with the fan she began to gleefully beat the wall outside the door, and to ring the bells hanging above the door.

"During the interval of one hour for supper, Mr. Thomas Blyton came in, and he was present at the next sitting. Katie showed herself as before. Once she said, 'Put out the light, and strike a match when I call.' This was done, and at the moment of the striking of the match, her face was again seen for an instant in a full light. She showed her face a second time in the same way. Once she said, 'Cook, don't gaze at me too fixedly; it hurts me.' On another occasion she said, 'The light hurts me; it makes me feel tired.' All along she was very careful in adjusting the amount of light, and the distance of the sitters from the curtains. Now and then she said, 'Sing, sing, all of you.' Singing evidently helped her as much as at an ordinary séance.

"She threw out about a yard of white fabric, but kept hold of it by the other end, saying, 'Look, this is spirit drapery.' I said, 'Drop it into the passage, Katie, and let us see it melt away; or let us cut a piece off.' She replied, 'I can't; but look here!' She then drew back her hand, which was above the top of the curtain, and, as the spirit drapery touched the curtain, *it passed right through*, just as if there were no resistance whatever.

"She then threw it out again, and again the yard of drapery passed through the curtain. It was a clear case of something which looked like solid matter passing through solid matter, and we all saw it. I think that at first there was friction between the two fabrics, and that they rustled against each other; but that when she said 'Look here!' some quality which made the drapery common matter was withdrawn from it, and at once it passed through the common matter of the curtain, without experiencing any resistance."

Mr. Blyton, in a published communication, confirms all that is reported as occurring in his presence, by Mr. Harrison. "At times, when speaking," says Mr. Blyton, "Katie's features were very natural and human. On our requesting to see a piece of the white drapery, the spirit held out a strip from the opening, resembling muslin in appearance. On her withdrawing her arm and hand, *this white spirit drapery disappeared through the curtain.* This passing of the drapery through the curtain was repeated several times."

As Miss Cook's mediumship grew in power, she was placed above the temptation of exercising it for gain. Mr. Charles Blackburn, of Manchester, with a wise liberality, and in the cause of science, supplied the means for this.

For a long time only a feeble light was permitted at the manifestations of spirit forms. The face of the spirit would be covered with white drapery, the chief use of which was said to be to economize the power by enabling the spirit to leave part of the head unmaterialized.

As the developments went on, Katie began to exhibit not only the whole of her bare face, but her hands and arms, in a strong light. In these early stages, Miss Cook was almost always awake during the manifestations; but sometimes, when the weather was bad, or other conditions were unfavorable, Katie would entrance her, the purpose of which was simply to increase the power, and to prevent the mental activity of the medium from operating as an interference. After a time Katie never appeared without the medium being in a trance.

Some sittings for recognizable faces were had in the presence of Miss Cook; but they began, as did Katie's manifestation, in a weak light, and were imperfect. They were abandoned, therefore, for the more marked phenomenon in which a certain success had been won. Two instances, however, in which recognizable faces were presented through Miss Cook's mediumship, occurred, and seem to have been well authenticated.

At a sitting at Hackney, Jan. 20th, 1873, Katie changed her face from white to black in a few seconds, several times; and to show that her hands were not mechanically moved, she sewed up a hole in the curtain. On the 12th of March, at Hackney, Miss Cook's hands being tied and sealed, Katie, with her hands perfectly free, walked out of the cabinet. A month or two later, several photographs were taken of Katie, under strictly test conditions, and by the magnesium light.*

Thus it was not till after many imperfect trials and partial materializations, accompanied with very gradual developments of increasing force, that the spirit Katie, in the full human form, and habited in white, as represented in her

*An account of these sittings, by Mr. J. C. Luxmoore, Justice of the Peace for the County of Devon, may be found in the London Spiritualist of May 15th, 1873.

photographs, came forth in the light from the cabinet, and walked about the room before a semi-circle of spectators.

Dr. J. M. Gully, formerly of Great Malvern, England, a thoroughly experienced physician and a careful investigator, under date of July 20th, 1874, writes me as follows :

"To the special question which you put regarding my experiences of the materialization of the spirit-form, with Miss Cook's mediumship, I must reply that, after two years' examination of the fact and numerous séances, I have not the smallest doubt, and have the strongest conviction, that such materialization takes place, and that not the slightest attempt at trick or deception is fairly attributable to any one who assisted at Miss Cook's séances.

"That the power grows with use was curiously illustrated by the fact that, for some time, only a face was producible, with, occasionally, arms and hands ; with no hair, and sometimes with no back to the skull at all—merely a mask, with movement, however, of eyes and mouth. *Gradually the whole form appeared*—after, perhaps, some five months of séances—once or twice a week. This again became more and more rapidly formed, and changed, in hair, dress, and color of face, as we desired.

"The voice came long before the whole form of the body, but was always husky, and as if there was a whispering catarrh ; save when she joined us in singing, when she gave out a *most lovely* contralto.

"The feel of the skin was quite natural, soft and warm ; her movements were natural and graceful, except when she stooped to pick up anything from the floor, when it seemed as if her legs as well as her trunk bent backwards.

"When that photograph* was taken, I held her hand for at least two minutes, three several times, for we sat three times for it on one and the same evening ; but I was constrained to close my eyes by reason of the intense magnesium light which shone directly upon me ; moreover she desired that

---

* The well-known published photograph, in which Katie is represented standing with Dr. Gully sitting at her side and holding her hand.

none of us would gaze at her whilst the lens was directed upon her.

"I believe that much information might have been obtained from her concerning the *outre-tombe*, but the circle seemed always bent on talking *chaff* to her, complimenting her, and indulging in ordinary inconsequential conversation; for only on one or two occasions was I (who hate all the nonsense that was said *to* and *by* her) able to put a few questions on the subjects about which every thoughtful Spiritualist is naturally anxious.

"It may be questioned whether these spirit beings *can* convey anything like an accurate idea of their state and powers; but I believe that, just as their power of physical manifestation augments with use, so would their power of mental communication increase were an intelligent curiosity always presented for their sympathetic reply. In fact, I believe that if less idle and more serious curiosity was felt by the circles, spirits of a higher and more powerful character would sympathetically come and teach by vocal words, written words, inspired words.

"So soon as a man has convinced himself of the reality of the spirit-presence, and the absence of all deception, he should, I think, use all his will power to place his own spirit in a state of reception for spirit knowledge, and feel assured he will get it. Physical manifestations are the alphabet of the subject, and if Spiritualism went no further it would do but little for humanity.

"But I quite believe in your suggestion, that, carried out to its consequences in thought and sympathy, it is destined to abolish a thick cloud of darkness which at present renders all religions more or less superstitious, and all philosophy a mere circle; and to substitute a light which will enable the mind in a body to hold communion with minds whose freedom enables them to see the workings of Great Cause and Great Effect, and so to bring forth a philosophic religion; whilst philosophy itself will be able to look ever onwards instead of going round and round, as it has done from Plato to Mill, tedious to study, and barren of result."

Similar materializations to those through Miss Cook had taken place not unfrequently in America, at séances where the light was very dim. Mr. Home, Mrs. Mary Hardy, Messrs. Bastian and Taylor, Mrs. Maud Lord, Mrs. Jennie Lord Webb, and others had, while sitting in the dark or in twilight, satisfied many of the presence of materialized spirits, who made themselves felt and heard, if they could not be distinctly seen. The materializations through Miss Kate Fox had satisfied Mr. Livermore, Dr. Gray, and Mr. Groute of the objective reality of the appearing forms.

But the bold and startling manifestations through Miss Cook, occurring in the light, and in the presence of a dozen or more spectators, were peculiarly impressive and satisfactory; and I give prominence to her case on this account. The manifestations, after the initiatory experiments had been made, were conducted under strict test conditions, and in the presence of persons of well-known character and intelligence, whose single object was the establishment of the truth; the apparition, being visible under the most powerful light, and solid to the touch, could be subjected to tests which were eventually supplied by scientific men and found satisfactory; and the medium, being exempted from all necessity of asking pay from the investigators, was comparatively independent and free in allowing the manifestations to take their course.

At a sitting at Mr. Luxmoore's, Nov. 18th, 1873, a witness, well known to me personally, Mr. Benjamin Coleman, was present, and from his account I have abridged the following:

The séance was given in the large drawing-room, in which an ordinary fire was kept burning throughout the evening. The small drawing-room, separated by sliding doors, was appropriated as a cabinet, and a dark curtain was hung between the open parts, by which all light was excluded. A lamp was placed on the table of the audience room, where there was a fire, and at no time was it dark. The fourteen ladies and gentlemen, who formed a horse-shoe circle in front of the cabinet, could see each other the whole evening.

A low chair was placed in the cabinet, upon which Miss

Cook, the medium, was seated; and Mr. Coleman and Mr. Blackburn were invited by Mr. Luxmoore to see her secured. Her hands were tied together with tape, the ends of which were sewn and sealed with wax; and then the tape was passed around her waist, and tightly knotted and sewn, and sealed again. The tape was then passed through a staple in the floor, leaving a slack of about a foot, and there knotted again. Thus it was impossible for Miss Cook to move from her seat more than a few inches.

The ties were all found secure, and the line of tape undisturbed, after the séance; and even had this precaution not been taken, the fact that, the instant Katie disappeared, the medium was found tied and differently clad, and asleep in her chair, would have satisfied any reasonable person that there was no trick or attempt to deceive. Whatever the figure of Katie might be, it evidently was not Miss Cook.

The figure of Katie entered the room. She was clad in a loose white dress, tied in at the waist, having long sleeves terminating at the wrists, with a close hood on her head, long lappets hanging over her shoulders, and her hair closely banded.

She at once saluted each of the company in turn, first asking the name of the only stranger unknown to the medium. Mr. Coleman asked Katie if she had shoes and stockings on. She said, "No," and at once drew aside her dress, and showed that her feet were naked; and to satisfy all, she raised one foot on to the dress of Mrs. Corner, in the most natural manner, and said, "Now you can all see that I have bare feet, can't you?"

There were pencils and sheets of writing paper on the table, and Mr. Coleman asked her if she would be good enough to write something for him. "Yes, I will," she said, taking a chair, and sitting down on it. "What shall I write?" Mr. Coleman said he was engaged in getting up a testimonial to Judge Edmonds, and perhaps she might have something to say to him.

Upon this Katie raised one knee, and commenced writing;

but, finding the position uncomfortable, asked for something hard "to rest the paper upon." This being supplied, she wrote off the following letter:—

"MY DEAR FRIEND—You have asked me to write a few words to you. I wish you every success with regard to Judge Edmonds's testimonial. He is a good man, and an earnest worker. Give him my affectionate greeting. I know him well, although he does not know me. My power is going, so with every good wish,

"I am your sincere friend, KATIE KING,
"*Properly* ANNIE MORGAN."

The letter was handed back to Mr. Coleman, who read it aloud, and then said to her, "I see you have not addressed it;" she took it back and deliberately folded it upon her knee, and wrote on the back, "Mr. Coleman."

On his requesting her to let him feel the texture of her dress, she replied by coming round past the back of Mr. Luxmoore's chair sideways, as there was barely room to pass, and holding up the dress to Mr. C.; he took it with both hands, and pulled it, and it was to all appearance, in substance, as if it were made of strong white calico. She then passed round the circle and shook hands, by gently touching the hands of each. Both her hands and her face throughout the séance were of a perfectly natural color, the reverse of pallid; her cheeks were red, and hands decidedly so; in fact, her whole appearance was that of a gentle and graceful young woman. She stooped down to pick up two sheets of paper which were in her way whilst crossing the room, and stepped aside to lay them on the table.

"This completed," writes Mr. Coleman, "the impression, which all must have felt, that we had been for an hour and a half holding intercourse with an intelligent living woman, who glided, rather than walked about, and who showed by her constant watchfulness of the medium, that *there* was the tie to which she was bound. It was altogether a marvelous exhibition."

Prince Emile of Sayn Wittgenstein, who was present at a séance at Mr. Luxmoore's, December 16th, 1873, published in the *Revue Spirite*, of Paris, an account of it, which was translated by Dr. G. L. Ditson, from whose version I quote most of the following:

"The gauze curtain of the cabinet was agitated, and a naked arm was thrust forth and made a sign. Then the right side of the hanging was opened, giving us a view of an apparition of ravishing beauty. She stood erect; the right arm was across her breast, the other fell at her side, holding the curtain. She seemed to review the persons present. It was the spirit of Katie, a thousand times more lovely than her photograph.

"I had before me a young lady of an ideal beauty, supple, elegant, and clad in most graceful drapery, with chestnut locks visible through her white veil. Her robe, trailing like that of an antique statue, entirely covered her naked feet. Her arms, of surpassing beauty, delicate, white, were visible to the shoulders. Their attachment to the body was finely statuesque; and the hands, a little large, had long, tapering fingers, rosy to the ends.

"Her face was pale and rather round than oval. Her mouth, smiling, showed beautiful teeth. Her nose was aquiline; her eyes were very large and blue, almond-shaped, shaded by long, heavy eyelashes, and having eyebrows delicately arched. And, to conclude, there was in this apparition the grace of a Psyche descended from her pedestal.

"Yet this rare feminine embodiment, this faithful reproduction of one many years dead, was soon to evaporate and disappear like a breath! One might mistake her, seen from a distance, for Miss Cook; but the apparition was large, with slender waist, while Miss Cook, though pretty, is much smaller, and her hands are not as large as Katie's. There could be no mistake: they were two distinct personalities.

"The apparition seemed to regard me with curiosity, and I saw in her something that reminded me of a spectre, and that was the eye. It was as beautiful as possible, yet it had a haggard, fixed, glassy expression; but in spite of that, with mouth smiling, with bosom heaving, she seemed to say, 'I am happy to be a moment among mortals.' She then remarked, in a sort of tremulous whisper, but with infinite grace, 'I cannot yet go far away from my medium, but soon I shall have more force.' When she was not fully understood, she repeated her words with infantile impatience.

"I asked to be favored with a sight of her foot; she gracefully raised her robe to comply with my request, and, when being solicited to show more of it, the robe was lifted to the ankle, and I saw a delicate foot, like that of an antique statue, white, plump, lovely as a child's, high and arched, the toes finely attached, and of a purity of design irreproachable; but all this *ensemble* was as if of one piece, and the real life was wanting.

"Katie King talked, laughed, chatted pleasantly with those present, calling each one by name with a roguish, infantile, defiant vivacity; gesticulating with her right hand as do the women of the Orient, with the movement of the fingers and curvature of the hand peculiar to that people; accenting her words with the most gracious movement of her head; often with gentle modesty gathering her veil about her neck; in a word, in everything, in her features, form, costume, gestures, giving an impression of the women of the Levant that could not be mistaken.

"A man of little intelligence, who was present, having addressed some rude words to Katie, she crumpled some paper in her hand, and threw it at him with an expression of disdain."

As an evidence of the spirit's clairvoyant powers, Prince Wittsgenstein sends the following to the London Spiritualist of July 10th, 1874, in a letter from Nieder Walluf, on the Rhine:

"A very striking fact, in direct writing, was recently obtained by Miss Cook, at my request, putting my sealed letter at night on her dressing table, with some pencils and sheets of paper near it. The letter, closely sealed by me, was further put into a second envelope by Mr. William Crookes, who also sealed it several times with his private signet.

"When it was sent back to me with Katie's answer, his seals, as well as mine, were quite intact.

"Katie copied the contents of my sealed letter to her, word for word, without a mistake or omission, on a separate sheet of paper. She also wrote an answer to me, with the following postscript:

"'I have given a copy of your letter, dear friend, to show you I have really read it. I must trust to your good nature to excuse any errors, as I have never done anything like this before.—A. Morgan, or Katie King.'"

Dr. George Sexton was for many years one of the most earnest of the secularist teachers, and an energetic lecturer against Spiritualism and all other forms of belief in a future life. After fifteen years of skepticism, during which, however, he did not disdain to investigate, the needful evidence came. In his own house, in the absence of all mediums other than those members of his own family and intimate private friends in whom mediumistic powers became developed, he got evidence of an irresistible character that the communications came from deceased friends and relatives.

Dr. Sexton's first attendance on the manifestation through Miss Cook, took place at Mr. Luxmoore's, Nov. 25th, 1873. The usual precautions for the satisfaction of skeptics were taken. Tied as she was, it seemed to him impossible for Miss Cook to remove from her seat more than a few inches. We quote the concluding portion of his testimony:

"The séance commenced, as is usual, with singing. The

lights were turned down, but not so low as to prevent our seeing each other most distinctly, and being eye-witnesses of all that was taking place in the room. The medium speedily became partially entranced, hands were shown at a small aperture at the top of the cabinet, and Katie gave indications of being present. Soon after, the curtain was moved aside, and the full form of the spirit, dressed in white, was distinctly seen by all present.

"Katie requested me to ask her questions, which I did continually for at least half an hour. These questions were mostly of a semi-philosophic character, having reference mainly to the laws and conditions under which spirits assume materialized forms, and such, therefore, as it is very questionable whether a young lady like the medium would have been able to answer. They were all replied to so satisfactorily that more than one well-known and highly-educated Spiritualist present stated that they had obtained information which they had previously often wished for, but could not procure.

"The spirit form came out of the cabinet several times during the evening, and walked about amongst the audience. She showed her feet, which were perfectly naked, and stamped them on the floor to prove that she was not standing on tiptoe, this latter fact being a very important one, seeing that she was at least four inches taller than Miss Cook. Her figure and complexion were almost totally unlike those of the medium. She came across the room to me, patted me on the head, and returned. I then asked her if she would kiss me. She replied she would try to do so. In a few minutes she again crossed over to me, and kissed me on the forehead three or four times. I may here remark that although the sound of the kisses were distinctly heard by all present, and the attitude of the figure seen, I felt no pressure of the lips whatever.

"Toward the end of the séance the spirit requested me to examine the cabinet to see that the medium was still fastened in her chair. Mr. Luxmoore lifted the curtain, and said, 'She is still there, lying down in the corner.' The curtain was then dropped again, and I, being on the opposite side of the room, had, of course, not seen into the cabinet. The spirit immediately inquired, 'Did Dr. Sexton see that?' I replied, 'No, I did not.' 'Then,' she said, 'come and look; I want you to see.'

"I at once crossed over to the cabinet, raised the curtain, and looked in. There I saw Miss Cook, sitting, or rather lying, in a trance on the chair in which she had been fastened, knots, seals, and all intact. The séance continued for something over an hour. I may remark that the spirit in the course of the evening wrote several short notes to persons present. The following was the substance of the one given to me:

'MY DEAR DR. SEXTON—I am pleased you have asked me questions.
'Yours, truly, ANNIE MORGAN.'

"Thus ended one of the most marvelous séances at which it has ever been my good fortune to be present."

Dr. J. M. Gully, from whose letter to myself I have already given an extract, was for many years at the head of the well-known water-cure establishment at Great Malvern, England, and is known to thousands of Americans as a skillful and scientific physician and a thoroughly estimable gentleman. He satisfied himself of the genuineness of the manifestations through Mr. Home, several years ago. The 28th of November, 1873, he was present at Mr. Luxmoore's, at one of Miss Cook's séances, of which he gives the following account:

"The spirit, Katie King, appeared this time dressed in a longer and more flowing white dress than usual, the sleeves reaching to the wrists and bound there, whilst over her head and face a beautifully transparent veil fell, giving to the whole figure an appearance of grace and purity which is not easily conveyed by words.

"The spirit greeted every one in the circle by name; then retired into the dark room, where she was heard moving heavy furniture about, and talking to the medium who was sealed and bound as usual. She then brought a large bowl into the circle and gave it to the hands of a sitter. Afterwards she brought a low chair, or prie-dieu, out of the dark room, and placed it wholly in the circle, sat down upon it, and desired that the sitters should sing, but not loudly, as she would try to join them, which she did with the clear contralto voice which she has several times exhibited. It is impossible to convey the impression of that voice issuing from an inhabitant of the *outre-tombe!*

She then begged that all would join hands in order that she might get all the possible power for what she wished to do, and whilst we, the sitters, did so, she retired for a minute or two to get fresh power from her medium, returned, and then deliberately walked around the entire circle (composed of fourteen persons) and touched each one in turn, some of the ladies on the cheek, the men on the hands; one man she told to put out his hand and she would show him that she could press it, which she did. The circle occupied a great portion of a large-sized drawing-room. She then desired to be questioned, and something like this colloquy took place:

"'Is it possible for you to explain to us what are the powers or forces you employ in materializing and dissolving your form?' '*No, it is not.*' 'Is it electricity, or does it bear any resemblance to it?' '*No; it is all nonsense what they talk about electricity.*' 'But have you no name or mode of conveying it?' '*It is more like will-power than anything else; in fact, it is the will which is at the bottom of the power I exercise.*' 'When you disappear where is it to?' '*Into the medium, giving her back all the vitality I took from her. When I have got very much power from her, if any one of you were to take her suddenly round the waist and try to carry her, you might kill her on the spot: she might suffocate. I can go in and out of her readily, but, understand, I am not her—not her double; they talk a deal of rubbish about doubles; I am myself all the time.'* 'When you dissolve, which part disappears the first, the body or the dress?' '*The body, of course; its material power goes back to her, and then the dress goes into its elements.*' 'Do you think one in the flesh can ever appreciate the powers you use in manifesting?' '*No; you never can.*' 'You speak of being yourself, and not a double of the medium—who were you when in the flesh?' '*I was Annie Morgan.*' 'Were you married?' '*Yes; but do n't talk of that.*' (At this she retired behind the curtain, apparently either hurt or grieved at the question, a state she has exhibited before when questioned about her married life.) She speedily returned, and was asked, 'Have you a husband now?' '*Of course I have.*' 'Can you give us any idea under what reign you lived?' '*I left the body when I was twenty-one years old, and I lived in the latter part of the reign of Charles I., during the Commonwealth, and to the early part of the reign of Charles II. I remember the high peaked hats of the Commonwealth and the broad hats of Charles I. and II.; the short hair of the men, but Cromwell's was not short.*'"

"At this point the time which had been agreed on as the utmost that could be given, having the health of the medium in regard, was reached, and, although the spirit expressed a desire to remain longer, she retired on Mr. Luxmoore's insisting on it, and the séance terminated.

"It is not always, nor even often, that the spirit Katie is in the humor to give us information of her present and past history, such as the above, and it has occurred to me that she declines it because she has been accustomed—too much, in my opinion—to jokes, and what might be called '*chaffing*' from the circle, and this probably is more to the taste of a spirit who, as she has herself stated, is not by any means in a highly spiritual sphere. But this may be mere speculation on my part."

Notwithstanding the confidence of these and many other intelligent parties in the genuineness of the manifestations through Miss Cook, the phenomena were so extraordinary that doubt, even among confirmed Spiritualists, would frequently be excited. That a spirit, palpably materialized or reincarnated, could come into the presence of mortals, that she should be undistinguishable in appearance from a human being, that she should allow herself to be touched, write letters before the spectators, converse fluently and audibly, and, in fact, show all the traits of an average and somewhat petulant young woman, and then disappear at once, on reëntering the cabinet, naturally awakened an amazement akin to distrust.

Although the faces of Miss Cook and Katie were much alike, it was found, on close examination, that there were marked differences, varying in degree at different times. The hair of the two was decidedly unlike; that of Miss Cook being dark, and that of the spirit of a light auburn or brown. That the hair of the latter was not false was proved by tracing it back to the scalp. This was done by Prof. Crookes, and also by Mrs. Florence Marryat Ross-Church. Specimens of the spirit hair have been subjected to the microscope, and found to be genuine *hair*, though rather coarse for a woman. The spirit-form was repeatedly measured and found to be, in its bare feet, taller by from two to four inches than Miss Cook. Other points of difference were noticed; but it is unnecessary to dwell upon them here, inasmuch as the distinctive individuality of Miss Cook and Katie was subsequently proved by irresistible tests.

Mr. Coleman suggested the theory that Katie was the double, or, as the Germans call it, the *doppelganger*, of the medium; but he was soon led by Professor Crookes's decisive experiments to abandon the idea.

While even among Spiritualists the element of skepticism was thus at work, an incident occurred at a séance at Mr. Luxmoore's, December 9th, 1874, which seemed to be, for the moment, a triumph of the skeptics. In violation of the conditions of the séance, Mr. Volckman rose from his seat and attempted to seize the supposed spirit. She glided from his grasp, however, and Miss Cook was soon afterwards found tied as she had been left.

This occurrence served only to confirm belief in the genuineness of the phenomena, for it drew forth testimonials from many in behalf of the reliability of the medium. Mr. Henry Dunphy, a barrister, and well known man of letters, who was present at the attempt, published in the February number of London Society (1874) an account, from which we quote the following:

"I was seated between Lady Caithness and Mr. Blackburn, holding a hand of each. The apparition appeared several times and came out into the centre of the room. It was arrayed in a long white dress with a double skirt, had naked feet, and wore a veil over the head and falling down below the waist. Count de Pomar asked whether he might approach it; and, having obtained permission, left the circle and walked straight up to it. Katie held out her hand, which he took, and subsequently returned to his seat.

"The apparition then advanced to the portion of the room farthest from the cabinet, when a person, who to me was a perfect stranger, jumped up, caught the figure round the waist, and held it, exclaiming 'It is the medium!' Two or three gentlemen present rushed forward and caught him, and a struggle ensued. I watched the result with considerable interest, and observed that the figure appeared to lose its feet and legs, and to elude the grasp, making for that purpose a movement somewhat similar to that of a seal in the water. Although the person who made the attempt was apparently well able to hold on to anything he might happen to clutch, the apparition glided out of his grip, leaving no trace of corporeal existence, or surroundings in the shape of clothing."

Mr. George Henry Tapp, of the Dalston Association of Inquirers, added his testimony to that of others on this occasion, and threw light on some mooted questions. He says that the points of difference between Katie and the medium were often remarkable, not only in regard to features, but as regards height, bulk, &c. The resemblance between the two was at times hardly perceptible. When he first saw the full form of Katie she stood five feet six inches high, with her naked feet flat on the floor. She was stout and broad across the waist and shoulders, quite a contrast to her medium, who was much shorter and *petite* in person.

Katie has frequently stood by Mr. Tapp, and leaned against him at séances for several minutes together, permitting him to thoroughly scan her face and figure in a good light. Once she laid her right arm in his outstretched hands, and allowed him to examine it closely. It was plump and shapely, longer than that of the medium. The hands, too, were much larger, with beautifully shaped nails, unlike those of Miss Cook, who was in the bad habit of biting her nails.

Holding the arm of Katie lightly in one hand he passed his other hand along it from the shoulder. "The skin," he says, "was beautifully—I may say, unnaturally—smooth, like wax or marble; yet the temperature was that of the healthy human body. *There was, however, no bone in the wrist.* I lightly felt round the wrist again, and then told Katie that the bone was wanting. She laughed, and said, 'Wait a bit,' and after going about to the other sitters, came round and placed her arm in my hand as before."

This time Mr. Tapp was satisfied. Sure enough, *the bone was there.*

In two instances he saw Katie with long ringlets reaching to her waist, the hair being of a light brown color; while the medium's hair was cut short, and was not curled, its color being a very dark brown, almost black. Katie's eyes were sometimes a light blue color, sometimes dark brown; and this difference was frequently noticed.

On one occasion Katie, on coming out of the cabinet, held up her right arm, which was of a dusky black color. Letting it fall by her side, and raising it again almost instantaneously, it was the usual flesh color like the other arm.

One evening Mr. Tapp made some jesting remark to Katie, when she suddenly struck him heavily in the chest with her clenched fist. He was startled, and, indeed, hurt by the unexpected blow; so much so, that he inadvertently caught hold of her right arm by the wrist.

"Her wrist," he says, "crumpled in my grasp *like a piece of paper, or thin cardboard, my fingers meeting through it.* I let go at once, and expressed my regret that I had forgotten the conditions, fearing that harm to the medium might ensue; but Katie reässured me, saying, that as my act was not intentional, she could avert any untoward result."

In conclusion Mr. Tapp bears the fullest testimony to the good faith and integrity of Miss Cook and her family.

That some abnormal power was at work in the manifestations through Miss Cook, no intelligent investigator seems to have denied. Katie would not be gone more than forty seconds at most from the circle, when the curtain of the cabinet would be drawn, and Miss Cook would be found waking from her trance. It was manifestly a physical impossibility for her to have changed her gown, put on her boots, dressed her hair and altered the color of it, and, in addition to all this, destroyed all trace of the "spirit's" flowing white robes, in less than a minute.

The question, therefore, reduced itself to this: Does the mysterious *force* do all these things, after having thrust forth the entranced medium to play the part of a spirit? What remained now to do in this investigation, was to establish still more conclusively, and by scientific tests, the separate identity of the two forms.

CHAPTER V.

Early in the year 1874, Prof. William Crookes, F. R. S., a well-known chemist, discoverer of the metal *thalium*, author of several esteemed scientific works, and editor of the Quarterly Journal of Science, undertook the investigation of the phenomena through Miss Cook.

In a letter dated 20, Mornington-road, London, Feb. 3d, 1874, Mr. Crookes writes: "Miss Cook is now devoting herself exclusively to a series of private séances with me and one or two friends. The séances will probably extend over some months, and I am promised that every desirable test shall be given to me. . . . Enough has taken place to thoroughly convince me of the perfect truth and honesty of Miss Cook."

Mr. Crookes began his investigations of Spiritualism as early as 1869. He endeavored to study the subject in its scientific aspect solely, without any bias from its sentimental or theological bearings. Under date of Dec., 1871, he says: "I wish to ascertain the laws governing the appearance of very remarkable phenomena, which, at the present time, are occurring to an almost incredible extent. That a hitherto unrecognized form of force—whether it be called psychic force or *x* force is of little consequence—is involved in this occurrence, is not with me a matter of opinion, but of absolute knowledge; but the nature of that force, or the cause which immediately excites its activity, forms a subject on which I do not at present feel competent to offer an opinion."

On the 6th of January, 1869, the London Dialectical Society appointed a committee to investigate the phenomena. Five-sixths of the members of it entered on their duties in the full conviction that they should detect a fraud, or dissipate a delusion.

The theories of self-delusion and imposture were soon dismissed by the committee as out of the question. The motions and sounds were undoubtedly real, and were certainly not caused by any trickery.

The committees' third and last explanatory conjecture, that, namely, of unconscious muscular action, which they had eagerly accepted on the authority of Faraday, they were compelled reluctantly to abandon, and to admit that there is a force, independent of muscular force, producing motion in heavy substances without contact or material connection, of any kind, between such substances and the body of any person present.

This mysterious force was found to be frequently directed by intelligence; and Sub-committee Number One reported unanimously that the one important physical fact thus proved to exist, *that motion may be produced in solid bodies without material contact, by some hitherto unrecognized force operating within an undefined distance from the human organism, and beyond the range of muscular action*, should be subjected to further scientific examination, with a view to ascertain its true source, nature and power.

Mr. Crookes constructed an ingenious apparatus, whereby not only could the existence of any force be demonstrated by delicate tests, but the amount and direction of it measured with perfect accuracy. Prof. Hare, of Philadelphia, and Dr. J. R. Nichols, a Boston chemist, had long before satisfied themselves, by similar tests, of the reality and independence of the force.

In his London Quarterly Journal of Science for January, 1874, Mr. Crookes published the result of further investigations, from which it would appear that he had made great progress. The occurrences to which he here testifies took place mostly in his own house, in the light, and with only private friends present besides the medium. He classifies some of the phenomena of which he became assured under the following heads:

1. The movement of heavy bodies with contact, but without mechanical exertion; 2. The phenomena of percussive and other allied sounds; 3. The alteration of weight of bodies; 4. Movements of heavy substances when at a distance from the medium; 5. The rising of tables and chairs off the ground without contact with any person; 6. The levitation of human beings; 7. Movement of various small articles without contact with any person; 8. Luminous appearances; 9. The appearance of hands, either self-luminous or visible by ordinary light; 10. Direct writing; 11. Phantom forms and faces; 12. Special instances which seem to point to the agency of an exterior intelligence; 13. Miscellaneous occurrences of a complex character.

The mediums for these phenomena were chiefly Miss Kate Fox and Mr. D. D. Home; and Mr. Crookes took such precautions as place trickery out of the list of possible explanations. Every fact, moreover, which he observed, is corroborated, as he admits, by the records of independent observers at other times and places.

"It will be seen," he says, "that the facts are of the most astounding character, and seem utterly irreconcilable with all known theories of modern science." Having satisfied himself of their *truth*, he saw it would be moral cowardice to withhold his testimony.

Mr. Crookes cautiously abstains from any confident theory in regard to the source of the phenomena. He is not yet prepared, like Mr. Wallace, to accept Spiritualism as the only theory that can cover *all* the facts. At first he was disposed to stop, in company with Serjeant Cox, at the half-way house of Psychic Force, or "*x* force," whatever that may be. We must not complain of him for this, for nearly all earnest investigators have had to tarry at this point for a while.

The theory of Psychic Force is by no means new. It was advocated, under the name of Odic Force, by the late Dr. E. C. Rogers, of Boston, with whom I had many discussions as far back as the year 1852, at which time he published a book on the subject. The theory was subsequently urged by Prof. Mahan and President Samson in America, and by Count Gasparin in France. Under its present name it was put forth by Mr. E. W. Cox, serjeant-at-law, a member of the Dialectical Society, author of a pamphlet entitled "Spiritualism answered by Science," and of an interesting psychological work in two volumes, entitled, "What Am I?"

The term "Psychic Force" may be regarded as a euphemism, useful in lessening the shock which the facts might impart to those who are disaffected by the term Spiritualism. Psychic force, if it means anything, means spiritual force, and the question, bluntly stated, is, whether spirits *out* of the flesh can have and exercise spiritual force as well as spirits *in* the flesh.

Does the medium, under the effect of "unconscious cerebration," send forth from the human organism a troop of visible, materialized forms, that can write, play on instruments, dance, sing, and converse rationally, the medium the while, as in the case of Mrs. Andrews, of Moravia, being herself aware of what is going on, though not that she herself is doing it? Or, are these materialized forms what they by speech declare themselves to be, manifestations by some independent spirit or spirits?

Was it psychic force that enabled Mr. Jencken's infant boy, when not six months old, to write, in the chirography of an adult, intelligible sentences?

Will psychic force explain an occurrence like the following, related by Mr. Henry E. Russell, and published in the London Medium of July 17th, 1874, in a notice of the mediumship of Mr. Charles Edward Williams, of London

"The writer has been often visited by Mr. Williams, and on many occasions when sitting with his family round a *harmonium*, the medium being deeply entranced upon an adjacent couch, and distinctly seen by every one in the room, the writer's father, many years since 'passed on before,' has drawn up a chair from a remote part of the room and joined the members of the circle, talking with them, singing with them, and selecting pieces of music to be played on the instrument. He has knelt down beside the writer's mother, as in prayer, has placed portions of his robes around the shoulders of some, and has drawn back their heads so as to lean on his breast, and stooping down kissed each of them before floating up to the ceiling, wishing them good night, and then dematerializing his form, or rather, apparently, vanishing from their sight, the medium at the same time being seen still extended on the couch. On such occasions several recognized spirits have been walking about and talking at the same time."

Truly the psychic force that could accomplish all this must be something more marvelous than the agency of a whole legion of spirits.

Of Mr. Russell, the witness of this remarkable occurrence, my friend, Benjamin Coleman, writes me, (July 21st, 1874): "Mr. Russell is a very reliable man, and the postmaster of Kingston, near Richmond."

The theory of a force unconsciously exercised by the medium, and producing *all* the various phenomena, is based only on a portion of the admitted facts. The higher phenomena, manifested in the actual appearance and tangibility of spirit forms, and the preterhuman rapidity of spirit action, are not included in the synthesis on which the theory is built. The best answer to this theory may be found in the facts to which I shall soon return.

Before I do this, however, let us consider what light, if any, Spiritualism throws on the great question of the ages, What is meant by *spirit*, and what by *matter?*

By *substance*, in metaphysics, is meant, not the equivalent of matter, but that which stands under phenomena. It is the fundamental fact of all existence. Spinoza defines it as self-existence; Leibnitz, as an active force like that of the strained bow; while Berkeley ironically tells us that it is the tortoise that supports the elephant that supports the world. We can never know it, for we know only phenomena, which are its appearances.

CHAPTER VI.

"What do you mean by spirit?" is the question with which the sanguine Spiritualist is often checked.

To reply intelligently he ought to know something of the efforts of human thought to throw light on the problem; but this knowledge can be had only by patient attention to certain results of philosophical speculation. These I will endeavor to present as briefly as possible; but the reader, if not in a mood for meditation, will do well to postpone their consideration for a more convenient moment.

Man has been described variously as a trinity, a duality, and a unity of two parts, physical and psychical.

Are there two substances?

"The arguments for the two substances," says Alexander Bain (1873), "have, we believe, lost their validity; they are no longer compatible with ascertained science and clear thinking."

This sweeping declaration is by no means admitted by many of the profoundest thinkers of the age.

Are there, then, simply degrees of one and the same substance? Or, are matter and spirit distinct entities?

The question is at the bottom of nearly all the controversies in philosophy and theology that have vexed human brains the last two centuries; and from the solutions, arrived at by different minds, emerges either Theism or Pantheism.

According to Mr. Herbert Spencer, the disputants on both sides are "equally absurd;" for they are both trying to fathom the "unknowable."

But one ought to know a good deal to have a right to say that.

My present object is to learn how far the question is affected by the facts of Spiritualism. Do we get from that quarter any new light?

Is immateriality a necessary quality of spirit? Locke says it is *not;* that the thinking substance in us, whether matter or not matter, is a spirit. This was the notion of the ancients, and is still the belief of uncivilized men. To their conceptions, naught is immaterial but what is naught.

By *soul*, and its correlative words in other languages, has been understood, generally, *the spirit while animating a human body*, and by *spirit*, the same soul as it is after that body's dissolution. But the use of the words is arbitrary and far from uniform.

Cicero and Virgil regard the soul as a subtile matter which might come under the name of *aura* (breeze), or *ignis* (fire), or *æther*, and this soul they both of them called *spiritus* (a breathing). In the Bible we find the same conception of spirit; though, that sometimes the scriptural use of the word will bear the interpretation of immateriality, is not denied.

Immortality is taken for granted, both in the Old Testament and in the language of Christ. Warburton's speculations to the contrary are now regarded as worthless. Belief in immortality entered into all the science, customs, actions and thoughts of the Egyptians. Could Moses, brought up in the palace of the Pharaohs, could the Israelites, so long dwellers in the land, have escaped the influence of the belief? Not only historical induction, but the text itself, refutes the supposition.

Repeatedly we find it prohibited in the Pentateuch to evoke the dead. In the Book of Samuel, the Witch of Endor calls up the shade of the prophet. Belief in spirits is equally implied in all the accounts of visions, spirit writings, hands and voices, apparitions, levitations, ascensions, and other preterhuman phenomena, so like those of Modern Spiritualism, throughout the Bible. Even Job, who often speaks as if the future life were left out of his calculations, has a spirit pass before his face, and hears a spirit voice.

Spiritualism does not use the terms *spirit* and *soul* as having only a negative meaning; as merely implying non-corporeity. Tertullian gives an account of a female medium who described a soul as corporeally exhibited to her view, and as being "tender and lucid, and of aerial color, and every way of human form."

Others, both seers and theologians, among the ancients, regarded man as a trinity of earth-body, spirit-body and spirit.

The Spiritualism of many of the early Christian Fathers seems to have been a sort of Organicism, explaining life by the properties of organs, and regarding matter, once organized, as sufficient to explain all the phenomena of man, whether we consider him as existing in the natural or in the spiritual body.

The primary conception of spirit seems to have been that of an attenuation of matter. Men must have become early aware that there are certain invisible essences of things. If wine is subjected to a boiling temperature, there is a separation of elements; but the finer part, disengaging itself from the grosser, may not be distinguished by all the senses until, by the aid of a distilling apparatus, the escaping spirit is liquefied and made visible.

Thus, the earliest conceptions of the relations of body and soul amounted to a sort of double materialism. Among primitive and uncivilized races this notion is universally prevalent. (See Tylor's "Primitive Culture," *passim*). We find it common when we go back as far as history and tradition extend. It was the belief of the Assyrians, the Babylonians, the Medes, and the early Christians, as it is now of the North American Indian, the Australian, the Hottentot and the Esquimaux. To its prevalence, all the traditions, all the religions, and all the narratives of navigators testify conclusively.

Among the Christian Fathers the conception of a soul-body, involved, larva-like, in the earth-body—a conception simple, obvious and aboriginal—was generally held up to the time of Gregory of Nyssa (331–394) and of Augustine (354–430). Before this, neither from Judaism nor from Christianity had the doctrine of immateriality received much countenance.

Even Augustine, embarrassed to decide how the immaterial soul can act on the dense matter of the body in producing movement, postulated a subtle corporeal substance, equivalent to a soul-body, which, as intermediate, may be affected and put in action by the mind.

Tertullian argues that what is bodiless is nothing; he predicates corporeity of Deity itself. The modern Christian notion that the soul is perfectly simple, incorporeal, and immaterial, was unknown to the early church.

It was not till Descartes (1640) taught the dogma of the immateriality of the soul, that it began to supersede the common belief. "To the best of my knowledge," says Coleridge, "Descartes was the first philosopher who introduced the absolute and essential heterogeneity of the soul as intelligence, and the body as matter."

"It is manifest," says Hallam, "to any one who has read the correspondence of Descartes, that the tenet of the soul's immateriality, instead of being general, as we are apt to presume, was by no means in accordance with the common opinion of his age."

And Descartes, let it be noted, in the effort to be consistent with his philosophy, made the declaration, still acquiesced in by many "Orthodox" teachers, but rejected totally by Spiritualism, that *there are no valid proofs of the soul's immortality except those founded on revelation.*

Spinoza, (1665,) who was largely under the influence of Descartes, having identified mind and matter, God and the universe, seems to have regarded the phenomenal facts of witchcraft, somnambulism and Spiritualism, as fatal to his Pantheistic system; and so he repudiated them all.

The soul, according to Spinoza, is nothing but a conscious body, and the body nothing but a soul having extension.

In his dread of dualism he rejects the positive facts, indicating pretermundane power, which were well known to many of his contemporaries. He might have admitted them, and still clung to his theory of a single substance, if the Cartesian notion of the soul's immateriality had not driven out of his head the double materialism of the early Christians. For there may be grades of matter, and still a single substance. But he strove to make everything tally unequivocally with his Pantheistic scheme.

Body and soul being, in his system, identical in substance, we may understand how they should be united in the terrestrial life, but how the soul, bodiless and unsubstantial, and parted from the one only substance, is going to get along any better under "the aspect of eternity" than under "the aspect of time," he does not make clear to us; nor does he explain why, the substance being one, death should not destroy soul as well as body.

In Spinoza's scheme the departed soul is indeed poorly off. The senses, the imagination, the human affections, all become annihilated with the death of the body. Reason only remains; there is light, but no warmth; intellect, but no love.

Thus, by depriving us, at death, of all that we have acquired, through the senses, during the earth-life, Spinoza virtually destroys our individuality, and leaves the soul, after separation from the body, equivalent, as Emile Saisset remarks, to "little more than a naked syllogism."

In failing to see that there may be, though impenetrable to sense, a duplicate and permanent ground of being in man, in which memory, affection and all knowledge may organically inhere, Spinoza was obliged to strip man of all those constituents essential to a conscious immortality. A glimpse of the spiritual body beyond the material would have saved him from many inconsistencies.

Among Spinoza's letters are several that passed between himself and a Spiritualist, though not a very enlightened one, of his day. To the phenomenal facts adduced by the latter, Spinoza replies petulantly: "I am indeed confounded to discover men of parts and ingenuity misusing their powers in attempts to persuade mankind of the truth of such absurdities."

Here Spinoza loses his temper, and scolds like a Cambridge professor at the thought of a spiritual manifestation.

"Had I only," he writes, "as clear a conception of a spectre as I have of a triangle or a circle, I should not hesitate to acknowledge that it was created by God."

To this his correspondent replies with some point: "Tell me, I entreat you, whether you have as clear an idea of a God as of a triangle?"

And Spinoza's answer is: "Yes; but if you ask whether I can form an image or picture of God as clear as that I form of a triangle, I answer No. For we cannot picture God to ourselves, but we can verily understand him."

This is a subterfuge unworthy of the great Spinoza; but with all his hair-splitting he does not parry the thrust of his correspondent. The latter, when pressed to explain his conception of a spectre, might have replied in words very like those of Spinoza himself, when qualifying his remark in regard to his conception of God. The retort would have been perfectly apt.

But let it be remembered that Spiritualism, in Spinoza's day, had to bear the burden of many gross superstitions, evident in the burning of witches and the prevailing *demonphobia;* and it is not surprising that, in his contempt for such wrongs and such cowardice, he should have undervalued and gradually taught himself to discredit the phenomena on which the belief in the agency of spirits was founded.

I come back to the great discussion stigmatized by Spencer as "absurd."

If the question is put, "What do you mean by spirit?" the obvious retort is, "What do you mean by matter?"

Materialism regards matter as the first and only existence, and mind as one of its modes or properties, like heat, electricity, or chemical action.

Idealism regards mind as the first and only existence, having matter for one of its modes; the conception of matter being only a mental synthesis of qualities.

Realism denounces the Idealist's notion of the non-reality of matter. "Metaphysics, in all its anti-realistic developments," says Herbert Spencer, "is a disease of language."

Even Helmholtz, the great German scientist, who criticises the human eye as a very bad piece of work, which he should have sent back for alteration if it had been produced by a human artificer, tells us that our senses report aright, and that things are what they appear; all which, considering the low character of the Maker in Helmholtz's estimation, would seem to be somewhat contradictory.

On the contrary, Plato, Plotinus, Kant, Hamilton, and other profound philosophical thinkers, tell us that we cannot know things in themselves; we can perceive only the appearances of things.

Mr. Spencer says that these great men did not believe their own speculations. Perhaps not; and yet there may have been some truth in them. We may be often wiser than we know.

The stupendous phenomena of Modern Spiritualism make us pause, and ask once more: What, then, is this mystery called matter?

All the conceptions of matter we get through the senses are modified, if not contradicted, by some of the well-attested proofs of spirit-power.

The materialized figure of Katie has been known to disappear instantly on reëntering the cabinet where Miss Cook was lying entranced.

In describing the remarkable phenomena through Mrs Anna Stewart at Terre Haute, Ind., Mr. Theodore F. Price of Monson, Ind., under date of March 4th, 1875, writes: "The doors of the cabinet were thrown open, and the spirit appeared holding the medium by the hand. Both spirit and medium advanced from the cabinet, now vacated by all things visible save the chair in which the medium previous to this had been seated. Said the spirit: 'Can you now all see the medium, and distinguish us both clearly? Are you all satisfied now that there is no deception about this?' Both spirit and medium remained standing in front of the cabinet for some minutes, the former asking that all should closely scrutinize the features of each." The light on this occasion was "clear and satisfying."

The spirit Florence that came through Miss Showers, at Mr. Luxmoore's house, in London, April 11th, 1874, dematerialized herself and her white robes almost instantly, so as to be invisible, and this three times in quick succession.

Mr. Alfred R. Wallace, in his "Defence of Spiritualism," gives the following account of some of the phenomena through Miss Nichol (afterwards Mrs. Guppy):

"The most remarkable feature of this lady's mediumship is the production of flowers and fruits in closed rooms. The first time this occurred was at my own house, at a very early stage of her development. All present were my own friends. Miss Nichol had come early to tea, it being mid-winter, and she had been with us in a very warm, gas-lighted room four hours before the flowers appeared. The essential fact is, that upon a bare table, in a small room closed and dark (the adjoining room and passage being well lighted), a quantity of flowers appeared, which were not there when we put out the gas a few minutes before. They consisted of anemones, tulips, chrysanthemums, Chinese primroses, and several ferns. All were absolutely fresh, as if just gathered from a conservatory. They were covered with a fine, cold dew. Not a petal was crumpled or broken, not the most delicate point or pinnule of the ferns was out of place. I dried and preserved the whole, and have, attached to them, the attestation of all present that they had no share, so far as they know, in bringing the flowers into the room. I believed at the time, and still believe, that it was absolutely impossible for Miss N. to have concealed them so long, to have kept them so perfect, and, above all, to produce them covered throughout with a most beautiful coating of dew, just like that which collects on the outside of a tumbler when filled with very cold water on a hot day."

At a meeting of the Marylebone Association of Inquirers into Spiritualism, in London, March 18th, 1874, Mr. Thomas Everitt said that he had known *as many as nine hundred and thirty-six words* to be written in a second by spirit-power. A pencil was used in this work; and that the writing was not done by some process analogous to lithography was rendered probable by several specified tests.

The flowing white robes of the spirit Katie would disappear instantly with the spirit-form, and yet, as we have learnt, she cut strips from her tunic and distributed them, and these have remained materialized, though the cut places were instantly made whole by the spirit.

Not only have inanimate objects been brought through

walls and ceilings into closed rooms, but living things. In the London Medium (Dec. 30th, 1870), a case is mentioned in which a dog and a cat were brought from Mrs. Guppy's house by the spirits, a distance of two or three miles. The names of eight witnesses to the occurrence are given.

The floating of the human body in the air has been a very common phenomenon. Dr. Davies narrated, at one of the Harley street meetings, in London, how he felt Mr. Home all over, while he was floating about in a semi-darkened room. Mr. E. B. Tylor (author of Primitive Culture), gave, in a lecture at the Royal Institution (1871), several instances of statements in historical records, that certain of the early fathers of the church were very often floated in the air. While holding the hand of a medium, in the dark, I have myself known her to be lifted in her chair and placed on the table. In the London Spiritualist (June 15th, 1871), will be found an account of a sitting at which Mr. Herne was floated in the air *in the light.*

Spirit music, in the absence of all human instruments, has been heard, not only by mediums, but by several persons at once, who were in their normal state.

Solid objects have been introduced in some unaccountable manner. "I have been present," says Mr. W. H. Harrison, "often in broad daylight, with Messrs. Herne and Williams, when solid objects, such as books and flowers, have fallen on us from above, where nothing but the whitewashed ceiling was to be seen."

Spirit photography, though genuine specimens are easily imitated, is now an admitted fact. I have received a remarkable photograph got by Mr. John Beattie, a retired photographer of Clifton, England. He had his own plates and apparatus, and superintended the whole process himself. A medium present would describe the form of the spiritual presence, and then the photographic impression would confirm the report. The figure in my copy, though almost grotesque, is yet human in its features, and sufficiently distinguishable. Mr. Alfred R. Wallace gives his testimony explicitly to the reality of spirit-photography. Lady Caithness, whom I knew in London, vouches (July 24th, 1874) for five recognizable spirit-photographs she and her son got through Buguet, the Parisian, to whom they went perfect strangers. Buguet took too many genuine spirit-photographs in London to leave it doubtful that he was a medium. Unfortunately he was tempted by want of money to supplement with fraud his insufficient and variable medial power, and subsequently, on being arrested in Paris, to abjure his mediumship. Once safe in Brussels, he addressed a letter (Sept. 27th, 1875) to the French Minister of Justice, confessing his apostasy.

In a letter from Florence, Italy, April 4th, 1872, to Professor Crookes, Baron Seymour Kirkup, an honorable man and sincere student of Spiritualism (see Hawthorne's account of him), relates that on a certain occasion he asked Annina Carboni, a spirit, to take a letter to her sister, Teresa, still in the earth-life, and residing at Leghorn. Paolina Carboni, another sister, was the medium. The Baron made a sketch of the letter, and Paolina copied it. In this letter Teresa is told to note the *exact minute* of its arrival, and to mention in her answer the exact time of sending it. "When Paolina," says the Baron, "had finished her letter, she went away, and I shut the door and remained alone. I folded the half sheet, and placed it at 6 P. M. on the piano, unsealed, and without an envelope. I watched it, expecting to see it go; but after two minutes, finding that it remained, I took a book, and after two minutes more I looked, and the note was gone. The door remained shut, and no one entered the room. At eight minutes past seven came three loud raps on the sofa. I went to the piano, to see—nothing. I returned to the table, and there on my book was a little triangular note, like Paolina's. It was a punctual answer to it, and I called Paolina to read it. The spirit had made two journeys of sixty miles each, besides waiting for the writing of the answer (fifteen lines), in the short time of one hour and fifteen minutes. As I remained on purpose totally alone, there could be no trick, no smuggling a prepared letter. . . . Another witness of my dear

Annina's exploit, is her mother, wife of a former English vice-consul at Rome. She has just come from Leghorn, where she was present when her daughter Teresa received and answered the letter of Paolina."

Subsequently to this, Baron Kirkup received still more striking evidences of the speed of the actual transmission of real, objective letters, to great distances, by spirit power.

The venerable S. C. Hall, honorably known in English literature, referring to the mediumship of Mr. D. D. Home, writes (1871): "I have held an accordion (my own property) in my hand, when delicious music was played on it, lasting several minutes. It has been taken from me, and carried to the end of a large room, playing there; I saw the stops moving and heard the music: I could only not see the power that produced the sounds. . . . Since this was written I have seen a hand moving the accordion up and down, and another hand acting on the stops. Two other gentlemen saw these hands also. The room was well lit. . . . I have seen a man (Mr. Home) taken from his seat by some power invisible, and conveyed about the room; and he has marked on the ceiling with a pencil, a mark that is still there. A red-hot blazing coal has been taken from a fierce fire, and placed (by Home) on my head, without singeing a single hair. I have seen nearly a hundred flowers — among them two large bunches of apple-blossom—thrown on my table; the medium, a lady (Miss Nichol), having been previously examined by two ladies on entering my house. I have repeatedly grasped a spirit-hand. I have seen lights that seemed phosphoric, to the number of, it may be twenty, at once, floating in all parts of a room. I have seen a heavy table floated to the ceiling. A grand piano has been raised from the floor, no visible person being within two yards of it. I have seen a hand-bell raised by a shadowy hand, and rung over the head of each person in the circle."

Mr. W. H. Harrison relates that on one occasion Katie, in the dark, gave the persons present something to feel, saying, "That is what we make the faces of. Do not pinch it." It felt like a piece of damp wash-leather. Next she said: "Feel this; it is true spirit drapery." The texture was certainly remarkable. As it was drawn over the fingers it felt as light and fragile as a spider's web; fine silk would be coarse and heavy in comparison. "Now feel it materialized," said Katie, and it felt like the heavy white drapery which ordinarily adorns the spirit heads.

But I need only refer to the facts I have already given in the narrative parts of this work, of the materialization and dematerialization of hands and entire human forms; of the extemporaneous production of appropriate clothing, ornaments, flowers, etc.; the passage of articles through solid matter; the production of drawings and writings with inconceivable swiftness, the motions literally equaling the quickness of thought; the apparent mastery of all material impediments.

It may be inferred from these phenomena that matter is to spirits something very different from what it is to mortals in the flesh; that our knowledge of it is, as the highest philosophy often asserts, simply relative and phenomenal; that a change in our organs of sense and perception would make matter other than what it now appears to us.

Leibnitz concluded that space is not something real, but only a subjective representation. Kant teaches that space and time are forms of our sensibility, pure intuitions, and have no corresponding objective reality. De Remusat, J. S. Mill, Bain, and others, believe that extension is a conception derived from our muscular sensibility.

These views, so astounding and even absurd to thinkers who have not yet risen into this rarefied air of speculation, accord with the teachings professedly got from personal communion with spirits by Swedenborg, the great Swedish medium and seer. But Swedenborg further teaches that the only possible existence, the sole ground of consciousness, for finite and derivative beings, must be phenomenal.

Mr. Herbert Spencer thinks that the experience hypothesis better explains the genesis of our conceptions of space and time. Whatever may be the genesis, the fact of their *relativity* may be realized by a few simple considerations :*

Suppose that while you are unconscious of any change, the whole world and all its contents should become enlarged a hundred times. Imagine the foot measure to be a hundred times longer, and everything increased to correspond.

When consciousness should return, things would appear to you *just as they did before their enlargement.* You would perceive no change. Your senses would be the measure of things as before. The relations and proportions of things would be the same. The whole outer world would be the same ; *how, then, to you can it be said to have any other existence or place than what your sensations and thoughts assign to it?*

If our organs of sensation, with the brain and the nerves, were formed and proportioned otherwise than they are, the whole visible world would not appear as it does now. If our eyes were so formed as to have telescopic and microscopic powers, or if they were as sensitive to impressions as the photographer's prepared plate, the whole creation would assume new aspects. Proximity and distance would affect us very differently ; and spiritual beings might be plainly seen.

A knowledge of optics soon teaches us that the report we get through the senses is often merely relatively correct. Yesterday I looked out of my window at a church steeple, which, in a peculiar light, just before an August sunset, and while a thunderstorm was brooding in a background of ebon cloud, appeared of a pure, snowy white. My wife and her brother looked also at the steeple, and it appeared a pure white to them ; and yet we all knew it was of a rather dark drab color.

Ever to the senses the limitations of the seeming are the end of all things. We *see* nothing leave the body at death, and, therefore, we fancy that nothing leaves it. The delusion is an inseparable accompaniment of our finiteness. Thus all human systems are necessarily imperfect. We can only make approximations to the truth.

---

* For a fuller illustration of the fact, see an excellent little work entitled "The Infinite and the Finite," by Theophilus Parsons. Boston: 1873.

CHAPTER VII.

Only He who can see all things in the universe at once can see any one thing in its true relations and, therefore, in the light of absolute truth, and as it actually is.

But because we do not see things as a Supreme Power may see them, or as spirits may partially see them, it does not follow that we do not see them aright under the limitations and relations to which we are here subjected, and so far as our external senses can aid us. Our mistake lies in supposing that these senses teach us all; that their report is a finality; whereas there are supersensual faculties in man, as indicated in the phenomena of somnambulism, clairvoyance, prevision, mediumship; and it is the business of man's aspiring intelligence to acquaint himself with these faculties, to study and interpret their revelations.

Thus one purpose of our subjection here to these limitations of sense and matter may be in order that, by our own efforts, we may rise above them into a higher atmosphere of truth. This discipline may be necessary to the growth of our spiritual and thinking faculties, since life without thought is a rudimental stage.

Materialism says truly that it is contrary to sound philosophy to introduce two entities to explain the phenomena of life when one will answer. It asks: As the vibrations of the light produce color, why may not the movements of the molecules of the brain generate thought and consciousness?

To this the Spiritualist may reply: Since we are as ignorant of the substance of matter as we are of that of mind, of course we cannot say that they may not be one and the same substance, supporting two very different sets of properties. Only, if this be so, then must matter have properties directly the reverse of those we usually ascribe to it. Even Hartley admits that it is the same thing whether I suppose that matter has properties and powers unlike those which appear, and superior to them, or whether I suppose an immaterial substance.

Whether we annihilate mind and make matter think, or whether we get rid of matter and substitute ideas, we are in an equal dilemma. The Materialist is as helpless as the Immaterialist or the Spiritualist in respect to the use of words. Materialism mocks at philosophy; but "to mock at philosophy," says Pascal, "what is it but to philosophise?"

Under the facts of Spiritualism we may regard it as still an open question, whether the unknown basis of matter may not be equivalent to the unknown basis of mind. Each may flow into existence from one divine creative substance; but that they result in two exhibitions of power, distinct not only in degree but in kind, and justifying the trichotomy of earth-body, spirit-body, and soul, the facts of this volume tend to show.

"To me," says Mrs. J. H. Conant, the well-known American medium, "the soul is the inner life, the principle eternal with God, a part of God; while the spirit is the covering or body of the soul, the intermediate body acting between the soul and the physical body in this life, and acting for the soul in the other life."

This was substantially the notion of Plato, who regarded terrestrial man as a trinity of soul, soul-body, and earth-body.

Such was the view of many of the early Christian Fathers, including Clement, Tatian, and Origen; and it is taught in the writings of Rivail (1804—1869), who, under the pen-name of Allan Kardec is identified with the history of Modern Spiritualism, and who derived his system from the teachings of spirits.

Andrew Jackson Davis, while he holds that the human spiritual structure is a result wrought out by the physical organization, believes in an uncreated principle of spirit; so that here, too, we have a trinity. The spirit's organism, according to Davis, is substantial and obeys laws, superior, but not antagonistic, to ordinary gravitation and the known physical forces.

Judge Edmonds says: "There is in man the emanation from God in the soul, the animal nature in the body, and the connection of the two in what I will designate as the electrical body. *Hence, man is a trinity.*"

The notion that spirit is merely an efflorescence of matter, that it is nothing until, in the words of Milton, "Body up to spirit work," is not consistent with these teachings, which regard spirit as the higher power, and matter as something which, if not distinct in essence, is at least subordinate, mediate and auxiliary.

In Swedenborg's system man is an organism, fitted by an earth-body to live in this world, and by a spirit-body to live simultaneously in the spirit-world, and vivified by continual influx from the divine creative source. In the dissolution of the earth-body the real man remains unimpaired in his individuality, except that his body and his surroundings are spiritual. Thus in this system, as in the others I have named, terrestrial man has, besides his twofold body, a divine influx, the equivalent of a soul.

"Either all matter," says Alfred R. Wallace, "is conscious, or consciousness is something distinct from matter, and in the latter case," which he claims to be true, "its presence in material forms is a proof of the existence of conscious beings, outside of, and independent of, what we term matter."

Admitting that "what we term matter" may not include all matter—since our senses do not tell us what matter is in itself, but simply what it is to us, constituted as we are—this view will be found not inconsistent with the theories I have named.

There is a skeptical philosophy somewhat active in our day, which would treat the subject of man's destiny as if all notion of causation could be excluded without doing violence to our reason. This school asserts, that for aught that we know to the contrary, anything may produce anything; astonishing phenomena may occur without basis, cause or reason, outside of some antecedent phenomenon; matter may produce mind since there is no need that a cause should be adequate to the production of an effect. "Every objectively real thing," says a writer of this school, "is a term in numberless series of mutual implications, and its reality outside of these series is utterly inconceivable."

But what scientific validity has an hypothesis like this? Does it not simply amount to a declaration that the problem is unsolvable and "unthinkable," and that we must abandon the attempt to meet the mind's legitimate demand for something to explain the derivation of intelligence and other phenomena?

"It is impossible," says the same writer, "to construct matter by a mere synthesis of forces."

But this, and his previous assertion, Spiritualism, by extending, or rather duplicating the realm of causation and introducing new and transcendent facts, consigns to the limbo of exploded dogmas.

Spiritualism gives us proofs of an intelligent Force, exerting itself both centrifugally and centripetally, repelling or attracting what, to our senses, is matter; using this matter as its slave, its toy, its vestment, and its ready instrument; finding in it, whether solid, fluid, or gaseous, no impediment; making it the plastic recipient of astonishing activities that seem to be independent of space and time, and ruled by an understanding will.

"Among the unquestionable rules of scientific method," says Jevons, "is that first law that *whatever phenomenon is, is.* We must ignore no existence whatever; we may variously interpret or explain its meaning and origin, but if a phenomenon does exist, it demands some kind of explanation. If, then, there is to be a competition for scientific recognition, the world without us must yield to the undoubted existence of the spirit within.

"A phenomenon which entirely fails to be explained by any known laws may indicate the interference of some wholly new series of natural forces. Thus the doctrine of the loadstone was anciently thought to contradict the law of gravitation; but there is no breach of that law."

Hence we may see how irrational are the notions of those who say that the law of gravitation is violated when a man is lifted by an unseen force, spiritual, but still natural, to the ceiling of a room. The phenomenon plainly has a cause, and the inquiry, What is that cause? is perfectly legitimate; although certain skeptics, when driven to the wall, reply, "Well, it proves nothing; there are plenty of things quite as mysterious!"

It proves this much at least: The limit which an atheistic Materialism would set up for us is swept away like mist by such a fact, and a new realm of causation is revealed for the exploration of thought. Science can no longer deny the existence of beings and things because they cannot be seen, weighed and measured.

Mr. John Beattie, whose investigations I have already mentioned, is of opinion that "spirit substance" is never photographed. His reasons are, that the spirit has power to attract to itself material envelopes or forms, upon which light may impinge, and which, in some cases of darkness, are self-luminous; that these exteriors only are photographed; that all forms of matter are merely the equivalents of motion-producing force; not compositions of final atoms, but coördinations of forces which may be re-combined or changed into their equivalents; and that thus the most enlightened Materialism must, when it arrives at its last analysis, merge in Spiritualism, and confess that behind all material play there exists the source of all force, namely, Universal Mind.

This last was the opinion of Plato, Plotinus, Bruno, Leibnitz, and many of the greatest thinkers.

The present tendency of science is to confirm their view by proving the unity of all forces and phenomena. But to this subject I shall again return.

"Instead of regarding spirit," says Fernand Papillon, "as a property of matter, we should regard matter as a property of spirit. Materialism is false and imperfect because it stops short at atoms, in which it localizes those properties for which atoms supply no cause, and because it neglects force and spirit, which are the only means we have, constituted as our souls are, of conceiving the activity and the appearings of beings. It is false and imperfect, because it stops half-way, and treats compound and resolvable factors as simple and irreducible ones; and because it professes to represent the world by shows without attempting to explain the production of those shows. . . . The source of differentiations cannot be in energy itself; it must be in a principle apart from that energy, in a superior will and consciousness, of which we have doubtless only a dim and faulty idea, but as to which we can yet affirm that they have some analogy with the inner light which fills us, and which we shed forth from us, and which teaches us, by its mysterious contact with the outer world, the infinite order of the universe."

Science tells us that the microscopic germ which evolves into a human being does not differ from the germ of the nettle, the reptile, or the beast. The chemical constituents are the same: oxygen, hydrogen, nitrogen and carbon, with about four per cent. of other elements.

What, then, causes the one germ to issue in a man and the other in a weed? "An *unknown something*," says Dr. Hitchman, "must be posited in addition to the physiological processes accompanying the phenomena." Since the difference is not in the *material* properties, it must be in what manifests itself as the *psychical;* in something not explained by the word *matter* unless we make that word comprehend what we mean by *spirit.*

Thus the ultimate form is predetermined in the embryo; and this fact harmonizes with the Hegelian doctrine of Nature, which teaches that for every form of existence we may find the motive in that which *apparently* follows. For example, we may say that matter exists as a theatre for life, and life as a manifestation of mind. But that for the sake of which a phenomenon takes place, must be, in truth, though not in appearance, prior to the phenomenon, and, moreover, it must be the substance and the truth of the phenomenon. The *psychical*, then, is the prior, the real, and the substantial; the *physical* is the dependent, the phenomenal and the changing.

St. Paul speaks from *appearances* when he says, "That was not first which is spiritual, but that which is natural." On the contrary, spirit is the senior, the causative and the essential.

"The demonstration," says Mr. G. H. Lewes (1873), "that thinking is a *seriation*, and that a series involves time, disproves the notions of ultimate unity and simplicity applied to a Thinking Principle."

But the facts of clairvoyance shiver this assumption. Not long since a peasant in Germany gave the following test: he would let you grasp a handful of beans from a bag, and then he would tell instantly the exact number in your hand.

The marvelous and instantaneous solution of complicate arithmetical problems by Zerah Colburn and other mathematical "prodigies" cannot be explained by the theory of a seriation of thought, as we mortals understand the word *seriation*.

The hypothesis of a spiritual organism is "untenable," according to Mr. Lewes, because it is the introduction of an *unknown* to take the place of the *knowable*.

But is not this a begging of the question; an assumption, contravened by the facts of Spiritualism; the assumption, namely, that our physical senses must be the measure of our entire organism?

When an inexplicable phenomenon is presented, what says the Materialist? Why, that we do not *know* all the resources and powers of Matter!

I readily admit the suggestion. We will suppose that it is unaided Matter which not only sees, feels, and thinks, but which produces the phenomena of clairvoyance, levitation, independent movement, materialization and dematerialization of forms.

Here, then, is a supposed *particular* matter, expressing itself in phenomena, of which we have no reason to believe that *matter in general* is capable. This *particular* matter, therefore, is truly "unknown" to us, so far as its power to produce the phenomena is concerned. So *unknown* is it, that, in order to distinguish it from matter comparatively *known*, we call it by the name of *spirit*.

Because we do this, it is not correct to say that we introduce an *unknown* to take the place of the *known;* for the matter that can produce the phenomena I have specified is not a matter that is known to us, and we are justified in distinguishing it by the name of *spirit* from the matter that we know.

The question whether this *spirit* is not a higher, subtler, and unknown form or grade of matter is distinct and perfectly legitimate.

But the objections which men of science often raise to the use of the word *spirit* will be found, under a strict analysis, to apply equally to the use of the word *matter*.

The late James F. Ferrier, though an acute metaphysician, used to lose his head when arguing against Spiritualism. In his day (1851) the phenomena had not attained their present development. Of Spiritualists, he says: "Oh, ye miserable mystics! have ye bethought yourselves of the backward and downward course which ye are running into the pit of the bestial and the abhorred?"

These are but wild and whirling words. Ferrier's mistake was in imagining that there is such a chasm between the mortal and the immortal, that spirits are not human still, taking with them the characteristics which constituted their individuality while in the earthly body.

Of matter he says: "It is already in the field as an acknowledged entity. Mind, considered as an independent entity, is not so unmistakably in the field. Therefore, as entities are not to be multiplied without necessity, we are not entitled to postulate a new cause, so long as it is possible to account for the phenomena by a cause already in existence; which possibility has never yet been disproved."

But the matter which sees without material eyes, and hears without material ears, and manifests supersensual knowledge, is *not in the field* as an entity. A simple fact of clairvoyance confutes Ferrier's assumption, and reintroduces the question which he would bar out.

Having a solid basis of facts on which to rest, Spiritualism can well afford to concern itself but little about the metaphysical disputes that have always agitated the human mind as to the nature of matter and spirit; as to whether there are two entities or only one; as to whether there is an underlying substance, apart from inhering qualities, or whether such a substance is a contradiction in thought, and only to be conceived of as inconceivable; as to whether time and space are forms of our sensibility, pure intuitions, or real things; as to whether extension is a conception got from our muscular sensibility, or something as real as it seems to us.

All these high and subtle questions do not affect the one dominant proof of man's continued existence. There are phenomena in abundance, which, if they do not enlighten us as to the nature of matter in itself, at least show that matter has its master in what we are obliged, in the poverty of language, to distinguish by the name of spirit.

One single decisive fact, says Dr. J. R. Buchanan (1873), "illustrating the mind's capacity for action independent of the brain, or its capacity for anything after the dissolution of the body, is worth a whole library of metaphysics."

What spirit is in itself, or in its substance, may remain one of the inscrutable secrets of Nature; but of spiritual power we may know something, just as we may know any natural fact. We know that a spirit can materialize and dematerialize a form, so as to manifest itself objectively to mortals in the flesh; and that it can do many inexplicable things with a celerity that can be only described by the word *magical*, though the process is undoubtedly in strict conformity with natural laws.

To the skeptic's question, "What do you mean by spirit?" we need therefore merely reply: "We mean by it something that we cannot intelligently express by the word *matter*."

Whether this something is simply some unknown matter, or whether its substance is distinct from that of all matter, are questions still open.

That spirit, though it may employ matter, for individualization and manifestation, is essentially distinct from it, and an entity independent of the conditions of space and time, seems, however, to be the belief of most Spiritualists; and so, unless they lapse into Idealism, and regard matter as something unreal, the Pantheistic view of things can be accepted only in company with a still higher truth.

Thus Spiritualism, if it neither discredits nor confirms the doctrine of two substances, at least makes doubly distinct the separation between the phenomena of so-called matter and the phenomena of so-called spirit. The two in one have been compared to the convex and concave of the same curve.

Plainly the domain of science does not extend to the region of first causes; and Spiritualism, though by its proofs of what inferior spirits can do, it helps us to the grandest conceptions of a Supreme Spirit, to whom all the facts of the universe are known, is yet unable to lift the veil from that Power which is at once Ground and Cause of the universe and its phenomena; impersonally immanent, (intra-mundane), automatic, evolutionary, and self-limited; personally transcendent, (supra-mundane), conscious, omniscient, absolute and omnipotent; the God in whom we live and move and have our being, and Our Father in Heaven; the God of Pantheism and, in his higher hypostasis, the God of Theism also.

CHAPTER VIII.

From these abstruse though not irrelevant considerations, the course of our narrative leads us back to Miss Cook.

She had begun to exhibit medial powers as early as 1870. In a letter to Mr. Harrison, dated May, 1872, she writes:

"I am sixteen years of age. From my childhood I could see spirits and hear voices, and was addicted to sitting by myself talking to what I declared to be living people. As no one else could see or hear anything, my parents tried to make me believe it was all imagination, but I would not alter my belief, so was looked upon as a very eccentric child. In the spring of 1870 I was invited to the house of a school-friend, whose name I am not at liberty to mention. She asked me if I had ever heard of spirit rapping, adding that her father, mother and self had sat at a table, and got movements, and that if I liked, they would try that evening."

Miss Cook, though at first somewhat "horrified" at the idea, got her mother's consent and sat with her friends. She soon found that the raps followed her. A message was given to her from what purported to be the spirit of her aunt; and then, she being left by herself at the table, it rose four feet. Miss Cook continues:

"I went home astonished. Mamma and I went a few days after. We had some excellent tests of spirit identity given us; *still we did not believe in spirits.** At last it was spelt out that if we would sit in the dark I should be carried round the room. I laughed, not thinking it would be done, and put out the light. The room was not perfectly dark, a light came in from the window. Soon I felt my chair taken from me. I was lifted up until I touched the ceiling. All in the room could see me. I felt too startled at my novel position to scream, and was carried over the heads of the sitters, and put gently on to a table at the other end of the room. Mamma asked if we could get manifestations at our own home. The table answered, 'Yes,' and that I was a medium. The next evening we sat at home; a table and two chairs were smashed, and a great deal of mischief done. We said we could never sit again, but we were not left in peace. Books and other articles were thrown at me, chairs walked about in the light, the table tilted violently at meal-times, and great noises were sometimes made at night. At last we sat again; the table behaved better, and a communication was given to the effect that we were to go to 74, Navarino-road, and that there was an association of Spiritualists there. Out of curiosity mamma and I went, and found we had been told quite correctly. Mr. Thomas Blyton came to a séance at our house; he invited me to a séance at Mr. Wilkes's library, in Dalston-lane. There I met Mr. Harrison. He came to see the manifestations at my home. By this time we were convinced of the truth of spirit communion. About this time I was first entranced; a spirit spoke through me, telling papa that if I sat with Messrs. Herne and Williams I should get the direct voice. I had several sittings with them, and finally succeeded in getting the direct voice, direct writing, and spirit touches. The presiding spirit of my circles is Katie, John King's daughter."

---

* Here is a touch of Nature, similar to that which Shakspeare makes manifest in the character of Hamlet. Just after he has seen and conversed with the spirit of his father, Hamlet talks of "that bourn from which no traveler returns." Just after Miss Cook has told us that she used to "see spirits and hear voices," she says, "still we did not believe in spirits." Perhaps, however, all that she here meant was that she did not believe they were active in this particular instance.

Of the subsequent developments, the sittings with Mr. Herne, and the final appearance of Katie in full form, I have already given an account.

Mr. Henry M. Dunphy relates that on one occasion, at a séance, Katie called for pencil and paper, saying she wanted to write a note. He produced a gold pencil-case with a double movement, one for producing the lead, and the other a pen. When handed to Katie, she unscrewed the little cap at the top, so as to scatter the leads on the carpet; she laughed, screwed on the top again, and then wrote the following message on a sheet of note-paper and threw it out: "I am much pleased that you have all come to-night at my invitation.—Annie Morgan."

On another occasion Mr. Dunphy inquired whether Katie would put on a heavy gold ring which he took off his finger and offered to her. This she immediately took out of his hand and placed on her own wedding finger, saying naively, "We are now engaged." On his subsequently reaching with his hand to receive the ring, Katie allowed him to touch hers, and afterwards told him to touch her lips, which he did with his hands, and she imprinted on them a kiss.

At another sitting, a passing remark having been made about lawyers, Katie asked whether her hearers knew what the Irish usher said when he was ordered to clear the court. "No," was the reply. "Well, then," said she, "he shouted, 'Now, then, all you blackguards who are not lawyers, leave the court.'"

Trivial and unspiritual as some of these acts and expressions may seem, I quote them as having a bearing on the question of the intellectual calibre of these materialized spirits.

Miss Emily Kislingbury, who has given considerable study to Miss Cook's mediumship, in a description of a séance at which she was present, Feb. 22d, 1873, remarks: "When Katie herself came and showed a fair-complexioned, large, massive face, and mouth set with brilliantly white teeth, I failed to see in it any resemblance to her medium; and my mother, who saw Katie for the first time, expressed her surprise that a comparison should ever have been made between them. I have, however, under more strict test conditions, seen in the spirit face a very striking resemblance to Miss Cook. . . .

"A slow tune was played with great expression inside the cabinet. . . . Katie asked me, to my astonishment, to sing the song beginning

'Du bist die Ruh', der Friede mild,'

and she would follow me. 'But,' said I, 'Katie, you cannot sing the German words.' 'Oh, can't I?' she said. 'My medium can't, but I am not so stupid ; you try me.' I sang the song through, and the same clear, bell-like voice again followed mine, pronouncing the German perfectly."

In the spring of 1873 a series of sittings was held for the purpose of getting a photographic likeness of Katie. The photographing was done by Mr. Harrison whose close and intelligent study of this remarkable case of materialization seems to have aided largely in the right development of Miss Cook's extraordinary powers. On the 7th of May a successful sitting was had, and no less than four photographs were taken. It is from one of the best of these that the engraving, which forms the frontispiece of this volume, was copied.

"In the photograph itself," says Mr. Harrison, "the features are more detailed and beautiful, and there is an expression of dignity and ethereality in the face which is not fully represented in the engraving, which, however, has been executed as nearly as possible with scientific accuracy, by an artist of great professional skill."

In a statement signed by Amelia Corner, Caroline Corner, J. C. Luxmoore, G. R. Tapp, and W. H. Harrison, we have a clear and interesting account, which I here slightly abridge, of the process of getting a photograph of Katie by the magnesium light :

"The cabinet doors were placed open, and shawls hung across. The séance commenced at six P. M., and lasted about two hours, with an interval of half an hour. The medium was entranced almost directly she was placed in the cabinet, and in a few minutes Katie stepped out into the room. The sitters, in addition to the undersigned, were Mrs. Cook and her two children, whose delight at Katie's familiarity with them was most amusing.

"Katie was dressed in pure white, except that her robe was cut low, with short sleeves, allowing her beautiful neck and arms to be seen. Her head dress was occasionally pushed back so as to allow her hair, which was brown, to be visible. Her eyes were large and bright, of a dark blue or gray color. Her countenance was animated and lifelike, her cheeks and lips ruddy and clear.

"Our expressions of pleasure at seeing her thus before us seemed to encourage her to redouble her efforts to give a good séance. By the light of a candle and a small lamp, during the intervals of photography, she stood or moved about, and chatted to us all, keeping up a lively conversation, in which she criticised the sitters, and the literary photographer and his arrangements very freely. By degrees she walked away from the cabinet, and came boldly out into the room.

"Katie usually leaned on the shoulder of Mr. Luxmoore, and stood up to be focussed several times, on one occasion holding the lamp to illuminate her face. Once she looked at the sitters through Mr. Luxmoore's eye-glass. She patted his head, and pulled his hair, and allowed him and Mrs. Corner to pass their hands over her dress, in order that they might satisfy themselves that she wore only one robe.

"As one of the plates was taken out of the room for development, she ran a few feet out of the cabinet after Mr. Harrison, saying she wished to see it; and on his return it was shown to her, he standing close to her and touching her at the time. While he was absent she walked up to the camera and inspected that 'queer machine,' as she called it.

"Just before one of the plates was taken, as Katie was reposing herself outside the cabinet, a long, sturdy, masculine right arm, bare to the shoulder, and moving its fingers, was thrust out of the opening at the top of the cabinet. Katie turned round and upbraided the intruder, saying that 'it was a shame for another spirit to interpose while she stood for her likeness,' and she bade him 'get out.'

"Toward the close of the séance Katie said that her power was going, and that she was 'really melting away this time.' The power being weak, the admission of light into the cabinet seemed gradually to destroy the lower part of her figure, and she sank down until her neck touched the floor, the rest of her body having apparently vanished, her last words being that we must sing, and sit still for a few minutes, 'for it was a sad thing to have no legs to stand upon.' This was done, and Katie soon came out again, entire as at first, and one more photograph was successfully taken. Katie then shook hands with Mr. Luxmoore, went inside her cabinet, and rapped for us to take the medium out.

"The séance had been given under strict test conditions. The only stipulation Katie made throughout was, that the sitters would not stare fixedly at her whilst she stood for her photograph.

"Before commencing, Mrs. and Miss Corner took the medium to her bedroom, and, having taken off her clothes and thoroughly searched them, dressed her without a gown, but simply with a cloak of dark gray waterproof cloth over her underclothing, and at once led her to the séance room, where her wrists were tied tightly together with tape. The knots were examined by the sitters respectively, and sealed with a signet ring. She was then seated in the cabinet, which had been previously examined. The tape was passed through a brass bracket in the floor, brought under the shawl, and tied securely to a chair outside the cabinet, so that the slightest movement on the part of the medium would have been at once detected.

"During the interval of half an hour, Mrs. Corner took charge of the medium, whilst she was out of the cabinet, and did not lose sight of her for one minute. The tying and sealing were repeated before the second part of the séance, and on each occasion of the medium leaving the cabinet, the knots and seals and tape were duly examined by all the sitters, and were found intact. The medium was tied and sealed by Mr. Luxmoore, whose signet ring was used."

In a separate communication Mr. Luxmoore writes:

"I carefully examined every part of the cabinet while Miss Cook was being searched by Mrs. and Miss Corner. Nothing could possibly have been concealed there without my discovering it. I should also mention, that, soon after one of the photographs had been taken, Katie pulled back the curtain, or rather rug, which hangs in front, and requested us to look at her, when she appeared to have lost all her body. She had a most curious appearance; she seemed to be resting on nothing but her neck, her head being close to the floor. Her white robe was under her."

Phenomena like these, as Dr. Wm. Hitchman aptly remarks, present a question "not to be settled at all by leading articles, but by positive experimental testimony." In this case such testimony has been given in abundance.

Previous to Prof. Crookes's taking the case in hand, Dr. Gully, Mr. Blackburn, Mr. Luxmoore, Mr. W. H. Harrison, and many other competent investigators had, at numerous séances, satisfied themselves fully that Katie and Miss Cook were distinct personalities.

"All who attended these séances," says Dr. Gully, "are aware with what anxious care arrangements were always made by which the smallest movements by the medium within were rendered detectable by the sitters outside, by means of tapes attached to the medium's body, and extended along the floor, and held by some one present; and, on one or two occasions, by the extension of the medium's own dark hair, not to mention the precise tying and sealing of the wrists. . . . These tests have abundantly satisfied me that the form which appears is not Miss Cook, but has a totally separate existence."

Notwithstanding these well-founded convictions there was a natural wish among Spiritualists that assurance should be made doubly sure, and in this wish no one joined more readily than Dr. Gully.

To determine the question whether Miss Cook was lying at rest inside the cabinet while Katie in her flowing robes was outside, Mr. C. F. Varley, F. R. S., the electrician of the Atlantic Cable, noted for his skill in testing broken cables, conceived the idea of passing a weak electrical current through the body of the medium all the time the manifestations were going on. He did this by means of a galvanic battery and cable-testing apparatus, which was so delicate that any movement whatever, on the part of Miss Cook, would be instantly indicated, while it would be impossible for her to dress and play the part of the spirit without breaking the circuit and being instantly detected.

Yet under these conditions the spirit-form *did* appear as usual, exhibited its arms, spoke, wrote, and touched several persons; and this happened, be it remembered, not in the medium's own house, but in that of Mr. Luxmoore, at the West end of London. For nearly an hour the circuit was never broken, and at the conclusion Miss Cook was found in a trance. Thus it was clearly proved that Miss Cook was not only in the cabinet, but perfectly quiescent, while Katie was visible and moving about outside.

Similar tests were soon repeated by Mr. Crookes in his own house with equally satisfactory results. Early in March he reported: "As far as the experiments go, they prove conclusively that Miss Cook is *inside* while Katie is *outside* the cabinet," and he further testified to Miss Cook's perfect honesty, truthfulness, and willingness to submit to the severest tests that he could approve of.

But the crowning proof was yet to come. On the 12th of March, 1874, during a séance at his own house, Katie came to the curtain, and called him to her, saying, "Come into the room and lift my medium's head up; she has slipped down." Katie was then standing before him, clothed in her usual white robes and turban head-dress. He walked into the library up to Miss Cook, Katie stepping aside to allow him to pass. He found that Miss Cook had slipped partially off the sofa, and that her head was hanging in a very awkward position. He lifted her on to the sofa, and in so doing had satisfactory evidence, in spite of the darkness, that Miss Cook was not attired in the Katie costume, but had on her ordinary black velvet dress, and was in a deep trance.

On the 29th of March, at a séance at Hackney, Katie told Mr. Crookes that she thought she should be able to show herself and Miss Cook together. Turning the gas out, he entered the room used as a cabinet, bearing a phosphorus lamp. This consisted of a six or eight ounce bottle, containing a little phosphorized oil, and tightly corked.

It being dark, he felt about for Miss Cook. He found her crouching on the floor. Kneeling down, he let air enter the lamp, and by its light saw the young lady, dressed in black velvet, as she had been in the early part of the evening, and to all appearance senseless. She did not move when he took her hand and held the light close to her face, but continued quietly breathing.

The remainder of the narrative I give in Mr. Crookes's own words:

"Raising the lamp, I looked around and saw Katie standing close behind Miss Cook. She was robed in flowing white drapery, as we had seen her previously during the séance. Holding one of Miss Cook's hands in mine, and still kneeling, I passed the lamp up and down, so as to illuminate Katie's whole figure, and satisfy myself thoroughly that I was really looking at the veritable Katie, whom I had clasped in my arms a few moments before, and not at the phantasm of a disordered brain.

"She did not speak, but moved her head, and smiled in recognition. Three separate times did I carefully examine Miss Cook, crouching before me, to be sure that the hand I held was that of a living woman, and three separate times did

I turn the lamp to Katie, and examine her with steadfast scrutiny, until I had no doubt whatever of her objective reality."

Of the points of difference between the two, Mr. Crookes says:

"Katie's height varies; in my house I have seen her six inches taller than Miss Cook. Last night, with bare feet and not *tip-toeing*, she was four and a half inches taller than Miss Cook. Katie's neck was bare last night; the skin was perfectly smooth, both to touch and sight, whilst on Miss Cook's neck is a large blister, which under similar circumstances is distinctly visible, and rough to the touch. Katie's ears are unpierced, whilst Miss Cook habitually wears ear-rings. Katie's complexion is very fair, while that of Miss Cook is very dark. Katie's fingers are much longer than Miss Cook's, and her face is also larger. In manners and ways of expression there are also many decided differences."

The exceeding whiteness of the drapery with which Katie came clothed was always noticeable; reminding the Scriptural reader of that passage in Mark: "His raiment became shining, exceeding white as snow, so as no fuller on earth can white them." The dress would vary in shape nearly every evening.

The fabric felt material enough. It did not melt away and disappear like the spirit fabrics felt by Mr. Livermore and Dr. Gray in the presence of Kate Fox. Miss Douglas took a specimen of the cloth to Messrs. Howell and James's, London, and asked them to match it; they said that they could not, and that they believed it to be of Chinese manufacture.

Whence came this white drapery? As we proceed in our narrative, it will be seen that Mr. Crookes satisfied himself thoroughly that it could not have been brought into his house and used by the medium.

Katie had announced, on several occasions, that her materializations through Miss Cook would cease the 21st of May, 1874. At one of her farewell séances, my friend, Mr. Coleman, whom I had some years before introduced to certain phenomena in Boston, was present. He took from his pocket a photograph; Katie received it from his hands, and exclaimed, "This is Dr. Gully and my likeness. What do you want me to do with it?" "Write," said Mr. Coleman, "your name, and any message you have to give me, on the back of it, that I may keep it in remembrance of this evening." Borrowing his pencil she wrote: "Annie Morgan, usually known as Katie King. To her dear friend, Mr. Ben. May 9th, 1874." When it was read aloud some one said, "That is too familiar," and she was reminded that there were others of the same name known to her; upon which she asked for the card to be returned, and wrote: "Mr. Ben is B. Coleman, Esq."

"During the evening," writes Mr. Coleman, "she frequently went behind the curtain to look after her medium, and once whilst she was there, Mr. Crookes raised the curtain, and he and I, and four others who sat by me, saw, at one and the same time, the figure of Katie, clad in her *white* dress, bending over the sleeping form of the medium, whose dress was *blue*, with a red shawl over her head." This exhibition was then repeated, and Mr. Coleman was fully satisfied that he saw both the living form of Miss Cook, and the materialized spirit-form of Katie.

The following remarkable incident, which Mr. W. H. Harrison and Mrs. Ross-Church (Florence Marryat) both confirmed in subsequent narratives, indicates the thaumaturgic power that was at work: "Taking up her skirt in a double fold, Mr. Crookes having lent her his scissors, Katie cut two pieces out of the front part, leaving the holes visible, one about an inch and the other two or three inches in circumference, and then, as if by magic, but without the conjurer's double boxes, or any attempt at concealment, she held that portion of the dress in her closed hand for a minute or two, and showed that the holes had disappeared, and that the dress was again entire. The pieces, a portion of which I have, are apparently strong ordinary white calico."

Of the repetition of this marvel at a subsequent séance, Mr. W. H. Harrison writes: "After she had thus cut several great holes in her dress, as she sat between Mr. Crookes and Mr. Tapp, she was asked if she could mend it, as she had done on other occasions; she then held up the dilapidated portion in a good light, gave it one flap, and it was instantly as perfect as at first. Those near the door of the cabinet examined and handled it immediately, with her permission, and testified there was no hole, seam or joint of any kind, where a moment before had been large holes, several inches in diameter."

Mrs. Ross-Church (Florence Marryat), a daughter of my old acquaintance, Captain Marryat, author of "Peter Simple," &c., was a witness of the same incident, and mentions it in an account of her experiences, which I shall soon quote.

The following is Mr. W. H. Harrison's account of the farewell séance, May 21st, 1874, in London, at which Katie appeared. There were present Mr. Crookes, Mrs. Corner, Mrs. Ross-Church, Mr. W. H. Harrison, Mr. G. R. Tapp, Mr. and Mrs. Cook and family, and the servant Mary:

"Mr. Crookes, 7.25 P. M., conducted Miss Cook into the dark room used as a cabinet, where she laid herself down upon the floor, with her head resting on a pillow; at 7.28 Katie first spoke, and at 7.30 came outside the curtain in full form. She was dressed in pure white, with low neck and short sleeves. She had long hair, of a light auburn or golden color, which hung in ringlets down her back, and each side of her head, reaching nearly to her waist. She wore a long white veil, but this was only drawn over her face once or twice during the séance.

"The medium was dressed in a high gown of light blue merino. During nearly the whole of the séance, while Katie was before us, the curtain was drawn back and all could clearly see the sleeping medium, who did not stir from her original position, but lay quite still, her face being covered with a red shawl to keep light from it. There was a good light during the entire séance.

"Katie talked about her approaching departure, and accepted a bouquet which Mr. Tapp brought her, also some bunches of lilies from Mr. Crookes.

"All the sitters in the circle clustered closely round her. Katie asked Mr. Tapp to take the bouquet to pieces, and lay the flowers out before her on the floor; she then sat down, Eastern fashion, and asked all to draw around her, which was done, most of those present sitting on the floor at her feet. She then divided the flowers into bunches for each, tying them up with blue ribbon. She also wrote parting notes to some of her friends, signed 'Annie Owen Morgan,' which she stated was her real name when in earth-life. She wrote a note for her medium, and selected a fine rosebud for her as a parting gift.

"Katie then took a pair of scissors and cut off a quantity of her hair, giving everybody present a liberal portion. She then took the arm of Mr Crookes and walked all round the room, shaking hands with each. She again sat down and distributed some of her hair; and also cut off and presented several pieces of her robe and veil. . . .

"She then appeared tired, and said reluctantly that she must go, as the power was failing, and bade farewell in the most affectionate way. The sitters all wished her God speed, and thanked her for the wonderful manifestations she had given. Looking once more earnestly at her friends she let the curtain fall and she was seen no more. She was heard to wake up the medium, who tearfully entreated her to stay a little longer, but Katie said, 'My dear, I can't. My work is done. God bless you,' and we heard the sound of her parting kiss. The medium then came out among us, looking much exhausted and deeply troubled.

"Katie said that she should never be able to speak or show her face again; that she had had a weary and sad three years' life 'working off her sins' in producing these physical manifestations, and that she was about to rise higher in spirit-life. At long intervals she might be able to communicate with her medium by writing, but at any time her medium might be enabled to see her clairvoyantly by being mesmerized."

Mrs. Ross-Church (Florence Marryat), who had been present at three of Katie's séances, on the 9th, 13th and 21st of May, 1874, in a letter to the London Spiritualist, wrote as follows:

"I will not recapitulate what so many have told of the appearance of the spirit 'Katie King,' nor of the means taken to prevent any imposition on the part of her medium. This has all been repeated again and again, and as often disbelieved. But I find Serjeant Cox, in his late letter on the subject of Miss Showers's mediumship, saying that could such an end be attained as a simultaneous sight of the apparition outside the curtain and the medium within, 'the most wonderful fact the world has ever witnessed would be established beyond controversy.' Perhaps Serjeant Cox would consider a sight of both medium and spirit in the same room and at the same time as convincing a proof of stern truth. *I have seen that sight.*

"On the evening of the 9th of May, Katie King led me, at my own request, into the room with her beyond the curtain, which was not so dark but that I could distinguish surrounding objects, and then made me kneel down by Miss Cook's prostrate form, and feel her hands and face and head of curls, whilst she (the spirit) held my other hand in hers, and leaned against my shoulder, with one arm around my neck.

"I have not the slightest doubt that upon that occasion there were present with me two living, breathing intelligences, perfectly distinct from each other, so far at least as their bodies were concerned. If my senses deceived me; if I was misled by imagination or mesmeric influence into believing that I touched and felt two bodies, instead of one; if 'Katie King,' who grasped, and embraced, and spoke to me, is a projection of thought only—a will-power—an instance of unknown force—then it will be no longer possible to know 'Who 's who, in 1874,' and we shall hesitate to turn up the gas incautiously, lest half our friends should be but projections of thought, and melt away beneath its glare.

"Whatever Katie King was on the evening of the 9th of May, she was not Miss Cook. To that fact I am ready to take my most solemn oath. She repeated the same experiment with me on the 13th, and on that occasion we had the benefit of mutual sight also, as the whole company were invited to crowd around the door whilst the curtain was withdrawn and the gas turned up to the full, in order that we might see the medium, in her blue dress and scarlet shawl, lying in a trance on the floor, whilst the white-robed spirit stood beside her.

"On the 21st, however, the occasion of Katie's last appearance amongst us, she was good enough to give me what I consider a still more infallible proof (if one could be needed) of the distinction of her identity from that of her medium. When she summoned me in my turn to say a few words to her behind the curtain, I again saw and touched the warm, breathing body of Florence Cook lying on the floor, and then stood upright by the side of Katie, who desired me to place my hands inside the loose single garment which she wore, and feel her nude body. I did so, thoroughly.

"I felt her heart beating rapidly beneath my hand; and passed my fingers through her long hair to satisfy myself that it grew from her head, and can testify that if she be 'of psychic force,' psychic force is very like a woman.

"Katie was very busy that evening. To each of her friends assembled to say good-by, she gave a bouquet of flowers tied up with ribbon, a piece of her dress and veil, and a lock of her hair, and a note which she wrote with her pencil before us. Mine was as follows: 'From Annie Owen de Morgan (*alias* Katie King) to her friend, Florence Marryat Ross-Church, with love. *Pensez a moi.* May 21st, 1874.' I must not forget to relate what appeared to me to be one of the most convincing proofs of Katie's more than natural power, namely, that when she had cut, before our eyes, twelve or fifteen different pieces of cloth from the front of her white tunic, as *souvenirs* for her friends, there was not a hole to be seen in it, examine it which way you would. It was the same with her veil, and I have seen her do the same thing several times.

"I think if in the face of all this testimony that has been brought before them, the faithless and unbelieving still credit Miss Cook with the superhuman agility required to leap from the spirit's dress into her own like a flash of lightning, they will hardly suppose her capable of re-weaving the material of her clothing in the same space of time. If they can believe *that*, they will not find the spiritualistic doctrine so hard a nut to crack afterwards. But I did not take up my pen to argue this point, but simply to relate what occurred to myself."

During the week before Katie took her departure, she gave séances at Mr. Crookes's house almost nightly, to enable him to photograph her by artificial light. In a letter dated July 21st, 1874, and enclosing two photographs, he writes me: "You may be interested in seeing one of my photographs of Katie, as she stood holding my arm; also one in which she is standing by herself." In the former of these the person of Katie, nearly to her ankles, dressed in her white robe, is taken; in the other, not quite so much of the figure is seen. In both photographs, the drapery is gracefully disposed; the countenance is placid, and the features finely formed, though it might not require much imagination to discover in their general expression a spectral look; the figure has all the distinctness of a veritable human being, there being nothing shadowy in the outlines.

Taken in his own laboratory, and under conditions the most satisfactory and unquestionable, these and some forty other photographs which he took, some inferior, some indifferent, and some excellent, confirmed all the previous tests which Mr. Crookes had got of the genuineness of the phenomenon. Frequently, at his own house, he would follow Katie into the cabinet, and would sometimes see her and her medium together, though generally he would find nobody but the entranced medium lying on the floor, Katie and her white robes having instantaneously disappeared.

During a period of six months Miss Cook was a frequent visitor at Mr. Crookes's house, remaining there sometimes a week at a time. She would bring nothing but a little hand-bag, not locked. During the day she would be constantly in the presence of Mrs. or Mr. Crookes, or some other member of his family; and, not sleeping by herself, there was no conceivable opportunity for any fraudulent preparation.

"It was a common thing," says Mr. Crookes, "for the seven or eight of us in the laboratory to see Miss Cook and Katie at the same time under the full blaze of the electric light. We did not on these occasions actually see the face of the medium, because of the shawl (which had been thrown over to prevent the light from falling on the face), but we saw her hands and feet, we saw her move uneasily under the influence of the intense light, and we heard her moan occasionally. I have one photograph of the two together, but Katie is seated in front of Miss Cook's head."

On one occasion Mr. Crookes was photographed with Katie, she having her bare foot on a particular part of the floor; their relative height was ascertained. Mr. Crookes was then photographed with Miss Cook under precisely similar conditions, and while the two photographs of himself coincide exactly in stature, etc., Miss Cook's figure is found to be half a head shorter than Katie's, and looks small in comparison.

"Photography," adds Mr. Crookes, "is as inadequate to depict the perfect beauty of Katie's face, as words are powerless to describe her charms of manner. Photography may, indeed, give a map of her countenance; but how can it reproduce the brilliant purity of her complexion, or the ever-varying expression of her most mobile features, now overshadowed with sadness when relating some of the bitter experiences of her past life, now smiling with all the innocence of happy girlhood when she had collected my children around her, and was amusing them by recounting anecdotes of her adventures in India."

The following particulars given by Mr. Crookes, as to the differences between Katie and the medium, will be found of interest:

"Having seen so much of Katie lately, when she has been illuminated by the electric light, I am enabled to add to the points of difference between her and her medium which I mentioned in a former article. I have the most absolute certainty that Miss Cook and Katie are two separate individuals as far as their bodies are concerned. Several little marks on Miss Cook's face are absent on Katie's. Miss Cook's hair is so dark a brown as almost to appear black; a lock of Katie's which is now before me, which she allowed me to cut from her luxuriant tresses, having first traced it up to the scalp and satisfied myself that it actually grew there, is a rich golden auburn.

"On one evening I timed Katie's pulse. It beat steadily at 75, while Miss Cook's pulse, a little time after, was going at its usual rate of 90. On applying my ear to Katie's chest I could hear a heart beating rhythmically inside, and pulsating even more steadily than did Miss Cook's heart when she allowed me to try a similar experiment after the séance. Tested in the same way, Katie's lungs were found to be sounder than her medium's, for at the time I tried my experiment Miss Cook was under medical treatment for a severe cough."

Of the final parting of Miss Cook and Katie, Mr. Crookes says:

"Having concluded her directions, Katie invited me into the cabinet with her, and allowed me to remain there to the end. After closing the curtain she conversed with me for some time, and then walked across the room to where Miss Cook was lying senseless on the floor. Stooping over her, Katie touched her and said, 'Wake up, Florrie, wake up! I must leave you now.' Miss Cook then woke and tearfully entreated Katie to stay a little time longer. 'My dear, I can't; my work is done. God bless you!' replied Katie, and then continued speaking to Miss Cook. For several minutes the two were conversing with each other, till at last Miss Cook's tears prevented her speaking. Following Katie's instructions, I then came forward to support Miss Cook, who was falling on to the floor, sobbing hysterically. I looked around, but the white-robed Katie had gone. As soon as Miss Cook was sufficiently calmed a light was procured and I led her out of the cabinet."

Thus ended this extraordinary series of séances, verifying the stupendous fact of the power of spirits to manifest themselves in a temporarily materialized human form. To Miss Cook's honesty and good faith Mr. Crookes bears witness in the strongest terms. Every test he proposed she readily submitted to; she was open and straightforward in speech, and never did he see in her conduct anything approaching the slightest symptom of a wish to deceive.

"To imagine," he says, "that a school-girl of fifteen should be able to conceive and then successfully carry out for three years so gigantic an imposture as this, and in that time should submit to any tests which might be imposed upon her, should bear the strictest scrutiny, should be willing to be searched at any time, either before or after a séance, and should meet with even better success in my own house than at that of her parents, knowing that she visited me with the express object of submitting to strict scientific tests—to imagine, I say, the 'Katie King' of the last three years to be the result of imposture—does more violence to one's reason and common sense than to believe her to be what she herself affirms."

When to these considerations is added the fact that the phenomena through Miss Cook have been recently paralleled and even surpassed by numerous similar well-attested phenomena, not only in England, but in America, what escape is there from the conclusion that they are wholly inexplicable under any theory of imposture or delusion?

CHAPTER IX.

By immortality I mean that exemption from death, of which we have the assurance in the spiritual body as a ground of continuous life. The spiritual organism is demonstrated not merely in the proof palpable, presented in the appearance of spirits in the human form, and by the attestations of spirits and mediums, but in the facts of clairvoyance, showing powers in the human being independent of the corresponding physical organs and requiring other and supersensual organs.*

Proofs of a future existence do not necessarily involve proofs of a perpetual existence. A discussion of the latter is not pertinent to my present purpose. But I may here remark that faith in our own everlastingness must depend largely on faith in the eternity of a supreme benign intelligence whence comes the order of the universe.

If we are at the mercy of blind, unconscious cosmic forces, of a mere "orrery," in the working of which neither mind nor love is active, we may feel, in the next stage of being as well as in this, that life is no assured possession. But to this subject I hope to return before I close.

The phenomena being admitted as actual and genuine, is it consistent with the laws of science to seek their cause?

"Of the efficient causes of phenomena," says J. S. Mill,

* For an abundance of facts proving clairvoyance, prevision, and many other supersensual phenomena, see "Planchette, the Despair of Science," by Epes Sargent. Boston: Roberts Brothers. It has not been thought necessary to repeat these facts in the present work.

"or whether any such causes exist, I am not called upon to give an opinion."

Mr. Mill acknowledges empirical causes only.

Well: the phenomena of Spiritualism force upon us the question of empirical causes; of causes fairly within the domain of science and experiment. When a solid figure in the human form, clothed and manifesting life and intelligence, melts away and disappears, and subsequently re-forms, before our sight, surely the phenomenon is one, the consideration of the *cause* of which is a legitimate inquiry of science. The philosophy of experience is the last which should deny this declaration; for to refuse to admit that there may be an empirical cause for the phenomenon in this case is purely an *à priori* assumption, to fall back on which is to abandon the whole philosophy of experience.

As the testimony in support of this amazing phenomenon cannot be too complete, I will quote, in addition to what I have already given, a description of their experiences by two highly competent witnesses. The first, Mr. A. B. Crosby, of Gold Hill, North Carolina, is, as I learn from my friend and neighbor John Wetherbee, a man scientifically educated, a graduate of Waterville College, and a careful observer. He writes to Mr. W., under date of August 7th, 1874, the following very clear and concise description of the phenomenon:

"I stopped on my way, at Philadelphia, and while there I saw the 'Katie King' manifestation, at No. 50 North Ninth street. There were about thirty persons present at the séance. The cabinet was a wooden partition across one corner of the room, the carpet of which extended to the extreme corner. There was a door in the partition and two apertures. Mr. and Mrs. Holmes, the mediums, sat outside the cabinet, and next to it, and were both in sight all the time. It is necessary for you to remember that, and also that the room was light enough all the time to see distinctly the persons present —about thirty. They sat in the form of a horse shoe, at each end of which sat a medium, which would be at each side of the cabinet. After some music and singing—about twenty minutes—we saw two delicate hands appear at the aperture over the door, then a face, rather dim, at the other aperture. After a short time, devoted to gathering strength from the circle, the door of the cabinet opened and a beautiful young lady, dressed in white, with a dark girdle and slippers, walked out into the centre of this circle. She had in her hands bouquets of flowers, which she held to the noses of many of the audience. She spoke to several in a weak voice. She went into and out of the cabinet several times; finally, she retired to the door of the cabinet and disappeared, gradually, until only a bright spot could be seen on the carpet. In less than a minute she began to reäppear, and in a short time walked out into the room apparently a veritable living person, as palpable as you or I; I think, for the time we saw her, that she was flesh, like us. I thought her person had a slight phosphorescent glow, because the shadows of the folds of her dress were very feeble, more of the character of a diffused light. I cannot conceive of what I saw being any trick; I *know* it was not, and you know what that means when I say it, and I am now a Spiritualist."

Dr. Raue, of Philadelphia, a physician of the highest standing, was present at the séance of August 9th, 1874. He assured himself by a close examination that there was no inlet or outlet to the cabinet. The two mediums remained outside among the spectators. After some music the curtains of the holes in the partition were raised, and several hands became visible. Soon a whole arm appeared, and as in salutation was waved to and fro in a graceful manner. Katie shook hands from the window with those who went up to it. She talked, too, repeatedly; for instance, she answered the question of "How do you like the present company?" by "I 'll tell you after awhile;" and, later, "I love you all." At another time she said, "I feel now as natural as when I was in earth-life." Her voice was mild and somewhat whispering. Of her issuing from the cabinet in a full materialized form, Dr. R. says:

"The door opened and Katie appeared, slowly moving her hands, as though saluting or declaiming, and clad in a tasteful white robe, and a mantilla of gauze or lace. Her waist was encircled by a belt, fastened with a gold clasp or buckle. At her throat appeared a gold cross, or similar ornament. Afterwards she emerged entirely from the closet, sat down upon a chair next to Mrs. Holmes, rose and receded slowly into the closet again.

"The question was then put to her whether she could not show us *how* she materialized herself, and was again answered by 'I will try.' After awhile the door of the closet opened once more, and we saw, in the right corner of it, a kind of gray mist, or cloud, from which, within a short time, Katie's whole figure was developed in a wonderful manner. Her disappearance was similar: it was a gradual fading and dissolving. The white figure *was not illumined by external light, but had a peculiar bluish-white and brilliant splendor, that seemed to come from within.* I do not believe that any mixture of earthly colors would be able to produce the same effect. The gold of the belt-buckle and the necklace appeared more golden than the finest gold."

Here was a proof palpable—but of what? Surely of immortal spirit, whether we call it psychic force, or independent spirit power. Admitting that there was no delusion—and the reader who has carefully weighed the testimony I have adduced will hardly adopt so insufficient a theory as that of fraud or deception—what can it be *but an intelligence and a will, exercising, through some centripetal and centrifugal use of the invisible constituents of matter, the astonishing power of materializing and de-materializing a human form with its appropriate clothing?*

An intelligence and a will! And this intelligence proclaims itself a spirit! And this will proves the claim by causing an animated body in human shape to vanish and reappear! If such a power does not answer the full signification which men in all ages have attached to the word *spirit*, as representative of the life of a man after the dissolution of his earth-body, I am at a loss to know what further evidence can be given under the present limitations of our human faculties.

But this spirit, we are told, is very unspiritual, and does not always speak the truth.

If a man having the Caucasian features and form, and speaking our language, were cast upon our shores from the sea, we should readily take his word for it that he was an escaped English or American mariner. He might prove in many other things untruthful and inconsistent, but we should have little doubt that he was a man, and of a certain nationality.

So when a man in the human form presents himself as a materialized spirit, and proves it, not only by the intelligence of his conversation and acts, but by dissolving and re concreting his corporeal envelope before our eyes, and by manifesting his powers, in other ways, as invisible force and intelligence, surely we have here a proof palpable, which no misrepresentations or mistakes, on his part, in regard to other questions, could impair, that he is what he claims to be, namely, what we understand by a spirit.

Skepticism, it is true, can find room for cavil even here, but so it can find room to cavil at the reality of our own terrestrial existence; and yet we go on, and eat, drink, sleep, think, and enjoy ourselves, in spite of all the subtleties by which it would prove that we are under a mistake.

That the phenomena have a cause, must be conceded as a postulate of human reason. The theories of imposture and delusion being dismissed, what sufficient cause can be assigned but that which the spirits themselves bear witness to, and that which human experience, in all ages of the world and among all tribes and nations, has accepted?

Although in December, 1874, charges of fraud were brought against Mr. and Mrs. Holmes, in consequence of which Mr. Owen and Dr. Child withdrew their confidence, the phenomena through Mrs. Holmes were satisfactorily tested throughout the year 1875, not only by Messrs. Lippitt and Olcott, but by Mr. J. M. Roberts, all gentlemen personally known to me. A Mrs. White, instigated, it is believed, by persons wishing to throw discredit on the phenomena, declared that she had been engaged by Mr. Holmes to play the part of Katie King. That she stood for a photograph of the spirit was true. Certain letters in Mr. Holmes's handwriting, which were not at first satisfactorily explained, gave color to her other claims. But it was in the end conclusively proved: *first*, that Mrs. White's word was entitled to no credit; *secondly*, that the manifestations could be produced without her or any other confederate; and *thirdly*, that the evidences of fraud were incomplete. For these reasons, and because the testimony of Mr. Crosby and Dr. Rauc has not been retracted, I have allowed it to stand as it appeared in the first edition of this work. Even Mr. Owen, after withdrawing the testimony he had given in behalf of the phenomena, declared that "the Holmes case, instead of disproving or casting doubt upon the phenomenon of materialization, does prove it conclusively."

The Holmes case made a great noise at the time, and was looked upon by the larger part of the uninformed public as invalidating all the phenomena; but it owed its importance to the reputation of Mr. Owen as a public man of tried integrity and an author of note. He had testified so earnestly to the facts that, although he remained as firm a believer as ever in the truth involved, the hostile newspapers, when he repudiated the manifestations in this single case, were jubilant over the event, and it was regarded as conclusive even against Spiritualism itself. Subsequent developments have shown how unwarrantable and exaggerated was the importance given to the affair. The materialization phenomena have so multiplied, have grown to be so complex and common, that the detection in fraud of any one medium, however conspicuous, cannot invalidate the general fact.

As our experience in dealing with these novel phenomena increases, moreover, we begin to learn that susceptible mediums, through sinister mesmeric influences exerted upon them either by operating spirits or by persons in a circle, may automatically do things which unskilled investigators at once set down as frauds sufficient to invalidate all proofs, however ample, of previous genuine phenomena.

These considerations may explain why it is that there are so few mediums who have not, at some time in their career, been charged with imposture.

Under date of Terre Haute, Ind., Oct. 27th, and Nov. 10th, 1875, Mr. Isaac Kelso, a well-known Unitarian clergyman, and an experienced student of the phenomena, gives an account of a sitting, at which Mrs. Anna Stewart was the medium. He says:

"The light is turned down, but not so far as to make it possible for any confederate to enter the cabinet without being seen. By-and-by one wing of the cabinet door slowly opens, and out steps a slight but beautiful figure, robed in pure white garments, looking a girl of about seventeen; not quite so tall as the medium, but with a step more elastic. Pausing an instant near the threshold, she says, 'Good evening,' in the softest imaginable tones, then, turning round, throws open the other wing of the cabinet door, showing us the medium sitting in a chair, apparently asleep, and deadly pale."

A stranger suggested to Mr. Kelso that it was a deception; whereupon the entranced medium lifted her arm and waved a white handkerchief. "Ah, the thing is a machine, moved by wires," persisted the skeptic in an undertone. Going at once to the medium the figure in white raised her to her feet, brought her out of the cabinet, and stood side by side with her. After describing a second apparition, that of a tall male figure, Mr. Kelso resumes:

"Finally the figure in white came out again. I requested her to give us the best proof she could that she was not a mortal like ourselves. After expressing a willingness to try, she called for a pair of scissors, which, being furnished, she handed to me; then kneeling down before me, requested that I should cut a lock of hair from her head. . . . The apparition threw her long raven tresses forward, allowing me to make my own selection. Cutting off a large lock, close to the scalp, I drew it carefully through my hand, then passed it to others; it was handed round; perhaps a dozen persons examined it; after this it was returned to the apparition, who remained in her kneeling posture close by me. Taking the hair into her hands, she stretched it out, laid it on a white handkerchief right under my eyes, and in full view of all the company, then folded the handkerchief over it. Having done this, she retired within the cabinet and closed the door, which placed her at the distance of at least nine feet from the hair.

"While the door was yet closed the handkerchief deliberately unfolded as if lifted by invisible fingers, and the hair began to move. I now placed the fingers of my right hand upon the carpet, slowly and carefully sweeping them entirely round the handkerchief, thus making it doubly sure that no fine thread or wire connected the hair in any way with the being from whose head I had clipped it. Very soon the lock of hair bounded from the handkerchief on to the carpet, and began moving toward the cabinet. Before it reached the threshold the apparition opened the door and came out. The hair leaped upon her white skirt, and slowly climbed to her shoulder; thence it sprang to her crown, and seemed to plant itself upon the very spot from which it had been taken."

A lady of my acquaintance, Mrs. H. B. Webster, a daughter of Croly, the poet, author of "Catiline," &c., after describing some phenomena that took place in Florence, Italy (July, 1874), through the mediumship of Mr. D. D. Home, remarks as follows:

"One asks one's self, of what nature can be the eyes and ears and the flesh and blood of the individual who can see eight or ten hands come out from under his own dining-cloth, while the hands of every visible individual present are staring him in the face, and can feel the living pressure of the flexible *human* fingers clasping him, and question for a single instant what they are? True it is that there are persons, clever and intelligent in all other respects, who, when their prejudices or preconceived ideas are thwarted, seem to have the faculty of shutting their eyes to all facts, and their minds to all logic, no matter how palpable. Thus a very distinguished and gifted Englishman told me the other evening, in the presence of several others, that at a séance with Mr. Home a hand and arm projecting from a white cloud descended from above in the full view of seven or eight persons, and first touching Mr. Home's head, then touched himself on the forehead. 'But,' said the gentleman in conclusion, '*What does that prove?* The hand might have been a *force.* Who assures me it came from a spirit?' To arguing of this description there is no answer possible, except, perhaps, that of Mr. Home himself, who remarked that *in such a case we may all be, ourselves, nothing but forces also!*"

Home's reply is apt and sufficient. To suppose that a mere force, independent of the will or knowledge of the medium exercising it, announcing itself as a distinct individuality and conducting like one, and yet nothing all the while but an emanation from the medium, can go forth from the latter, incarnate itself partially or wholly, clothe itself appropriately and instantaneously in garments woven apparently out of nothingness, converse, argue, sing, walk, dance, write, play on instruments, and then suddenly vanish, *while the* medium, in the possession of all his faculties, is looking on and believing it a separate personality—is obviously to suppose something far more miraculous and incredible than a direct manifestation by a returning spirit.

It may be asked: "Under the theory of a spiritual body coexistent with the natural, may not the spirit of a person still in the earth-life manifest itself thus objectively?" That it can do so we have good reason to believe; but if it can thus separate itself from the living earth-body, why should the dissolution of the latter limit the spirit's power of manifestation? Ought not its power to be increased rather than diminished by the severing of a tie which must be more a limitation than a help?

The proof palpable of immortality is the culmination of other cognate proofs, in themselves a sufficient assurance of the existence in man of a supersensual, spiritual nature.

Death is not disorganization, but change. The caterpillar does not lose himself in passing to the butterfly, neither does man lose himself in leaving a physical organism for a spiritual.

There is undoubtedly a force, call it psychic, odic, or spiritual, which is a property of man's duplicate organism. It may be manifested in various ways during the earth-life of the individual; it may be the agent in many phenomena not explicable by the agency of the normal powers of terrestrial man; but there is a large class of phenomena which are more rationally explained by the intervention of spirits that have parted from their mortal bodies.

The testimony of the spirits themselves and of entranced and clairvoyant mediums, from whose organisms they borrow a certain power facilitating manifestation, must carry some weight; nor is the fact that both spirits and mediums are fallible and often deceptive, sufficient to impair wholly the value of such assurance.

But apart from this testimony, we have all the proof that our senses can give, and in addition, the proofs of an intelligence and a power that cannot be credited to our known and normal faculties.

Mrs. Louisa Andrews, from whose testimony in regard to the materialization phenomena I have already quoted, records the following incident: "At a late sitting in Moravia, where there were many in the circle anxiously hoping to see friends and relatives, a young man appeared whom no one knew. After showing himself for a moment, he spoke, giving his name as Freeman Kelly. No one recognized the name or the face. He then spoke again with apparent effort, saying, 'I passed away in Ithaca;' and he added, in a low but very impressive voice, '*Let all men know that this is true.*'

"On my return to Ithaca, I found, on inquiry, that a man bearing this name, and described as resembling the spirit we had seen, died last spring (1872). He had promised some friends living in this place that if he should go first, and if spirit returns were possible, he would come and testify to the fact. These friends were not present when he redeemed his promise, but received his communication through the lips of those who heard it."

Dr. Edwin Lee, in his "Report upon the Phenomena of Clairvoyance" (London, 1843), mentions the case of the prediction of the death of the King of Wurtemberg by two different somnambulists; the one having foretold the event four years beforehand; the other, in the spring of the same year having mentioned the exact day, in the month of October, as also the disease (apoplexy). "The exact coincidence," says Dr. Lee, "of the event with the predictions, is not doubted at Stuttgard; and a fortnight ago Dr. Klein, who is now in England, accompanying the Crown Prince of Wurtemberg, having been introduced to me, I took the opportunity of asking him about the circumstance, which he acknowledged was as has been stated, saying, moreover, that his father was physician to the King, who, on the morning of the day on which the attack occurred, was in very good health and spirits."

Mr. Clark Irvine, a respectable lawyer of Oregon, Holt County, Missouri, of whose visit to Dr. Slade I have already spoken, in the third chapter of this work, writes me some particulars of this and other experiences, which include some noteworthy facts. He was wholly unknown to Dr. Slade, the medium, and came upon him unprepared. While he sat in a chair in the light and Dr. Slade sat at some distance from him, Mr. Irvine felt an invisible spirit hand which he grasped. He held on to it tightly, and the hand, after pulling violently, gave a few spasmodic jerks and then seemed to melt away, his fingers gradually closing together as though holding some dissolving substance.

While himself holding a slate close up under and against the top of a small table, Mr. Irvine got "almost immediately, with more than mortal speed, in writing," a communication signed "Your grandmother, Tabitha M. Irvine." If he had ever known that she had an M in her name, he had surely forgotten it; but on reference, some days after, to an old family Bible he learnt that the M was correctly inserted. Bear in mind that all the while the writing was going on, Slade was sitting at some distance and did not even know the name of his sitter.

While Mr. Irvine held an accordion, in broad daylight, in such a way that he could look closely on the keys, the side of the instrument opposite his hand began to be violently pulled out and pushed back with great rapidity, the keys rose and fell, and the tune of "Home, Sweet Home" was played. Mr. I. could not himself play the instrument, nor could he have even started the tune. Slade sat some distance opposite with his hands clasped behind his head as a spectator. Mr. I. then requested, *mentally*, that the tune should be changed to "Hail Columbia," and this was done without a word having been uttered.

"From the most positive disbelief in a future state," writes Mr. Irvine, "I was converted by the overwhelming tests I received on this occasion.

"On the evening of the same day I visited Mr. Charles Foster. At his request, while he was in another room transacting some business, I wrote down about twenty names of various persons dead and alive, but among the names four of dear friends deceased and much thought of, and folded the paper closely up. I had given Foster my name on entering the room. He placed his hand on the paper, and exclaimed, 'The spirit of Leonard Bartlette is standing there. He says he is an uncle of yours.' This was in truth one of the names I had written, though why I should have done so was singular, as I had not in many years thought of it. 'What was the cause of his death?' 'He says he fell from his wagon.' 'That was not so.' 'How then?' 'He was killed by a saw log rolling down on to him as he was walking along a bank.' Foster laughed. 'What do you laugh at?' 'Why, this spirit says he himself was on the ground and knows all about it, and you were not. Are you quite sure you are right?' 'Yes, as sure as a man can be of things he gets from the report of friends.' Some acquaintance of Foster's had entered during the séance; and this man now exclaimed: 'Charley, you old humbug, you are caught this time, and I am glad of it.' Foster looked serious and said: 'I can't help it; mistakes are made, and lies are told, but——' And then brightening up, and speaking with renewed confidence, he said: 'See here; this spirit knows what he is about; he is truthful; you are wrong, and he is right.' He then described the man's appearance accurately, and asked me to learn if I were not in error.

"On returning to Missouri, I stopped in Ohio, and asked my mother the cause of her brother Leonard's death. She replied: 'Why, he fell from his wagon of course!' After full investigation it appeared that I had never heard a true account of the accident. It took place some twenty years ago, when I was in Louisiana; a friend wrote me there that my uncle had been killed by a saw log, and this statement I had never thought to question."

Whence, under the circumstances, could Foster, ignorant as he was, have got his information if not from the spirit whose appearance he accurately described?

The Rev. Samuel Watson, of Tennessee, a well-known clergyman and author, says (1874): "In full daylight, at three o'clock in the afternoon, I have seen the materialized spirit forms of my former wife, with whom I had lived twenty-six years; and the father of my present wife, who had been a Methodist preacher; and I saw a number of other spirits, some of whom were also recognized as friends. I insist upon the reality of these facts, and upon their value as indicating the communion of the departed with those still on earth."

I have just had an interview (Sept. 2d, 1874) with the Rev. R. S. Pope, of Hyannis, Mass., one who in his very aspect and presence brings the credentials of a man of ample intelligence and perfect truthfulness He tells me that he was at Moravia with his wife, both of them strangers to all the persons there, and their very names unknown. They saw his mother and his two sons, all deceased. The last two came night after night every evening for a week. They spoke to him, they proved their identity to the complete satisfaction of himself and his wife. "I saw them," says Mr. Pope, "face to face as distinctly as I see you now. They were visible to all the spectators. There could be no delusion. It was a reality. My mother, who came first, proclaimed to the company my name (till then unknown to all); and my son Milton said, 'Preach this truth when you go home'—thus revealing my profession. My mother had on her head a cap of a luminous whiteness. *Solid light* will best express its appearance." Mr. Pope was a total disbeliever in Spiritualism when he went to Moravia. He came home thoroughly convinced of its fundamental truth, and he proclaimed his experiences publicly to his people. Previous to sitting for the phenomena he had satisfied himself thoroughly, by examining the room and the cabinet, that no human contrivance could produce the manifestations. In the course of his conversation with me, Mr. Pope said: "As I could not believe these things on any man's testimony, so I do not ask you to believe them on mine." Three of his parishioners, he told me, had been to Moravia and satisfied themselves by similar objective phenomena of the survival of deceased friends and relatives.

Facts like these, combining the proof palpable of immortality with those inductive proofs derived from the exhibition of mental and physical powers wholly transcending all that is known to belong to mortal man, must be considered in connection with a vast collection of similar facts, attested by many thousands of sincere, intelligent persons in all parts of the world, not only at the present time especially, but in all past times.

When so considered they lead irresistibly to the conviction that the dissolution of the earth-body leaves a man unimpaired in all those essential qualities and characteristics which constitute his identity and his individuality.

If this view contradicts some of the exalted ideas we may have formed of the spiritual state, let us not therefore shrink from the facts. Mere sentiment will soon reconcile itself to the actual.

"Suppose I *do* find the unseen to be the haunt of ungrammatical ghosts," says Mr. St. George Stock, "what then? It has its high life, I suppose, as well as its low. This world itself is vulgar or practical according to the light in which we look at it. Do not reject well attested narratives merely because they sound grotesque. He is not a faithful lover of truth who would not go through dirt to meet her. 'One vision of her snowy feet is worth the labor of a life.'"

"True fortitude of understanding," says Paley, "consists in not suffering *what we know* to be disturbed by what we do *not* know. The uncertainty of one thing does not necessarily affect the certainty of another thing. Our ignorance of many points need not suspend our assurance of a few."

This advice cannot be too closely pondered by Spiritualists. The one great fact that they *know* must not be disturbed by the innumerable questions which even a child's skepticism can raise, and satisfactory answers to which cannot be readily given. Remember that this is a rudimental stage of being, and that we have all the future before us in which to think, study and work. We have reached the sublime summit from which we can surely see that man survives the corporeal dissolution. Let that immense and ever-fertile truth enter into our convictions, and possess them thoroughly, and help to shape our every act, thought and affection, and we may well be content to postpone all minor problems.

CHAPTER X.

The late Robert Chambers, the well-known Scottish publisher and author, was a thoughtful investigator of the spiritual phenomena. During his last visit to America, I introduced him to the séances for physical manifestations, given by Miss Jenny Lord,* and he was thoroughly satisfied as to their remarkable and genuine character.

In his introduction to the autobiography of Mr. D. D.

* Now Mrs. J. L. Webb, and resident in Chicago. She gives remarkable tests of spirit power and identity. I have myself received some through her quite recently. Mr. S. S. Jones, of the Religio-Philosophical Journal, relates the following: "On the evening of June 13th, 1874, we with others attended one of Mrs. Webb's séances. Through her mediumship a spirit will materialize a hand, and write by it visibly. During the séance a spirit by our side wrote a communication on paper, folded it up and placed it in our hand. Immediately, another spirit controlling Mrs. Webb's organs of speech, addressed us by name, saying, 'There is a spirit standing behind you; he looks as if he was seventy or eighty years old when he died. He was a large man and a mesmerizer. He it was who wrote and placed the communication in your hand just now.' We held it until the gas was lighted, and then, to our joy, found it was from our old and esteemed friend, Dr. Underhill" (with whom Mr. Jones had had some slight differences of opinion, resulting in one or two unkind letters and a coldness, about a year before the doctor's decease). "It read as follows: 'Good evening, Mr. Jones. You will pardon a few errors in the past. You remember. Success to you. SAMUEL UNDERHILL.' The communication was given under absolute test conditions, such as would admit of no fraud or collusion on the part of any person present, and not only that, but no one present knew of any letters of unpleasantness having been received from Dr. U. by us."

Home, the well-known medium, Mr. Chambers has the following pregnant and suggestive remarks: "The idea is now arising that the cause of the undiminished darkness overhanging all that relates to a state of existence after this life, may be, *that the right track has never yet been entered on; that the facts really affording in this direction materials for induction have hitherto been disregarded;* that they nevertheless abound; and that a higher enlightenment will cause attention to be turned to them and reveal their profound significance."

How true is all this! In ancient times, before the positive and inductive sciences, which the nineteenth century has developed, had opened new realms of thought and discovery, men hardly discriminated between the ordinary phenomena of Nature and those which indicate a direct spirit origin. Both classes of phenomena being equally mysterious to the ignorant, a misleading superstition, fatal to all scientific progress, drew men away from the rational exploration and study of occurrences indicating spirit power and prevision. We must except such great thinkers as Plato, Aristotle, Cicero and Plutarch; but the general scientific culture was not sufficient to make their explanations level to the popular understanding.

In mediæval times, when witchcraft was rampant, men were no better off. A narrow but imperious theology, and a state-craft, bound in priestly fetters, made it dangerous for a man to prosecute researches into the "ill-famed land of the marvelous."

If even in our own day so enlightened a man as Professor Tyndall* is yet so besotted with prejudice as to attempt to warn off investigators by denouncing Spiritualism as "degrading" (as if the knowledge of any fact of God's universe were *degrading!*), how can we wonder at the persecution which checked all rational inquiry into spiritual phenomena two centuries ago!

---

* "The overbearing minister of Nature," says the late Prof. De Morgan, "who snaps you with *unphilosophical!*" *unscientific! degrading!* "as the clergyman once frightened you with *Infidel*, is still a recognized member of society, *wants taming, and will get it. He wears the priest's cast-off garb, dyed to escape detection.*"

There truly has not been a time in the world's history till now when it was wholly safe for a man to investigate the facts, really affording, as Robert Chambers remarks, *materials for induction in relation to a state of existence after this life.*

Bear in mind, and learn humility from the fact, ye scientists of the year 1975, that, even in our day, the four leading professors of Harvard University tried to put a stop to all investigation into these astounding and now established phenomena by denouncing "any connection with spiritualistic circles, so-called" as corrupting the morals and degrading the intellect; as tending "to lessen the truth of man and the purity of woman;" that Professor John Tyndall, as late as 1874, spoke of Spiritualism, (a veritable *science*, by the testimony of such men as Wallace, Fichte, Flammarion, Varley, and Hare,) as "degrading;" and that Professor T. H. Huxley, as late as 1869, wrote a letter to the Dialectical Society, in which he says: "Supposing the phenomena to be genuine, they do not interest me."

If learned professors, in the full blaze of the science of the latter half of the nineteenth century can be so befogged by their petty prejudices and preconceptions, as to try to blot out the *facts* of Spiritualism, surely it will be easy for us to find charity in our hearts for the clerical and legal authorities who advocated the slaughter of witches, but little more than a century ago!

Before concluding the testimony of our day as to the materialization phenomena, I must not omit an account of the Eddy family. Some ten years ago I satisfied myself by personal investigation of the genuineness of their mediumship, and my convictions were not impaired by subsequent reports that two of them had turned against Spiritualism, and were professing to make antagonistic exposures.

It appears that in some Western town, finding themselves utterly destitute of money and of the means of raising it, friendless and longing for home, they were tempted by some unscrupulous adviser to give exhibitions for the "exposure" of the phenomena of Spiritualism. This they did, and they got audiences and funds from the foes of Spiritualism, which they could not get from the friends. But the poor mediums were as helpless as was the ancient heathen medium, Balaam, when called upon to curse: "How shall I curse whom God hath not cursed, or how shall I defy whom the Lord hath not defied?"

No one of the marvels wrought by spirits could be exposed or explained by any practical exhibition of trick or skill on the part of the two Eddys; and those persons who had hoped to see Spiritualism finally shown up and exploded, went home in a sadder but wiser mood.

We must exercise the largest charity for the moral weakness that led to such an attempt by the mediums. Only he who has experienced the suffering of extreme destitution is qualified to estimate their temptation.

In a letter to the N. Y. Sun, dated Chittenden, Vermont, the village where the Eddy family reside, Sept. 2, 1874, Col. Henry S. Olcott, a well-known journalist of New York, gives an account which carries internal evidence of sincerity, competency, and careful observation of the phenomena. The diagram on the following page will give an idea of the room where most of the occurrences which he relates took place.

The apartment is forty-eight by sixteen feet, with three windows on each side. At the west end is a raised platform the width of the room, about two feet high by four broad, reached by three steps of about ten inches rise. Between the kitchen chimney, which is in the middle, and the right hand wall is a small cupboard or closet, lathed and plastered, with a very narrow door, six feet and one inch high, opening from the platform, and a single window for purposes of ventilation. This closet is the cabinet in which the medium sits. A light hand-rail runs from side to side of the room at the edge of the platform.

The Eddy family, originally twelve in number, are now reduced by marriage and death to five—three sons and two daughters. The great-grandmother on the female side was condemned to death in Salem in 1692, for witchcraft. She escaped the gallows, however, by being rescued from the jail by her friends.

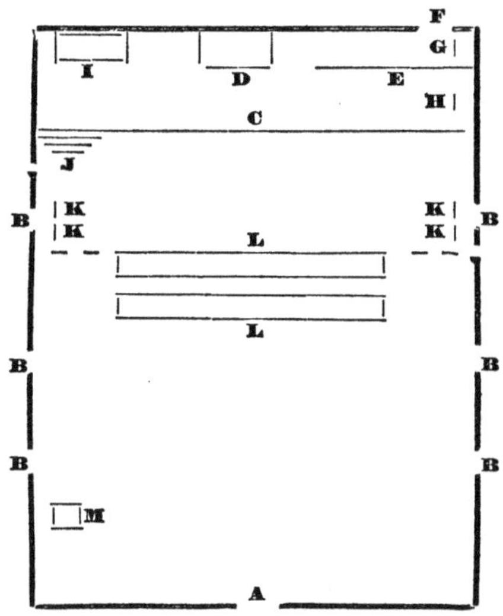

A—Entrance door; B B B—Windows; C—Platform; D—Chimney; E—Cabinet; F—Window; G—Chair where medium sits; H—Chair outside cabinet; I—Table; J—Steps; K K—Chairs; L L—Two benches; M—Small stand on which a kerosene lamp stands.

Chittenden, where the Eddys reside, is seven miles north from Rutland, and they live in a gloomy farm-house a century old, shaded by trees whose dense foilage makes the dark brown structure appear more sombre and inhospitable.

"There is nothing about the Eddys or their surroundings," says Col. Olcott, "to inspire confidence on first acquaintance. The brothers Horatio and William, who are the present mediums, are sensitive, distant, and curt to strangers, look more like hard-working, rough farmers than prophets or priests of a new dispensation, have dark complexions, black hair and eyes, stiff joints, a clumsy carriage, shrink from advances, and make new-comers feel ill at ease and unwelcome. The house is dark, rough, and uninviting, the appurtenances of the rudest, the astounding stories of what the Eddys do excite suspicion and invite distrust, and it would not be strange if a majority of persons attending only one séance should leave, as did a gentleman who came here with me, persuaded that it was a colossal humbug.

"I thought about as much myself at first, and it was not until a second and third opportunity had been afforded me to enter the circle room, to inspect the cabinet before and after the performances, and I had informed myself from perfectly trustworthy sources as to their antecedents, that I became willing to put my name to this tale and say that, whatever the source of the marvels may be, it is certainly not the chicanery or legerdermain of a pair of expert thaumaturgists. It suffices to leave each to form his own doctrine and join with Cicero, who in describing the different kinds of magic says: 'What we have to do with is the facts, since of the cause we know little. Neither are we to repudiate these phenomena, because we sometimes find them imperfect.'"

Col. Olcott says:

"The Eddys can get no servants to live in the house, and so have to do all the housework—cooking, washing, and everything—themselves, and as they charge nothing for séances, and but $8 per week for board, there is small profit and much work in taking boarders. They are at feud with some of their neighbors, and as a rule not liked either in Rutland or Chittenden. I am now satisfied, after a very careful sifting of the matter, that this hostility and the ugly stories told about them are the result of their repellant manners and the ill name that their ghost-room has among a simple-minded, prejudiced people, and not to any moral turpitude on the part of the mediums. They are in fact under the ban of a public opinion that is not prepared or desirous to study the phenomena as either scientific marvels or revelations from another world.

"Many points noted in my memorandum book as throwing suspicion upon the Eddys I omit, because upon sifting them I found there was an easy explanation, and I cheerfully admit that my impressions of the brothers, as to their honesty in the matter of the manifestations, as well as their personal worth, have steadily improved since the first day. I am satisfied, moreover, that they have not the ability to produce them if they should try, which they do not, nor the wardrobe nor properties requisite to clothe the multitude of forms (estimated at over 2,000) that during the twelvemonth last past have emerged from the cabinet and stalked the narrow platform.

"After some singing and dancing, the persons present at the séance are invited to seat themselves on the benches, and William Eddy hangs a thick shawl over the door of the cabinet, which he enters, and sits on the chair G. The lamp is turned down until only a dim light remains; the sitters in front join hands, and a violinist, placed at the extreme right of the row and nearest the platform, plays on his instrument. All is then anxious expectation. Presently the curtain stirs, is pushed aside, and a form steps out and faces the audience.

"Seen in the obscurity, silent and motionless, appearing in the character of a visitor from beyond the grave, it is calculated to arouse the most intense feelings of awe and terror in the minds of the timid; but happily the idea is so incomprehensible, the supposition so unwarrantable, even absurd, that at first most people choose to curiously inspect the thing as a masquerading pleasantry on the part of the man they saw a moment before enter the cabinet. That the window of his closet is twenty feet from the ground; that no ladder can be found about the premises; that there is no nook nor corner of the house where a large wardrobe can be stored without detection; that the medium totally differs in every material particular from the majority of the phantoms evoked; that the family are barely rich enough to provide themselves with the necessaries of life, let alone a multitude of costly theatrical properties, avails nothing, although everybody can satisfy himself upon these points as I did.

"The first impression is that there is some trickery; for to think otherwise is to do violence to the world's traditions from the beginning until now; besides which the feeling of terror is lessened by the apparition being seen by each person in company with numerous other mortals like himself, and the locked hands and touching shoulders on each side soon beget confidence. If the shape is recognized it bows and retires, sometimes after addressing words in an audible whisper or a natural voice, as the case may be, to its friends, sometimes not.

"After an interval of two or three minutes the curtain is again lifted, and another form, quite different in sex, gait, costume, complexion, length and arrangement of hair, height and breadth of body, and apparent age, comes forth, to be followed in turn by others and others, until after an hour or so the session is brought to a close, and the medium reäppears with haggard eyes and apparently much exhausted.

"In the three séances I have attended I have seen shapes of Indian men* and women and white persons, old and young, each in a different dress, to the number of thirty-two; and I am told by respectable persons who have been here a long while that the number averages about twelve a night. The Eddys have sat continuously for nearly a year, and are

* "Quite a number of Indian spirits," says Dr. G. L. Ditson, "materialize themselves every night at the Eddys'; for Mrs. Eddy was, it is said, a noble, generous-hearted woman, who cherished the most friendly intercourse with these red men when in the flesh, and one severe winter kept in her house a whole family of them that might otherwise have perished."

wearied in body and mind by the incessant drain upon their vital force, which is said to be inevitable in these phenomena.

"For want of a better explanation I may as well state that they claim that the manifestations are produced by a band of spirits, organized with a special director, mistress of ceremonies, chemist, assistant chemist, and dark and light circle operators."

Col. Olcott describes these spirits, and of one of them, an Indian girl, he says:

"Honto is about five feet five inches high, a well-made, buxom girl, of dark copper complexion, and with long black hair. She is very agile and springy in gait, graceful in movement, and evidently a superior person of her class. At my second séance, she in my presence reached up to the bare white wall and pulled out a piece of gauzy fabric about four yards long, which parted from the plastering with a click, as if the end had been glued to it. She hung it over the railing to show us its texture, and then threw it into the cabinet. At either end of the platform she plucked, as if from the air itself, knitted shawls, which she opened and shook, and passed behind the curtain. Then descending the steps to the floor of the room, she pulled another from under Horatio Eddy's chair, where I had seen nothing but the bare floor a moment before. Then returning to the platform, she danced to the accompaniment of the violin, after which she reëntered the cabinet and was gone. Let it be noticed that this creature had the shoulders, bust and hips of a woman, a woman's hair and feminine ways, and that she was at least four inches shorter than William Eddy, who measures five feet nine inches, and weighs one hundred and seventy-four pounds."

Col. Olcott here quotes what was certified to by Mrs. Cleveland, an old lady of the neighborhood; but as there has been a misunderstanding about money between her and the Eddys, and she has since spoken equivocally in regard to her experiences, I have ruled out her testimony as of no importance either way, though her original declarations were probably true, as any one may learn on close inquiry.

The testimony of Mr. E. V. Pritchard of Albany is of a very different weight. For months he pursued his investigations at Chittenden. Repeatedly, day after day, the materialized figure of his deceased mother, an aged woman, would come out, put her arms about his neck, kiss him audibly, and lead him to a seat. Mr. Pritchard testifies that he could see every wrinkle of her face, the color of her eyes, and all the details of her dress, to the very ribbon in her old-fashioned cap. Once, as she receded toward the curtain, she began to sink to the floor just as "a piece of butter would melt down on a hot plate," and her figure dwarfed till it was not above eighteen inches in height. Mr. P. had seen the same thing happen once to Honto.

Since his long-continued experiences Mr. Pritchard has had no cause to have any misgiving as to the genuineness of the phenomena. To satisfy myself of this, I requested Dr. G. L. Ditson of Albany to call on him and learn what he could. Under date of Jan. 18th, 1876, Dr. Ditson writes me:

"Neither Mr. Pritchard nor his sister, Mrs. Packard, has had any misgivings in respect to the genuineness of the William Eddy manifestations. Lately Mr. Pritchard has been to 'Cascade,' Mrs. Andrews's home, and has had his faith confirmed—his faith in the actuality of the materialization of his spirit-friends; for *his mother appeared there exactly as she had at Chittenden*, wearing the same cap and ribbon, and the same dress in which she had so often showed herself at the Eddys'. Mr. P. staid about a month at Mrs. Andrews's. In the circle he was only about five or six feet from his mother's apparition, and, as the light was good (much better than at Chittenden), he could see her quite distinctly. She bowed to him also, and when he was quite satisfied that it was his mother, he said, 'Is that you, mother?' She replied in a loud whisper, 'Yes, my son.' Neither Mr. P. nor Mrs. Packard, who lived in the Eddy house for months, lay any stress on the reports from Mrs. Cleveland. They saw nothing that looked like fraud, and their opportunities were unequalled."

Col. Olcott resumes his narrative:

"Of the thirty-two spirit forms I have seen, more than three-fourths were recognized by persons present as near relatives. The first evening, my eyes not being accustomed to the light, nor my powers of observation trained to watch details, the spectral shapes came and went in a confusing manner; but the second and third séances found me prepared to scrutinize the phenomena with deliberation.

"The reader will please remember that owing to my inhospitable reception, the suspicions excited by the place and its surroundings, and the astounding claims put forth by the spiritual press as to the Eddy manifestations, I was on the alert to detect fraud and expose it. As each phantom came into view I observed its height against the door jamb, its probable weight, its movements, apparent age, style of wearing the hair, and beard if a man, the nature and elaborateness of its costume, and the external marks of sex, as regards form—all the while having in mind the square, Dutch build and heavy movements of William Eddy. I saw men, women and children come one after another before me, and in no one instance detected the slightest evidence of trickery.

"Among the remarkable tests of identity coming under my notice was the appearance of a young soldier of about twenty years of age, the son of Judge Bacon of St. Johnsbury, Vt., whose death occurred under painful circumstances in the army, and whose name or existence even had not been mentioned by his father to any person about the place. The spirit was clothed in a dressing-gown, light trousers, and a white shirt with turn-down collar. He was instantly recognized. The night that Mr. Pritchard was sitting on the chair H, two of his nephews, dressed differently, wearing their beards in different ways, differing in height and appearance in a marked degree, stepped forth and shook hands with him. I sat within five yards of them, and saw them with entire distinctness.

"The gentleman of whom mention has been previously made, Mr. E. V. Pritchard,* of Albany, is a retired merchant, whose credibility must be well known in that city at least. He came to the Eddys' in May, expecting to remain only a few days, but his experiences have been so satisfactory that he is still here. He first saw the spirit of his brother's son, who was killed in the army, and afterward his mother, his sister's husband, two of her sons and one son-in law, and his brother's son. He has seen four or five female spirits carrying children in their arms, and, setting them on the floor, lead them about by the hand. He has seen the children in some cases clasp their arms about their mothers' necks. Once an Indian woman brought in her papoose, swaddled in the Indian fashion, and he heard it cry. An Indian girl brought in a robin perched on her finger, which hopped and chirped as naturally as life.

"Mr. P. saw a mother spirit walk to the front of the platform and hold her babe over the railing toward the audience, so that they could see it kick its little legs, move its arms and hear it crow. Again, on another evening, three little girls, apparently four, six and eight years of age respectively, stood side by side in the door of the cabinet, and the eldest calling to her mother in the audience, spoke her own name, 'Minnie.' No William Eddy in this instance, surely. Mr. Pritchard has heard the spectres speak in all voices, from the faintest whisper to a full, natural voice. As regards costumes, he has seen the forms clothed in what appeared to be silk, cotton, merino, and tarletan, soldiers in uniform, one navy captain in full uniform, and wearing his side arms, women in plain robes and richly embroidered, Indian warriors in a great variety of costumes, some barefoot and others shod in moccasins. Once a pipe was lighted and handed to Honto, who walked about smoking it, and at each whiff her bronze face was illuminated so that every lineament was shown. She came and smoked in his very face to give him a perfect view of her own.

"Out of the mass of testimony I have noted in my memorandum I will only quote in addition what Mr. Bacon says, as this, added to what has preceded, should suffice to at least

---

* Dr. G. L. Ditson, of Albany, the well-known writer and Spiritualist, says of Mr. Pritchard, in whose company he witnessed the phenomena at the Eddys': "His veracity and good judgment no one will question who knows him."—E. S.

clear William Eddy from the suspicion of producing the phantom shapes by changes of voice and dress. John Bacon 2d of St. Johnsbury, Vt., is an associate Justice of the county court of Caledonia county. He came here August 22d, 1874, to see the phenomena. The first evening he saw the spirit of his father, who died forty-eight years ago. Recognized him by his shape. The form was dressed in dark clothes, with a standing shirt collar and white shirt. He was bare-headed. Standing erect he towered to the height of six feet one inch, and called his son by his Christian name, speaking in his familiar tones. His breathing was distinctly perceived in the act of speaking. Besides him the Judge has seen one sister, fifty-three years of age at the time of her decease, and another of only three years; his wife's father and mother (the latter wore a light dress and a white cap; she is a very short woman, not above five feet in height); and finally his own son, whose death has elsewhere been alluded to. By actual count kept he has seen sixty-six different spirits to date (Sept. 2d, 1874)."

According to Col. Olcott he had an interview with Andrew Jackson Davis before going to Chittenden, and in reply to Col. Olcott's question how he could account for the impartation of life to these temporary organisms, so that the heart can be felt to beat and the other physical operations be carried on, Mr. Davis said he had no explanation to offer, and left the riddle for the disciples of Comte and Tyndall to solve. He said that Varley, the English electrician, wrote to him recently to ask where was the connecting link between matter and spirit. He replied that it was just upon the plane of these materializations, where spirit descended toward matter, and matter ascended toward spirit, the point of contact would be found. There are: 1, solids; 2, fluids; 3, atmospheres; 4, ethers; 5, essences (the imponderable distilled out of the whole universe of matter). Matter is at its climax of progress there. Then takes place the alliance of spirit, and at this sensitive place occur all these apparitions. The spirit lifts matter up to this point, and by reducing its temperature and motion he evolves the apparition. The reversal of this action produces the vanishment of the shape. All forms and potencies exist in the atmosphere, and by the action of spirit upon them all these and any other desired results are attained.

Mr. Davis is disposed to regard all these materialization phenomena as "feats of jugglery by expert spirits, numbers of whom are deeply versed in chemistry and the other natural sciences." The phenomena, he thinks, are "necessary to convince nine-tenths of the world's people, that *death does not kill a man.*" He considers Katie King and the Eddy ghosts as of no importance as individual identifications; they are simply important as establishing the general doctrine of immortality.

But Mr. Davis does not regard himself or any other seer as infallible. His opinions must be taken with the qualifications he himself suggests. There are many intelligent witnesses who wholly dissent from the notion that there are no "individual identifications" in these materialization phenomena. They see no reason why the proofs of identification are not as strong in the case of materialized spirits as in the case of those spirits who manifest themselves only to the clairvoyant vision. The question of identification is equally difficult in all its phases.

"Vain is it," says Dr. John P. Gray, "to rely on the integrity and childlike honesty of the seer's outer-life character as a protection against illusion on this topic of identification; the world's history is full to overflowing of the recorded contradictions of seers."

There is still a long distance, it would seem, between the highest spirits and the Infinite Intelligence; and it is time that we were made to realize this important truth. In exposing the error of the common notion as to the infallibility of men when they have passed out of their earthly surroundings, Spiritualism is doing a service next to that of proving immortality. The hiatus caused by passing from the mortal to the spiritual state is not so serious as is generally supposed.

"You complain," says Shorter, "that the spiritual communications you receive are not to be implicitly trusted. Well, perhaps that is the very lesson they are chiefly designed to teach you." No one has done more than Mr. Davis to guard us from too hasty a confidence; and his cautions as to the materialization phenomena should be carefully heeded.

CHAPTER XI.

In this chapter I propose to consider the spirit-body; the testimony which seers and others offer on the subject, and which the phenomena of Spiritualism seem to confirm.

But some preliminary observations in regard to the weight to be attached to the revelations of seers are here in place.

Experience in Spiritualism soon teaches us to regard no spirit, seer, or revelator as infallible. There have been great mediums who have believed themselves the direct vehicles of the highest divine inspiration; but it would seem to be a divine law that human reason must be left free. The seer who plays the theosophist, and claims infallibility, is often blindest when he thinks himself most illumined. Humility is ever the best ground for our high researches. To get a sight of the stars by daylight we must go to the bottom of a well.

Swedenborg (1689–1772) was a great medium and seer; but I cannot believe he wholly escaped the influence of some of the deluding spirits, against whom he warns us. When he describes Quakers and Moravians as lingering in infernal wretchedness in the other world, merely on account of certain speculative beliefs held in this, I can see only inconsistency with those teachings which he gives us in his humbler yet higher moods.

But Swedenborg's testimony, when it accords with reason and with facts, must not be regarded as weakened, because he sometimes seems to err and give way to fantasies the most revolting. Though not infallible, he is oftentimes a divine teacher. It is when he claims infallibility, and threatens those who discredit him with some nameless spiritual injury, insanity, or loss, that we must question his illumination.

The imperfection of all individual revelations, through Messiahs and seers, is well explained by the Rev. James E.

Smith* (1854), who says: "Though the works of God are perfect, in universals, they are not so in particulars. This glorious truth contains the very seed of wisdom. The superficial opinion is, that every individual, or particular divine production, must be perfect, in the common sense of the word; and what is not perfect, men ascribe equivocally to Nature, or any other cause but God—a habit of mind which, logically developed, leads a man to its natural ultimate, practical and theoretical atheism; for, seeing nothing around him that is absolutely perfect, or free from defect, he seeks for the cause in an imperfect agent, and goes no further when he has found it.

"Were God's particular works all and alike perfect, there would be neither learning nor progress, no improvement, no amendment, no desire to improve or amend, and therefore no industry, no activity, no motive whatever even for action. God's works are a graduated scale of better and worse. Perfection belongs to the whole collectively; never to any of the parts.

"*No individual revelation whatever can be perfect, any more than any other individual or particular work of God.* There never was an age without prophets. They exist now, as real and genuine, though not as eminent and authoritative as ever. Prophets abounded in Israel. Prophecy then ceased, or rather they ceased to compile prophecies. Not understanding the nature of the mystic phenomena, they established *a creed, which prevails to this day, that revelation has ceased*, and that modern pretenders to inspiration are either madmen or impostors—the only intelligible mode of avoiding the difficulties which presented themselves to their minds—a mode still resorted to by Jews, Christians, Philosophers, Deists and Atheists, to account for all spiritual visitations, such as the mission of Mahomet or Swedenborg, which they cannot understand for the reason above given, their belief being that even

*Born in Glasgow, 1801, died in 1857. He was a Spiritualist long before 1848; and subsequently satisfied himself of the genuineness of the phenomena, through Mrs. Hayden, the excellent American medium. He wrote "The Divine Drama of Civilization," and edited the Family Herald.

a particular and local revelation from God *can never be characterized by any imperfection or any contradiction.*"

"Some persons ask," says Kardec, "Of what use are the teachings of the spirits if they offer to us no greater certainty than human teachings? The answer is easy: As we do not accept the teachings of all men with equal confidence, neither must we the teachings of all spirits. God has given us reason and discrimination to judge of spirits as well as of men. Surely the fact of our meeting in the world with bad men is not a reason for withdrawing ourselves from society. There are spirits of all degrees of goodness and of malice, of knowledge and of ignorance, all subject to the law of progress."

We must judge of their communications precisely as we would of those that come through channels mortal and terrestrial. We must learn to separate the wheat from the chaff, the spirit from the letter, the essentially divine from the enveloping finite. To ask why men were not created perfect, is equivalent to asking why they were created at all.

Among the truths to which Swedenborg, in company with all great seers, bears witness, is that of the spirit body. He tells us that thought implies a thinking substance, as much as sight or hearing implies a seeing and hearing substance; that it is as absurd to contemplate thought as something independent of the substance of the soul or spirit, as it is to contemplate sight or hearing independent of the substance of the eye or ear.

It is remarkable with what unanimity mediums everywhere and at all times have insisted on describing spirits as in the human form, and in representing man, in all the stages of his existence, as an organized being. This doctrine of a spirit body seems to be inseparable from all forms of Spiritualism. The oldest Magi, the wise men of Persia, believed in it. Hesiod and Homer teach it. Surely the attributes of mind will not be lessened in dignity by being indissolubly connected with an organism.

A spirit body, composed of elements imponderable and invisible in reference to our physical senses, is, as we have seen, in the second chapter of this work, a legitimate scientific conception, involving no chemical difficulty. Even all the constituents of our present earth-body may be held in solution, in a state invisible and impalpable, in the atmosphere; and how far matter may gain new properties or part with old ones by differentiations and transformations, ruled by spirit power, we are yet to learn.

"Let us distrust," says Chaseray, "our imperfect senses, since there are so many substances which we can neither feel nor see. Let us not be precipitate in denying the duality of the human being because the scalpel of the anatomist cannot reveal to our sight a principle eminently subtle. Man is not driven to annihilation even under the hypothesis of materiality." Chaseray thinks that the spirit body may some day be proved by science.

Even Cabanis (1757–1807), the great physiologist of France, who sees nothing but organism, who regards the brain as "an organ specially designed for the production of thought as the stomach and intestines are for digestion, and the liver for the filtration of the bile," and from whom Carl Vogt has borrowed some of his own rash expressions in opposition to the immortality of the soul—even Cabanis concludes by admitting that "a principle or vivifying faculty" is needed to account for the phenomena. He elsewhere tells us that for those who would establish the persistence of this principle or "cause," after the destruction of the living body, it may suffice to know that "the contrary opinion cannot be demonstrated by any positive arguments."

Spiritualism proves that the "contrary opinion" is wholly untenable; that there is a *somewhat*, not explicable by the known qualities of matter, which is the *antecedent of the organization;* that there can be no such thing as a gradual transition from known matter to thought, seeing that life is in every case *prior* to organization.

The notion of certain Spiritualists that the spirit body is evolved out of the physical is therefore a reversal of the order of things. "To make A the offspring of B, when the very existence of B as B presupposes the existence of A, is preposterous in the literal sense of the word, and a consummate instance of the hysteron proteron in logic."*

It is due to the memory of Cabanis to add, that in a posthumous letter, published by Dr. Bérard, he abandons his materialistic opinions and recognizes formally the necessity of a spiritual or immaterial† principle.

Dr. Georget, another celebrated French materialist, author of the "Physiology of the Nervous System" (1821), was led by the phenomena of clairvoyance and somnambulism, to reverse his whole philosophy and to proclaim, in his will, that he had arrived at a "profound conviction, founded upon incontestable facts," that there exists "an intelligent principle, altogether different from material existences; in a word, the soul and God."

The examples of Professor Hare, Dr. Elliotson, and many others, converted by the phenomena of Spiritualism from a life-long adherence to materialism, are further illustrations of the power of facts.

To name the great men, ancient and modern, who have entertained a belief in a corporeal principle surviving the physical body, would be an interesting but an endless task. Plato, in strict conformity with Modern Spiritualism, declares that "the apparitions of the dead are not mere groundless imaginations, but proceed from souls themselves, surviving in luciform bodies."

We have already seen that the Christian Fathers were divided in opinion in respect to the soul; some, who were Platonists, maintaining that it is an immaterial principle, devoid of all concretion, but invariably associated with a thin, flexible, and sensitive body, visible to the eye; while others, among whom Tertullian may be regarded as the chief, main-

* Coleridge's Biographia Literaria.

† One of Henry More's antagonists (1659) tells him that the word *immaterial* signifies nothing but a negation. More replies: "A negative particle, in composition with a word that denotes imperfection, implies positiveness and perfection, as in *infinite*, *immortal*, and the like; these remove the imperfections in *finiteness* and *mortality*, and imply something positive of a better nature. And so does *immaterial* remove the imperfections of discerpibility and impenetrability, and implies the contrary.'

tained that the soul is simply a second body. This they did to serve their theological notions in regard to the future punishment of the unregenerate. The abler writers, including Clement and Origen, taught the Platonic doctrine. Both parties, however, concurred in the fact of the spirit body.

"Even here in this life," says Cudworth, "our body is, as it were, twofold, interior and exterior; we having, besides the grossly tangible bulk of our outward body, another interior spiritual body, which latter is not put into the grave with the other."

"The primitive belief," says Herbert Spencer, "is that every dead man becomes a demon (spirit), who remains somewhere at hand, may at any moment return, may give aid or do mischief, and is continually propitiated. Hence among other agents whose approbation or reprobation is contemplated by the savage as a consequence of his own conduct, are the spirits of his ancestors."

This was meant as a reproach to Modern Spiritualism! I accept it as a confirmation that its fundamental fact is well known to men in a savage as well as to those in a civilized state.

In his "Physical Theory of Another Life," Isaac Taylor says: "What the Christian Scriptures specifically affirm is the simple physiological fact of two species of corporeity for man: the first that of our present animal and dissoluble organization; the second, a future spiritual structure, imperishable, and adorned with higher powers and many desirable prerogatives."

Thus the pneumatology of the New Testament as well as of the Old teaches the fact of a future spirit-body, and I may add that in many passages it assumes that the spirit-body is a present fact; as when the damsel Rhoda (Acts, xii.) told how Peter stood before the gate, and her hearers would not believe it, but replied, "It is his angel"; and as when Paul says, "There is a natural body and there is a spiritual body" —is *now*, not *shall be*.

The heathenish doctrine of the resurrection of the natural

body, so long an excrescence on rational Christianity, is now rarely preached except in a qualified sense that makes it less repulsive to scientific thought.

"The soul," says Lavater, "on leaving its earthly frame is immediately clothed in a spiritual frame withdrawn from the material. The soul itself, during its earth-life, perfects the faculties of the spiritual body, by means of which it will apprehend, feel, and act in its new existence."

It is not improbable that matter, as its elements become more subtile, is more suited for high organic forms. The body which is unfolded by natural processes from an egg contains in itself, even before the shell is broken, chemical substances which no test can discover in the egg or in the air. May there not be in man's constitution an anterior germ of spiritual vitality, from which, cotemporaneous with the growth of the physical, a spirit-body is developed?

"By the facts of somnambulism," says A. J. Davis, "the double nature of man is proved to a demonstration. From the universal exhibitions of a system of duality or twofold organization, it is but common sense to infer that the outer organs of vision, like all the other senses, are but the external form of interior correspondential principles, as words are the forms of thought."

The true and genuine body must be that which retains and preserves its organical identity amid the changes and the flux of matter, which the physical frame is constantly undergoing. The power which connects the gases, earths, metals, and salt into one whole, which penetrating them keeps them together, or dismisses some and attracts others, must be that divine and forming principle, the soul, binding the seeming duality of physical body and spiritual body in the strictest unity, so far as the exterior which changes, decays, and passes, can be bound to the interior which abides as the continent of man's individuality for the next stage of being.

But why not a duality of beast and plant, as well as of man? What of the lower animals? Do *they* have this inner, invisible body, the abiding principle of their external frames?

Yes, the psychical principle is that which controls all organic forms. But as to what becomes of the psychical individualization when organisms lower than the human are dissolved, we have only speculation and analogy for our guide. Seers and spirits are at variance on this inscrutable question. According to some the psychical element is permanently individualized only in man. As unripe seeds do not germinate, so the inferior forms of intelligence render up the psychical element at death to return to that source from which it was separated in organization.

But the higher Spiritualism teaches, that the psychical element of all animals, if not of all plants, is imperishable in its individualization. It is not necessary to suppose that the lower animals will have, in their remote future states, the same forms they had here. They may rise to higher forms of being, and, in some mysterious way, there may be a progress for them having some analogy with our own.

There is surely room enough for all, since the capacities of God's universe are limited only by his own infinity. Even for the innumerable germs that *seem* to perish, and of whose apparent waste atheistic Skepticism* has so much to say, there may be a provision by which all that is essential in them is not wasted, but returned with improved power to Nature's measureless receptacles.

Sir J. E. Smith (1759–1828), the distinguished botanist, was of opinion that in the vital principle we have a glimpse of the immediate agency of the Deity. He says: "I can no more explain the physiology of vegetables, than of animals, without the hypothesis of a living principle in both." What can this principle be but that one deific force, to which universal science is conducting us?

Charles Bonnet (1720–1793), the great Swiss naturalist, says: "The common opinion which would consign to an eternal death all organized beings, man alone excepted, would

* "See," says Strauss, "the small apples and pears fallen ere they were yet ripe; know that if the spawn of fish invariably attained full growth, all the rivers and seas would not suffice for them!" But does it follow that because Strauss does not see how such apparent waste is compensated, that there therefore *is* no compensation in the laboratories of Nature?

impoverish the universe. It would precipitate forever into the abyss of nothingness an innumerable multitude of sentient creatures, capable of a considerable increase of happiness, and which in repeopling and embellishing new earths, would exalt the adorable beneficence of the Creator."

This, I am disposed to think, is the general sentiment of Spiritualists, as it was of Leibnitz, Bishop Butler and Agassiz, on the subject of a future for the lower animals.

Bonnet believed further, that man's future body exists already with the body visible; and he believed that science would some day have instruments which would enable it to detect this body, formed as it probably is of the elements of ether or of light. Is not his prediction partially verified in the power of the photographer's apparatus to catch the impression of spiritual forms which our normal vision cannot detect?

This spirit-body, according to Bonnet, will not require those daily reparations which the animal body exacts, but will subsist undoubtedly by the simple energy of its principles and its mechanism. It will be superior to those laws of gravitation which limit grosser bodies. It will obey with ease and astonishing promptitude the slightest behests of the soul, and will transport us from world to world with a facility and a speed equal to that of light. By its superior powers we shall exercise without fatigue all our faculties, because the new organs through which the soul will unfold its motive force will be better proportioned to the energy of that force, and will not be subject to the influence of those disturbing causes which continually conspire to check and impede our activity in our present physical bodies. Our attention will seize at once and with equal clearness a very great number of objects, more or less complicate; it will penetrate them intimately, separate partial impressions from a general knowledge, and discover without effort resemblances the most delicate. Our genius will then be proportioned to our attention, for attention is the mother of genius.

But the development of these enlarged powers will probably be very gradual; it will be in proportion to our own efforts, our own aspirations and attainments. If we have led a sluggish, sensual life on earth, we must not hope that the spirit-body will at once make up for our delinquencies or convert a sinner into a saint, a blockhead into a Kepler or a Newton.

The student of spiritual phenomena is continually astonished by the vast amount of testimony, past and contemporaneous, in confirmation of them. The testimony of the past has a new interest and significance now that it is confirmed by marvels of daily occurrence.

In his remarkable account of "Spirit-rapping, healing, music, drawing, and other manifestations in Sunderland, England, in 1840, through Mary Jobson,"* my friend W. M. Wilkinson observes: "Enough there is to prove that all natural objects exist only by reason of a spiritual creative force, which projects and sustains them in the realm of matter, which we call the world, and that to have a manifestation of this spiritual force, it is only necessary that some conjoint conditions of mind and body should be so arranged as to be favorable to that end. The person in whom this occurs is called a medium."

Melancthon† says: "I have myself seen spirits, and I know many trustworthy persons who affirm that they have not only seen them, but carried on conversations with them." Luther bears testimony equally strong to the existence of the departed in spiritual forms; so do Calvin, Knox, Wesley, Oberlin. St. Augustine mentions saints by whom he was visited, and states that he himself had appeared to two persons who had known him only by reputation. At another time he appeared to a famous teacher of eloquence in Carthage, and explained to him several most difficult passages in Cicero's writings.

---

* See the London Spiritual Magazine, September, 1874.

† "De Anima Recogn.," Wittenberg, 1595, p. 317. Melancthon relates that Luther was visited by a spirit who announced his coming by "a rapping at the door." Richard Baxter (Saints' Everlasting Rest, Chap 7) says: "Yea, goodly, sober Melancthon affirms that he had seen such sights or apparitions himself." Baxter adds: "I have received undoubted testimony of the truth of such apparitions." For Wesley's experiences, see "Planchette," p. 31; for Oberlin's, ib., p 259. Oberlin, in his Memoirs, declares that for nine years he had constant interviews with his deceased wife. Luther's works *passim* show the entireness of his belief in apparitions.

Thus Augustine's testimony is in support of the theory that the spirit-body can be separated from the physical, even during the earthly lifetime of the individual.

Accounts, like the following, of the action of spirits in interposing to influence mortals at critical times, are very numerous. A famous German jurist, Counsellor Hellfeld in Jena, an hour before midnight was on the point of signing the death-warrant of a cavalry officer. His clerk was present. All at once they both heard heavy blows fall on the window as if the panes were struck with a cavalry whip. The judge delayed his action in consequence, and substituted a minor punishment; and before the year closed a criminal was caught who volunteered the confession that he was the perpetrator of the crime for which the innocent cavalry officer had been punished, and had been near to being executed.

It is not true that the intelligence exhibited by the supposed spirit is always measured by that of the medium. The instances to the contrary are innumerable. Witness the case of Mrs. Fox-Jencken's infant boy, less than six months old. Among the Camisard prophets (1686–1707) were many infant trance-mediums, who spoke in language altogether above their capacities. We hear of a boy fifteen months old who spoke in good French, "as though God were speaking through his mouth." Jacques Dubois says he has seen more than sixty children between three and twelve years of age, who exhibited similar powers. "I knew at Tyés," says Pierre Charman, "a man whose little boy, only five years old, prophesied, predicted disturbance in the church, exhorted to repentance, and always spoke in good French." The annals of witchcraft are crowded with similar phenomena, perfectly well authenticated.

Mr. E. B. Tylor, in his "Primitive Culture," shows how ancient are the phenomena of the instantaneous untying of complicate knots by spirit skill. This preternatural unbinding is vouched for by no less a personage than the crafty Ulysses himself on board the ship of the Thesprotians:

"Me on the well-benched vessel, strongly bound,
They leave, and snatch their meal upon the beach.
But to my help the gods themselves unwound
My cords with ease, though firmly twisted round."

In his "Theory of a Nervous Ether" (1873), Dr. B. W. Richardson suggests that there exists, in addition to a nervous fluid, a gas or vapor, pervading the whole nervous organism, surrounding as an enveloping atmosphere each molecule of nervous structure, and forming the medium of the influences transmitted from a nerve-centre to the periphery, and from the periphery to a nerve-centre.

Here we are brought by the latest inductive science close upon the confines of the spirit-body. Every investigator whose prejudices do not incapacitate him from looking into the facts, begins to see that some higher series of causes, hitherto denied by modern science, must be conceded in order to account for those phenomena of Spiritualism, inexplicable on any known principles.

"I have come to the conclusion," says J. H. Von Fichte (Stuttgardt, 1871), "that it is absolutely impossible to account for these (the spiritual) phenomena, *save by assuming the action of a superhuman influence.*"

"The spirit-body," says a spirit communicating through M. A. (Oxon.), "is the real individual; and though for a time it is clothed with fluctuating atoms, its identity is absolutely the same when those atoms are dispensed with. It is preserved after the death of the earth-body in precisely similar sort as it exists now, veiled in grosser matter." But these changing atoms, which the spirit-body attracts to itself, are according to this authority, no real part of the personality.

Spiritualism makes us realize that we are under the scrutiny of any spirit who, from curiosity or affection, may desire to know our deeds and our thoughts. In this tremendous fact, is there no incentive to right thinking and right doing?

"There is a wonderful world of spirit," says Leifchild, "and there are hierarchies of ministering spirits. Surely they form a great cloud of witnesses, who, though they sit aloof, intently watch our earthly course, and encourage us by their unseen but not always unfelt presence. With the speed of thought they interfuse their holiness into *our* thoughts. They shine into our earthly homes like morning beams, and they beautify our departure in death with the heavenly splendor of an evening Alp-glow.

"Blessed and blessing hierarchies! Not one of your innumerable cohorts can be subject to annihilation. You multiply by human death, you increase by spiritual selection, you obtain liberty through the grave, you gain light by looking on the countenance of the Divine. Not one single act of your beneficent ministry to man is altogether lost; every one is a celestial force. You have been often misapprehended and not seldom vulgarized. Distorted Science has denied you, scornful Naturalism has derided you, foolish Superstition has degraded you. Nevertheless you live, and you live for us. Were our eyes duly purged, we should behold you daily; were our ears rightly attuned we should listen to you hourly."

In Kardec's system the spirit-body is a fluidic vaporous envelope which he calls the *périsprit.* This, he says, he has neither invented nor supposed in order to explain phenomena; its existence has been revealed to him by spirits, and observation has confirmed it. It is supported, moreover, by a study of the sensations among spirits, and above all by the phenomenon of tangible apparitions, which would imply, according to the contrary opinion (that, namely, of the identification of the spirit-body with the spirit or soul), the solidification and disintegration of the constituent parts of the soul, and consequently its disorganization. It would be necessary, besides, to admit that this matter which can fall under the scrutiny of the senses is itself the intelligent principle; which is no more rational than to confound the body with the soul, or the clothing with the body. As to the intimate nature of the soul, it is unknown to us.

"When we call it *immaterial*," says Kardec, "we must understand the word in the relative and not in the absolute sense, for absolute immateriality would be nothingness; now the spirit is surely something, one might say that its essence is so superior that it has no analogy with what we call matter, and that for us it is immaterial."

Bacon's theory of the soul is like that of nearly all the great seers and mediums. [See page 86.] He, too, regards man as a trinity of earth-body, spirit-body, and spirit. As is God, so also, according to Bacon, is the spirit (spiraculum), which God has breathed into man, *scientifically incognizable;* only the physical soul, which is a thin, warm, material substance, is an object of scientific knowledge.

"Two different emanations of souls," says Bacon, "are manifest in the first creation, the one proceeding from the breath of God, the other from the elements." No knowledge of the rational soul (the spirit) can be had from philosophy; but in the doctrine of the sensitive, or produced soul (the spiritual body), *even its substance*, says Bacon, *may be justly inquired into.* "The sensitive soul must be allowed a corporeal substance, attenuated by heat and rendered invisible, as a subtle breath, or aura, of a flamy and airy nature, and diffused through the whole body."

Thoroughly acquainted with the spiritual phenomena of his day, and of antecedent times, Bacon teaches unequivocally the doctrine of the spiritual body and of the three-fold nature of terrestrial man. He says: "But how the compressions, dilatations and agitations of the spirit, which, doubtless, is the spring of motion, should guide and rule the corporeal and gross mass of the parts, has not yet been diligently searched into and treated."

"And no wonder," he adds, "since the sensitive soul itself," by which he means the spirit-body, "has been hitherto taken for a principle of motion, and a function, rather than a substance. But *as it is now known to be material*, it becomes necessary to inquire by what efforts so subtile and minute a breath can put such gross and solid bodies in motion."

"This spirit of which we speak," continues Bacon, "*is plainly a body*, rare and invisible, quantitative, real, notwithstanding it is circumscribed by space."

Bacon admits the facts of clairvoyance, or divination, and distinguishes between that proceeding from the internal power of the soul, as "in sleep, ecstasies, and the near approach of death," and that which comes from influx through "a secondary illumination, from the foreknowledge of God and spirits."

Never was I more impressed by Bacon's greatness as a sagacious interpreter of natural facts, than when I found him thus anticipating the highest conclusions of Modern Spiritualism, both on the subject of the spiritual body and on the distinction between the knowledge that is explicable by a theory of psychic force, and that knowledge which must come from "the illumination of God and spirits."

The questions raised by Dr. Rogers, Count Gasparin, Serjeant Cox and others, as to whether odic force or psychic force may not explain all the phenomena of Spiritualism, are here, with the discrimination of one who had studied all the facts of divination, and who speaks with unquestionable authority, decided in conformity with the views of Spiritualists.

It is true that Bacon adopts or reännounces opinions on this subject that may be found in Plutarch; but this does not detract from his merit as an original observer. He had verified the facts which Plutarch knew. In regard to mediumship, Plutarch explains how the violent ecstasy of inspiration results from the contest of two opposite emotions, the higher divine or spiritual emotion communicated to the medium, and the natural one proper to the medium himself; *just as an uneasy struggle between the natural and the communicated motion is produced in bodies to which, while by their nature they gravitate to the earth, a gyratory movement has been communicated.*

"Everything pertaining to the Deity," says Plutarch, "in and by itself, is beyond our power of perception, and when it reveals itself to us through some other agent (or medium), *it mixes itself up with the proper nature of that medium.*"

Here we have it explained why Swedenborg, Harris, Davis, and all other mediums, as well as inferior spirits, mix up errors with their communications of truth. Were it otherwise (could we accept any teacher as really infallible), would not our mental freedom be impaired, and much intellectual effort paralyzed?

Kardec's spirits merely repeat the teachings of Bacon as to the nature of the *périsprit*, or spiritual body. It constitutes for the spirit a fluidic, vaporous envelope, which, though invisible to us in *its* normal state, and in *our* normal state, does not the less possess *some of the properties of matter*. A spirit, then, is not a point, an abstraction, but a being, limited and circumscribed, to whom are wanting only the properties of visibility and palpability to resemble human beings. Why, then, can it not act on matter? Does not imponderable light exercise a chemical action on ponderable matter?

Newton tells us that the effluvium of a magnet can be so rare and subtle as to pass, without any resistance or any diminution of its force, through a plate of glass, and yet be so potent as to turn a magnetic needle beyond the glass. Why, then, may not the will-power of a spirit suffice to produce (as we know that it *does*) the most amazing effects upon matter?

We can now realize the profound meaning in that remark of Joubert: "*To create the universe an atom of matter sufficed.*"

Nothing is made out of nothing; but the sovereign power of God is not nothing: it is the source of matter as well as of spirit.

Even so orthodox an authority as the Catholic World (New York, 1874,) says: "Nothingness is to be considered, under God's hand, as a *negative potency of something real.*"

And if an equally high Protestant authority were needed, I might quote Christlieb (1874), who says: "Although God is spirit, he has, nevertheless, a nature which we may term substantial. *It is designated as light and fire.*"

The creation out of nothing is virtually abandoned by admissions like these; and they render some form of Pantheism inevitable. It must be a form involved in that of Theism, as the less is in the greater. Bruno, the martyr philosopher, who was burnt at the stake in 1600, tells us truly: "If you think aright you will find a divine essence in all things." But he adds that, though it is impossible to conceive Nature separated from God, we can conceive God separated from Nature. God, he tells us, is *superessentialis, supersubstantialis.* Though He caused the universe, He is not limited by it. In this conception lies the truth which must reconcile the pantheistic demand of science and the theistic demand of theology and faith.

According to Swedenborg, that which underlies matter and is its substance, flows forth from the Divine substance. But mind causes, or rather coöperates to cause, the form, incidents, and appearance, under which we give to this substance the name of Matter. This is not a false appearance; it is a reality, but of it we can know nothing, save from the action of mind on the impressions made by this substance on the mind through and by means of the senses. The importance of this truth lies in the rational belief it permits us of a body, a home, and a world, when we leave this world. If material substance is but the effluence from and of the Divine substance, caused to affect us in a certain way in this world, the same effluence may provide for us a spiritual body and a spiritual world.*

The matter of the spirit-body is flexible and expansible; it changes at the will of the spirit, who can give himself such or such an appearance at his pleasure. It is because of this property of his fluidic envelope that the spirit who wishes to be recognized by friends on the earth can present the exact appearance he had when living; re-producing even the bodily scars or malformations by which he was marked.

Spirits, says Milton,

"—In what shape they please,
Dilated or condensed, bright or obscure,
Can execute their airy purposes,
And works of love or enmity fulfill."

"It is an extravagant conjecture of mine," says Locke, that spirits can assume to themselves bodies of different bulk, figure, and conformation of parts."

---

* See "The Infinite and the Finite," by Theophilus Parsons; p. 15.

Spirit hands may be the visible and tangible parts of an invisible intangible being; but sometimes they are tangible without being visible, and sometimes visible without being tangible. The instantaneous disappearance of materialized bodies or parts of the bodies, proves that the matter of which they are composed is eminently subtle, bearing some resemblance, perhaps, to those substances that can pass alternately from the solid to the fluid, or gaseous state, and *vice versa.* Here a new order of facts is introduced, and science may some day discover a new law for their explanation.

"Is it not in the most rarefied gas, in the most imponderable fluids," asks Kardec, "that industry finds its most powerful motors?" What is there, then, strange in admitting that a spirit, by the aid of his spirit-body, can raise a table?

"Being able to take all appearances," says Kardec, "the spirit presents himself under that by which he would be most readily recognized, if such is his desire. Æsop, for example, as a spirit is not deformed; but if he is evoked as Æsop, he will appear ugly and humpbacked, with the traditional costume. . . . If the simply visual apparition might be attributed to illusion, the doubt is not permitted when you can grasp it, handle it, when it seizes you and holds you fast. However extraordinary these phenomena may be, all the marvelous disappears when we learn that far from being contrary to Nature's laws, they are only a new application of them."

By its nature and in its normal state, the spirit-body is invisible, and it has that property in common with many fluids which we know exist, and yet which we have never seen; but it can also, the same as other fluids, undergo modifications that render it perceptible to the sight, whether by a sort of condensation or by a change in the molecular disposition; it then appears to us under a vaporous form.

By further condensation the spirit-body may acquire the properties of solidity and tangibility; but it can instantaneously resume its ethereal and invisible state.

We can understand this state by comparing it with that of invisible vapor, which can pass to a state of visible fog, then become liquid, then solid, and *vice versa*. These different states of the spirit-body are the result of the will of the spirit, and not an exterior physical cause, as in our gases.

According to Kardec, when the spirit appears to us he puts the spirit-body into the state necessary to render him visible. In order to do this, his will is ordinarily insufficient; for the modification of the spirit-body is effected by its combination with the fluid of the medium; but this combination is not always possible, *which explains why the visibility of spirits is not general.* It is not enough that the spirit desires to be seen; it is not enough that a person desires to see him; it is necessary that the two fluids should combine, and that the medium's supply should be sufficient; perhaps, also, that there should be other conditions to us unknown at present.*

Another property of the spirit-body and which pertains to its ethereal nature, is penetrability. Matter is no obstacle to its passage through everything, even as the light passes through transparent bodies. This is why no closing can shut out spirits; they visit the prisoner in his cell as easily as they do the man in the open fields.

In regard to the materialization of articles of clothing, ornaments, flowers, &c., Kardec questioned the spirits closely, and here is the result: The spirit acts on matter; he draws from the universal cosmic matter the elements necessary to form, at his will, objects having the appearance of various bodies which exist on the earth. He can also by his will effect an intimate transformation of elementary matter, and impart to it certain properties. This faculty is inherent in the nature of the spirit, who often, when necessary, exercises it without thinking, as an instinctive act. The objects formed by the spirit have a temporary existence; he can make and unmake them at will. These objects may become visible and tangible to earthly persons; and *could* be made to have a character of permanence and stability; but this, according to Kardec's informant, is contrary to order, and is not done.

* See "The Book on Mediums, by Allan Kardec;" an excellent translation of which into English by Emma A. Wood has been published by Colby & Rich, Boston, Mass. I have been indebted to it in these quotations from Kardec.

It *was* done, however, in the experiments at which Professor Crookes, Mr. Harrison, and many others were present; and some of the cloth which Katie cut from her tunic still remains materialized. It was said by the spirit, however, that a special effort was needed to give the cloth this character of stability.

From the facts here brought together, it may be inferred that the spirit-body is not a mere hypothesis; it is proved by the phenomena and the inductions of Spiritualism; by the objective appearance of spirits themselves in bodies; by the testimony of clairvoyants who can see spirits in the human form; by the phenomena of somnambulism and clairvoyance, indicating supersensual powers, requiring organs other than those of the physical body; by all the analogies which reason and experience supply; and by the belief of men in all ages and climes, a belief founded on the actual reäppearance after death of deceased relatives and friends.

Add to these considerations the facts of double consciousness, pointing to a double organism; also the marvels of memory, in which faculty impressions inhere and persist which are inexplicable under the theory of materialism, involving a constant flux and removal of the molecules of the organs of thought. Only the existence of a spiritual body can account for these things.

CHAPTER XII.

The existence of a single elementary substance or force, from which, by differentiation, transformation, and the adjustment of proportions, all the varieties and properties of matter are produced, is an hypothesis to which the whole drift of contemporary science is bringing us nearer with every fresh accession of knowledge.

We know that a very slight change in the arrangement of

elemental particles converts wholesome food into poison. Two harmless substances, combined in certain proportions, can produce a deleterious one. Without changing the proportions, a slight change in the molecular arrangement changes properties; makes the opaque transparent; the palatable, unsavory.

"Since the spirit," says Kardec, "has by his simple will so powerful an action on elementary matter, it may be conceived that he cannot only form substances, but can denaturalize their properties, will having herein the effect of a re-agent."

If, as Liebig, Dumas, and other chemists have asserted, all plants and animals are solidified air, why may not all matter be the product of solidified forces, having their origin in the essence and ultimate reason of things—in that force and necessity which derive all their virtue from the Divine Idea? This is no fanciful inquiry; its practical interest and importance are brought nearer to us every day by the advance of science.

The phenomena here recorded show that matter is not altogether the stuff which our senses would make it appear. "The force which every being is possessed of," says Vera, "as well as the *form* or law according to which it acts and displays its powers, lies in its very nature, *i. e.*, in its idea. The difference of forces is owing to the difference of ideas. Matter is a force, and the soul is a force, and, as forces, they are the product of one and the same idea, and both produce similar effects; for instance, the soul moves the body, and a body moves another body. Their difference is to be found in their specific elements, or in what constitutes their special idea; for instance, space, and time, extent, attraction and repulsion, &c., for matter; imagination, will, thought, &c., for the soul."*

As idea is force, and the source of all forces, so if there be no diminution in the quantity of force, it is because its principle, its idea, suffers no deterioration.

---

* See A. Vera on "Ideas as Essence and Force," in the St. Louis Journal of Speculative Philosophy for July, 1874.

If a materialized spirit—by which I mean a spirit animating a visible, tangible body—can make the matter thus embodied dissolve and then at once reäppear by an effort of the will, it is not difficult to conceive that the universe itself may be a concretion of forces, the trunk-force of which is in the Divine Idea.

While Spiritualism is in harmony with many of the facts on which the Darwinian theory is based, it supplies a new order of facts from which we infer that the idea must ever precede the organism; and that the attempt to prove that this idea is developed through immense periods of time by purely physical means and processes is a fallacy. "Living beings," says Stirling, "do exist in a mighty chain from the moss to the man; but that chain, far from founding, is founded *in* the idea, and is not the result of any mere natural *growth* into this or that. That chain is itself the most brilliant stamp and sign-manual of design."

"Even granting," says Vera, "that the germ be endowed with an inexhaustible power of begetting similar individuals, or that it should contain, like some infinitesimal quantity, an infinite number of germs, such hypotheses will explain neither the initial germ, nor the unity of the species, nor even the grown-up and complete individual. . . . The idea must constitute the common stock, and the ultimate principle to which the individual, the species, and the genus, owe their origin and existence."

"*Thought is a motion of matter,*" says Moleschott. But this is no more of an explanation than it would be to try to account for the sentiment and the charm in a melody of Mozart's by saying, "It is a motion of matter." All that science can fairly hypothecate is, that *Thought is accompanied by a motion of matter;* for, were the head and brain so transparent that this motion could be seen, the mystery of thought would be as far as ever from being solved.

"*No thought without phosphorus,*" says Moleschott.* He

* Locke must have had a presentiment of the appearance of a Moleschott on our planet, for he says: "A chemist shall reduce Divinity to the maxims of his laboratory, explain morality by sal, sulphur and mercury. Let

might as reasonably have said, *No thought without rhubarb.* Spiritualism proves that there can be thought without any brain which a mortal chemist can analyze. Liebig's sarcasm is perfectly just when he says, that the bones should produce more thought than the brain, if Moleschott's asseveration is true. "The honor of the discovery that phosphorus exists in the brain," says Liebig, "belongs not to me, but to Dr. Moleschott; and in my Chemical Letters I have declared it to be a mistaken idea, not based on a single fact."

To Liebig's remark, "We know nothing of the origin of an idea," Büchner's reply is, that "None but a mind prejudiced in favor of a superstition" could make such an assertion; and yet all the light which Büchner himself can throw on the origin of an idea is to repeat Moleschott's assertion, that *thought is a motion of matter;* an assertion which, whether true or false, could never be proved, even if we were to exclude those spiritual facts which disprove it utterly.

"We do not know," says Materialism, "all the powers of matter, its magical and spiritual nature, and its life eternal."

Then if we do not know them, how can any one say that they are not what is meant by spirit? The physiologist of mind, who would trace it to *simple brain motion*, is compared by Ferrier to the unheeding woodman who severs the bough on which he stands; for "*being* cannot be meaningless; its essence must be conscious intelligence."

Mr. Tyndall would trace all the phenomena of mind and matter to the potencies of atoms. He allows Theism, however, to entertain its little hypothesis, and leaves it an open question whether atoms may not have had a Divine Creator.

"Abandoning all disguise," he says, "the confession I feel bound to make before you is, that I prolong the vision backward across the boundary of the experimental evidence, and discern in that matter which we, in our ignorance, and not-

---

a man be given to the contemplation of one sort of knowledge, and that will become everything." With the sanguine positiveness of a youthful scientist, Moleschott (1862) says: "It is not reflection, but obstinacy, not science, but faith, which supports the idea of a personal continuance after death." Why not be consistent, and call this obstinacy a defect of phosphorus in the brain?

withstanding our professed reverence for its Creator, have hitherto covered with opprobrium, *the promise and potency of every form and quality of life.*"*

I agree with Mr. Tyndall that there is nothing very alarming in the mild and contradictory materialism that would not exclude the postulate of a Creator behind and beyond matter. His "confession" is not a startling one, either to the Materialist or the Spiritualist; for it is an attempt to sit at the same time on the stools of both; nor is it striking for its novelty.

Spiritualism casts no "opprobrium" on matter, since it holds that individualized mind must, in the next stage of being, continue to manifest itself through an organism, and this organism must be something.

If Mr. Tyndall means merely to repeat Locke, and say that all that he would suggest is, that matter may be *divinely* impressed, with the power of generating mind, then he at once spiritualizes matter, and lowers the flag of materialism.

But this is not what he means. When he tells us that matter may contain "the promise and potency of every form and quality of life," what he means, obviously, is that, among other qualities of life which mere matter may evolve, is that of mind. Now this idea has been often put forth, long before Mr. Tyndall's day, and as often answered. By no one has it been answered better than by Schelling (1775–1854), who said of the attempts, in his day, to make matter account for *all* the phenomena of life: "To explain *thinking* as a material phenomenon, is possible only in this way: that we reduce Matter itself to a spectre—to the mere modification of an Intelligence whose common functions are thinking and matter."

Coleridge, who was accustomed to borrow from Schelling, expresses the same idea thus, and his words fully answer all that Mr. Tyndall has to say about matter: "As soon as ma-

*On reconsideration Professor Tyndall modified this expression. The revised form of it is as follows: "By an intellectual necessity I cross the boundary of experimental evidence, and discern in that matter which we, in our ignorance of its latent powers . . . have hitherto covered with opprobrium, the promise and potency of *all terrestrial life*."

terialism becomes intelligible, it ceases to be materialism. In order to explain *thinking* as a material phenomenon, it is necessary to refine matter into a mere modification of intelligence, with the two-fold function of *appearing* and *perceiving*. Even so did Priestley, in his controversy with Price." (Even so would Tyndall do now!) "He stripped matter of all its material properties; substituted spiritual powers; and when we expected to find a body, behold! we had nothing but its ghost—the apparition of a defunct substance!"

"To say that matter is the principle of all things," remarks Paul Janet, "is simply equivalent to saying, We do not know what is the principle of all things—a very luminous science indeed! Even in its claim that matter is eternal, Materialism has to beg its premises, and to proceed wholly on a metaphysical, *à priori* assumption. If Materialism does not explain matter, much less does it explain mind and thought."

The ignorance which philosophical science is always compelled to avow, in regard to first causes, makes dogmatic atheism impossible for the truly scientific mind. The skeptical attitude is legitimate; the coarse confidence which denounces all belief in a Supreme Being, is the proclaimer of its own insufficiency and charlatanry. Mr. Tyndall is far from this.* If he chooses to call by the name of Matter the unknown *something* that produces Mind, he is at perfect liberty to do so. Others may prefer to call it by the name of Spirit. In the "prolongation of his vision backward" he has got as far as atoms. But we have seen that the Materialism which stops at atoms is false and imperfect, since it would localize, in them, properties for which atoms supply no cause. If atoms are the ultimate reality, the one real sub-

*Since this was written, Prof. Tyndall has disclaimed atheistic intentions. He says: "Were the religious views of many of my assailants the only alternative ones, I do not know how strong the claims of the doctrine of *materialistic atheism* upon my allegiance might be. Probably they would be very strong. But, as it is, I have noticed, during years of self-observation, that it is not in hours of clearness and vigor that this doctrine commends itself to my mind; that in the presence of stronger and healthier thought it ever dissolves and disappears, as offering no solution of the mystery in which we dwell, and of which we form a part." Let us hope that Prof. Tyndall will, even in this life, outgrow his bigoted opposition to the facts of Spiritualism. In those "hours of clearness and vigor," of which he speaks, does he never feel a little shaky in the arrogant position he has assumed toward the testimony of such men as Wallace and Crookes?

stance, then there is no place for spirit, no future for man; an assumption wholly disproved by the facts of this volume.

In the fullness of time Modern Spiritualism has come forth to demonstrate that the atomic *theory* must be supplemented by the spiritual *fact*. That same Spiritualism which Mr. Tyndall, in his unscientific spleen, dismisses as "degrading," shows by its phenomenal evidences, as here recorded and authenticated, that there is a power using these atoms at its pleasure, ruling them, instead of being ruled *by* them.

Mr. Tyndall refers to certain "rash and ill-informed persons" as "being ready to hurl themselves against every new scientific revelation." Alas! Is he himself one of these *rash, ill-informed* persons? So it would seem; for, chafe as he may, and sneer as he may, *the facts of Spiritualism are now facts of Science;* and he is so "ill-informed" as not to have found it out, and so "rash" as to put himself on the record against them.

He conducts us as far back as atoms, and there sets up his board, labeled, *No Thoroughfare.* But Spiritual Science disregards his warning and passes on; *whither*, the next chapter may show.

CHAPTER XIII.

Modern Science, including, as it does, Modern Spiritualism, helps us to a conception of a force behind and beyond atoms.*

The unity of all phenomena was the dream of ancient philosophy. To reduce all this multiplicity of things to a single principle has been, and continues to be, the ever-recurring problem. Water, air, fire, the primary elements, were sever-

* For the facts and some of the language of this chapter, see the untranslated works of Emile Barnouf, especially his "La Science des Religions;" the "Unity of Natural Phenomena" of Emile Saigey; the "Constitution of Matter" of Fernand Papillon; and the papers on "Matter, Ether, and Spirit," by the late Israel Dille, which have appeared in Brittan's Quarterly Journal of Spiritual Science. My principal indebtedness is to Barnouf.

ally and collectively imagined, by the great thinkers of antiquity, as the original factor.

To the question of a unity of substance, Greek science repeatedly applied itself.

The innumerable varieties in forms, qualities, and habits, in both the vegetable and animal kingdoms suggest the existence of forces adequate to the production of all the differentiations in nature. Hence to mount to the scientific conception of a single force as the originator and regulator of all these minor forces is the legitimate effort of all profound thought on the subject.

It was this craving for unity, which led the white men of Asia, the ancient Aryan race, to the conception of God as the one substance, immanent in the universe. At first they were polytheists, but with the progress of thought their number of gods diminished, and the authors of the Veda at last arrived at the conception of a unity of forces, of a Divine Power as the ultimate substratum of things. They regarded the beings of the world as, in effect, composed of two elements : the one real and of a nature permanent and absolute, and the other relative, flowing, variable, and phenomenal; the one spirit, the other matter, but both proceeding from an inseparable unity, a single substance.

The unity of physical forces is the point on which Science has its eyes now fixed. Materialism is not more eager than Spiritualism for the proof. Already has it been demonstrated that heat, electricity, light, magnetism, chemical attraction, muscular energy, and mechanical work, are exhibitions of one and the same power acting through matter. That all these forces may be transformed into motion, and by motion reproduced, is now something more than an hypothesis. *Hence the deduction that all physical phenomena have one and the same primordial agent as their original generator.*

Chemistry, by its theory of equivalents, is tending to unity. Few intelligent chemists now regard the elements ranked as simple as being simple any further than the present imperfection of our instruments compels us to class them as such

The employment of the balance has demonstrated that in the chemical transformations of bodies, nothing is created, nothing is lost.

Hence the sum of the material elements is constant, and, as it is impossible to conceive a limit to the universe, this sum is infinite ; and thus the aspects so various which matter presents consist only in the *forms* it successively takes on according to the combinations of its chemical elements.

But the substance of things evades all chemical testing ; and so the simple bodies of chemistry are themselves only forms, more or less elementary, the agglomeration of which produces compounds.

If by the theory of equivalents these forms should be some day reduced to unity, *chemistry* will be entitled to infer, with some reason, the substantial unity of the universe.

Neither the primitive cell, regarded as an elementary form of life, nor any principle known to science, suffices to explain life itself, or that power of action which is in the living being at all the epochs of its existence, and consequently in the cell. In addition, therefore, to the material and sensible elements, there must be in it a principle inaccessible to observation ; and it is this principle which is the agent of life, the impelling cause of vital motion and of all differentiations.

But the reduction of all living forms to unity, that is, to the cell, is an indication that the vital agent is itself a form of the one primitive force, and thus *physiology* tends to unity by the way of morphology ; and this reduction of organs to unity may be proved for plants as well as for animals.

The unity of the principle of life and thought is another conclusion, to which science is tending in the department of physiology. Every primary germ owes its evolution to the spirit or idea involved. If the cell is the most elementary form of the living being, the principle of life which it encloses cannot be developed except in so far as the form at which it ought to arrive *resides in it already in the state of idea.* This idea expands with the life, ramifies with it, accommodates itself to the means and conditions which the general order of the universe imposes; and *thus the study of the psychical nature of man* points also in the direction of unity. Spiritualism, through all its facts, is suggestive of unity.

The embryo is preserved by intelligent processes of which neither itself nor its parent knows anything. This intelligence is a property of the life by which they live.

This life, what is it but the pervading efflux of the deific love and life vivifying all nature and sustaining the animal and vegetable world as well as the world of mind?

Should it be objected that this proves too much; that it involves the identity of the vital principle of animals and vegetables, let us not shrink from the conclusion. The essential unity of all spirit and all life with this exuberant life from God is a truth from which we need not recoil, even though it bring all animal and vegetable forms within the sweep of immortality.

The universe is not dead. Think you this earth of ours is a lifeless, unsentient bulk, while the worm on her surface is in the enjoyment of life? To an inquiry whether the soul is immortal, Apollonius, one of the greatest of the ancient mediums, replied, "Yes, immortal—but like everything."

These suns, systems, planets and satellites are not mere mechanisms. The pulsations of a divine life throb in them all, and make them rich in the sense that they too are parts of the divine cosmos. Dissolution, disintegration and change are not death while an immortal principle survives.

"Science," says the Duke of Argyll, "in the modern doctrine of the conservation of energy and the convertibility of forces, is already getting a firm hold of the idea, that all kinds of force are but forms of manifestations of one central force issuing from some one fountain head of power. Sir John Herschel has not hesitated to say, that '*it is but reasonable to regard the force of gravitation as the direct or indirect result of a consciousness or a will existing somewhere.*'"

In support of the identity of life and spirit, the Spiritualist will find some unexpected allies. Even so orthodox a teacher as President Noah Porter comes up to the vindication of the grand truth, and in vindicating it he has to lend his support to the inevitable doctrine of a spiritual body.

"The soul," he says, "beginning to exist as the principle of life, *may have the power to create other bodies than the physical for itself, or it may already have formed another medium or body in the germ, and may hold it ready for occupation and use as soon as it sloughs off the one which connects it with the earth.* . . . The evidence of observation and of facts is decisive that the soul begins its existence as a vital agency, and emerges by a gradual waking into the conscious activities of its higher nature."

The soul which has had enough divine intelligence to prepare for itself a body in this world may be trusted to have ready a fitting substitute when death loosens the physical tie. If from a little microscopic cell, by successive differentiations, it may evolve man's complex organism, surely it may, from its higher point of being, evolve future organisms suited to its more advanced states.

But it is not merely Protestant theology that concurs in this view of the soul as the vivifying principle, active not only in the formation and functional processes of the body, but in the exercise of man's conscious activities. The highest Catholic authority teaches the identity of the vital and the psychical principle. By a brief dated April 30th, 1860, the Pope declares that the doctrine of the substantial unity of the principle of life and that of thought is *according to faith*, and he condemns any contrary opinion as inconsistent with Catholic teaching.

Both Plato and Aristotle had taught this doctrine. They tell us that the life comes from the soul; from that which feels and thinks. "No," says Descartes; "the soul is that which thinks; consequently we must not attribute to it vital phenomena of which it has no consciousness." To this objection Leibnitz replies that we certainly do have confused, indistinct perceptions of which we are not conscious at the time. Leibnitz plainly refers to what in our day Dr. Carpenter calls *unconscious cerebration.*

G. E. Stahl (1660-1734,) going somewhat further than Leibnitz, and anticipating the doctrine of unconscious cerebration, shows that there are mental operations independent of consciousness. He teaches that the true principle of life is the soul. Were this soul blind and unintelligent, it would do no more and no better than matter itself; but if it is capable of directing the movements of the body towards an end, it is because it is intelligent; in what then does it differ from the rational soul or spirit? True, in our normal state, it may not have a consciousness of all its acts; but from this it does not at all follow that it may not perform them.

The facts of double consciousness, apparent in the phenomena of somnambulism, mesmerism, and Spiritualism, confirm these views. They show that the nature of the soul is complex; that this complexity may include the vital processes; and that both intelligence and life may be the resultants of a single force.

"No proof of the soul's immortality," says Papillon, "is so strong as that we draw from the necessary simplicity and eternity of all the principles of force. Nothing bears witness so powerfully to the majestic reality of a God as the spectacle of those diversities, all harmonious, which rule the infinite range of forces, and bind in unity the ordered pulses of the world."

There is a principle of moral and intellectual unity, and we call it *reason.* Were all the facts of observation established as absolute truths, admitted by science, discussion would cease and there would be no more diversity of opinion. Now *psychology* demonstrates that the two or three general formulas or principles of reason are but the analytical development of one single idea, to which we may give what name we see fit, but which religion and philosophy almost unanimously call *the idea of God.*

"This idea," says Burnouf, "constitutes the basis of thought in all its degrees. In man it leads to the highest regions of speculation; to all animals it gives the means of motion, of alimentation, of reproduction; to every living thing it gives the general form of life. It resides in the cell; it gives unity to the infinite movements and to the innumerable shapes of the universe."

"All existence," says Oersted, "is a dominion of Reason. The laws of Nature are laws of reason, and all together form an endless unity of reason, one and the same throughout the universe."

Thus in physical science, in astronomy and chemistry, for the inorganic world, and in physiology and psychology for the world of living beings, the tendency at this moment is toward unity, and all the analyses of science, physical and psychical, converge in this direction.

"What do we know of an atom, apart from force?" asks Faraday. "You conceive a nucleus, which may be called *a*, and you surround it with forces, which may be called *m*; to my mind, your *a*, or nucleus, vanishes, and substance consists in the energy of *m*. In fact, what notion can we form of a nucleus, independent of its energy?"

Thus is scientific thought forever shadowing forth the hypothesis that matter, in its last analysis, must be resolved into force; and thus we find it is no chimerical dream to suppose that the deific idea constitutes at once the essential form and the substance of things.

If the prospect is that in this all-embracing unity matter and spirit will be made to appear as phenomenal manifestations of one divine substance, let us not be alarmed. Pantheism is true as far as it goes, but it must be supplemented by Theism before the whole truth can be apprehended; nor is there contradiction in this. The notion of a creation out of nothing is now so modified by the most advanced Christian theologians, that it is virtually abandoned. At once intramundane and supramundane, immanent and transcendent, God appears, more and more to the modern conception, as both automatic Nature and absolute Spirit.

"The difficulties of thought," says Picton, "the silence of the heavens, the actual breathing, deathless beauty of creation, command us, with an inspiration which the age will not resist, to see God not so much as the meditative Designer who makes, but rather as the Eternal Power which constitutes and is the All in All."

As we draw nearer to a principle of unity, we draw nearer to a conception of God. What relations has Spiritualism to this conception? The answer was given when we found that Spiritualism, like every other science, teaches the unity of all forces and all phenomena. But the question shall have a further consideration.

CHAPTER XIV.

The thinking spirit being itself of a divine, an immortal nature, the search after God seems inseparable from the development of our moral and intellectual faculties. Having, at least in our lower and normal state of consciousness, no explanation within ourselves of our existence, we rise to the conception of an infinite, uncaused, intelligent Power, having his reason for being within himself, and from whom the principle of our limited being is mysteriously derived.

What bearing do the facts of Modern Spiritualism have on this theistic conception?

D'Holbach (1723–1789), author of "La Système de la Nature," and still perhaps the most famous of all atheistic writers, says: "It is necessary to fall back on the doctrine, *so little probable*, of a future life and of the immortality of the soul, in order to justify a belief in Divinity."

Even in D'Holbach's view, the one belief necessarily involved the other. He could not well see how a Spiritualist could be an atheist. But he did not make allowance for all the inconsistencies of human thought.

"That we are to live hereafter," says Bishop Butler, "is just as reconcilable with the scheme of atheism, and as well to be accounted for by it, as that we are now alive is: and therefore nothing can be more absurd than to argue from that scheme that there can be no future state."

Bishop Butler is right. Strange as it may seem, there are atheistic seers and atheistic spirits.

At the first glance a belief in spirits would seem to facilitate belief in a Supreme Spirit, author and ruler of all; and so it does. For one of the principal arguments of speculative atheism is annihilated by the very fact of the existence of a spirit, exercising clairvoyant powers, and independent of the material impediments of space and time. But history shows that a sincere belief in spirits and a future life may exist independently of any belief in a God. The old polytheism was largely a belief in mere spirits; and the uncivilized tribes who believe fully in spirits are often found without a notion of any other deities than their departed ancestors and great men.

Man, however, as he advances in culture, is forced to struggle with the theistic idea. That such a problem as the existence of a God is placed before him is itself an earnest of his immortality; a promise written in the very texture of his being that his profound questionings shall some day be answered.

"Great," says Aimé-Martin, "is the creature to whom it is allowed to imagine questions to which a God only can reply."

So stupendous seems the question of a God in its proportions to our faculties as normally limited, that it is not surprising so many reverent minds should shrink from it altogether. "It is when we acknowledge that we do not know God, that we know him best," says St. Denis, the areopagite. "That which I conceive," says Fichte, "becomes finite through my very conception of it; and this can never, even by endless exaltation, rise into the Infinite."

But broader views of man's complex nature lead us to realize that the unfathomable exists in the human soul as well as in the nature of God; that we do not see the *whole* of man in his normal and material limitations; that he has powers and a hidden intelligence, altogether unexplained by any experience-theory, or any theory of hereditary transmission, or of knowledge got through the physical senses; and we begin to have glimpses of actual relations of the finite to the Infinite. We learn, upon reflection, that it is not less difficult to comprehend how a finite, derived and dependent being can exist, than to form a conception of an absolute, omnipotent and omniscient God.

To say that we bring God down to some measure of anthropomorphism by the very conception of him, is simply to beg the whole question, and to deny the inference which the phenomena of clairvoyance and Spiritualism abundantly authorize—the inference, namely, that man has in himself an element relating him to the Infinite.

The same motive that would keep us from studying the infinite, ought to deter us from studying the finite, since the infinite is everywhere involved in it, and both are, in themselves, inscrutable. In every bud there is a mystery. Nothing, in its essence, can be known. The growth of a blade of grass is as unintelligible to us as the existence of a Supreme Being.

From our own imperfections we are led to ask, Does not the finite and dependent require the infinite and absolute? Does not derivative being require the conception of the Underived? Does not an effect require a cause; and, in the regress of causes, must we not stop at the uncaused Cause, the one Being who has within himself his reason of existence?

In the eloquent words of Descartes: "We are the imperfect; we are the finite; we are the caused. There must be One who is the complement of our being, the infinity of our finitude, the perfection of our imperfection; a mind which gives us that which we have not from ourselves."

The late Emile Saisset has given so beautiful a paraphrase of these ideas, that I cannot resist the temptation of translating it here from the French:

"I turn my thoughts in upon myself, and I say, Whence comes it that I cannot help thinking on God? I exist, I live, I love to exist and to live; I find around me thousands of objects capable of pleasing and of interesting me; what need I more for satisfying my soul, and why do I search for something beyond?

"Why? It is, too well I see, because I am imperfect, and surrounded by imperfection. When I consider my being, I see it flow on like a rapid wave; my ideas, my sensations, my desires all change from hour to hour, and around me I find no being that does not pass from movement to repose, from progress to decline, from life to death. Amid these vicissitudes, even as one wave is pushed on by other waves, I roll onward in the immense torrent which is sweeping all things to unknown shores. Change, unceasing change, is the universal law, and such is my condition.

"And the more I reflect, the more I see that this condition attaches to the very nature of things. Within me and without, all being is changing *because it is limited.* Here am I, shut up in a corner of space and time; in vain do I stretch all the springs of my frail corporeal machine; I can take in only the small number of objects which are proportioned and near to me. I think; but among the innumerable truths of which I catch a glimpse, I can seize only a few, and even those on condition of concentrating my thought in a narrow circle, outside of which I see confusedly, or see not at all. I love, but my power of loving, which goes forth easily toward everything suggestive of some perfection, open or secret, can attach itself only to objects fragile, changing and perishable, none of which give me what they had promised. Everywhere is *limitation.* Within me is an indefinite power of development which aspires to display itself in a thousand different senses, and which, encountering everywhere limitations, sometimes strives vehemently to overleap them, and sometimes falls back weary, sinking and discouraged. This is why I change unceasingly, and why everything around me changes: it is because we are all—guests of this world, great or small, thinking atoms, or blades of grass, or grains of sand—we are all, in different degrees, and under forms infinitely variable, *incomplete beings*, striving for completion, and approaching it only partially and imperfectly.

"But why am I incomplete, and why under such a form, to such a degree, in such a time, in such a place? Why, indeed, do I exist, instead of not existing? I am ignorant. *And this proves to me invincibly that I have not within myself my reason of existence;* that my being is not the primal and absolute being, but a being relative and borrowed.

"Now, every time that I regard my being as radically incomplete and incapable of existing by itself, I see dawning upon my soul the idea of *the perfect one.* I conceive of him as accomplished in all the infinite powers of his being. While I strive to reässemble, in this brief, fleeting span of time, the dispersed fragments of my life, and to develop some of my faculties, he, concentred in an immutable Present, enjoys the absolute plenitude of his being eternally unfolded. Everywhere I meet limits, whether in the beings who surround and press upon me, or in the number, form and degree of my own faculties. But he is the being without limitations, the being unique and above all, the being to whom nothing can be wanting. All the potencies of life are in him—not only those of which I know something, but the infinite number of which I know nothing. Unequal and bounded in incomplete beings, they are there, the prey to struggle, to negation and to disaccord. In him, all is infinite, positive, full, equal, unique, harmonious. This plenitude, this harmony, this unity of all the potencies of being—this is the good supreme, the first, the absolutely fair, the being of beings, God.

"This idea of the perfect being commands my admiration. How vast it is—how sublime! But is it not too far from me? Not at all. It is intimately near. Plunged in the movement of things that pass, I yield for an instant to the seduction of their attractions. In the spirit of pride and self-reliance, I may at times be dazzled and misled by the sentiment of my energy, of my knowledge and my powers; but this is when I regard only the surface. As soon as I enter into and examine myself intimately, I am dismayed at my utter feeblness, my inconsistency, the incurable fragility of my being; and I feel that it would vanish away, had it not its support in the one veritable being. There is in this no effort of mind, no circuit of thought, no reasoning; it is a sudden, spontaneous, irresistible sense of my imperfect soul, referring itself to its eternal principle, feeling itself to live and to be through him.

"When I come to reflect and to reason upon these two objects of my thought, the being imperfect that I am, and the being perfect by whom I exist, I see that to suppress either one of these two terms would be an insensate enterprise. I find them at the end of all my analyses, at the beginning of all my reasonings. They form, in their indissoluble union, the permanent ground of my consciousness.

"Can I think of the duration that is flowing, always preceded and always followed by another duration, without conceiving of eternity? Can I represent to myself a certain space, enveloping a smaller space, and enveloped by a larger, without conceiving of immensity? Can I contemplate the finite being, the mobile, the developing, without conceiving of the infinite, the immutable, the accomplished? These two ideas suggest, the one the other, and are enchained by a necessary relation. Prior to the being imperfect, there is the being perfect; prior to that which exists only in a manner temporary, local, relative, there is that which exists fully and absolutely. Behold that which is simple, clear, evident; it is a natural axiom, the first of axioms; it is the supreme law of my reason. Shall I attempt to destroy by an artifice of my reason what Nature has so profoundly graved in my consciousness?

"No! Man without God is an enigma, an inexplicable chimera. He has no longer a mission on this earth, nor a hope in worlds beyond. In losing his divine ideal, in essaying to take himself for his ideal, he falls below himself, and in having wished to make himself God, he ceases to be man."

But all theistic speculation is dismissed as unscientific and unprofitable by the experience-philosophy of J. S. Mill, Herbert Spencer, G. H. Lewes, and others. They tell us that science deals only with observed phenomena ; that cause, in the scientific sense, is the name given to the required conditions that antedate phenomenal changes ; and that the human mind has no right to reason about real cause and final purpose in the universe.

But the experience-philosophy is shattered, from turret to foundation-stone, by the facts of clairvoyance and of Spiritualism ; for the experience-philosophy rests on the assumption that *we have no ideas independent of experience ;* whereas the facts of this volume demonstrate at every step* that we have ideas that come to us through no gate of the senses, through no experience, and through no "inheritance from preceding organisms."

In regard to this last expression, it should be borne in mind that in the philosophy of both Mr. Spencer and Mr. Lewes, the *innateness* of ideas that are seemingly independent of experience, is explained by the doctrine of inherited forms of thought, shaped by the accumulated experience of preceding organisms. Spiritualism accepts this as a partial, but not as an entire truth.

Innumerable well-authenticated instances of prevision and clairvoyance have been cited, in which a knowledge transcending all that mere experience could supply is clearly manifested. Spiritualism opens to us a new world of observed phenomena, indicating supersensual powers ; phenomena that have been scientifically tested and proved by thousands

* Phenomena of daily occurrence prove my position. Hardly was the ink dry on the above sentence, when I received a letter from a sister in Davenport, Iowa, in which she writes (Sept. 28th, 1874),—"Bishop Lee died on the 26th inst. Some two months ago he got up in the night, and took a bath. In returning to his room he stepped off a long flight of stairs, and landed at the foot with a tremendous crash, as he was very heavy. He was slightly bruised, and his right hand a little lamed. Mr. H. and myself called on him two days after, and while telling us of the fall, the bishop mentioned this coincidence. He had a letter in his hand, just received from his son Henry, living at Kansas City (several hundred miles distant). Henry wrote : 'Are you well? For last night I had a dream that troubles me. I heard a crash, and standing up said to my wife, *Did you hear that crash? I dreamed that father had a fall and was dead.* I got up and looked at my watch, and it was *two o'clock;* I could not sleep again, so vivid was the dream.' The bishop remarked that the dream must have occurred at the very hour of the same night of the accident, for his own watch showed *quarter past two*, making it at the same moment, allowing for difference of time. The fall finally caused the bishop's death. His hand became intensely painful, and gangrene set in, which, after two weeks of suffering, terminated his life." Will Mr. Lewes please explain, by his experience-philosophy, how Henry Lee was made aware of the accident to his father?

of competent witnesses. The sphere of Causation must be enlarged to take in these new facts, or rather these old facts confirmed in the light of moderm science.

So inevitable is this conclusion, so astounding is the prospect of the introduction of a body of phenomena which must revolutionize philosophy, and awaken many self-complacent scientists to a mortifying sense of their stubborn ignorance, that the Tyndalls, Huxleys, and Carpenters of our day can undervalue our facts only by denying them outright; a mode of warfare which may serve our assailants for a time, but which must terminate in their utter discomfiture at some not distant day. Through Dr. Büchner of Germany, the Materialism claiming to be scientific tells us that "the phenomena of clairvoyance are now proved to be idle fancies;" that "the perception of external objects without the aid of the physical senses is an impossibility," and that "all that we know comes through those senses."

Thus one of the leading representatives of the atheistic Materialism of our day bases his theory largely on the denial of facts which all Spiritualists know to be true, and which are already in the keeping of experimental science!

The limits, then, which are set up by that system of philosophy that has regard solely to experience and to associations got through the physical senses, are found to be arbitrary, and contrary to known facts. Spiritualism, by its inductions, leads us to realize that the visible universe is not all; that the unseen must vastly exceed the seen.

But does Spiritualism prove a God?

Spiritualism is science, though science of a unique and transcendent character; and "Science," says Chevreul, "can neither prove nor disprove a God; though the reasoning by which it would prove a God is more in conformity with its own experimental methods than that by which it would disprove a God."

Since God has in himself alone the reason and necessity of his own being—since he is the one absolute substance—he cannot be proved, for the proof of a thing must be in something higher than itself. "If the existence of God could be proved," says Jacobi, "then God would be derived from a ground before and above him."

We must accept Him, then, as a postulate of the reason and of the heart; of the reason, because of the intelligence in Nature and in the mind of man, and because the producing Cause of the Universe must be higher than any of its manifestations; of the heart, because of the love which mounts from the endeared finite objects on whom it is tenderly fixed, to One in whom those objects have their reason of being and their only earnest of unending life. How many, after a great bereavement, can say, "Never was faith in Providence, never was the hope of another and a higher life so clear a certainty, so intense a reality as it has become since sorrow made it, to me, a spiritual necessity! I want no argument now!"

A knowledge of immortality cannot be barren in its relation to the question of the divine existence. "It is an error," says Fichte, "to say that it is doubtful whether or not there is a God. It is not doubtful, but the most certain of all certainties, the one absolutely valid objective truth, *that there is a moral order in the world.*"

"A single aspiration of the soul," says Hemsterhuis, "after the future, the better, the perfect, is a demonstration more than geometric of Divinity."

"To tell me that I do not and cannot know what substance is, that I never can know anything but phenomena, neither convinces me of illusion, nor drives the thought of ultimate eternal reality from my mind. My ignorance is precisely of that kind which asserts its own incomprehensible object. . . We cannot mark phenomena without thinking of substance. We cannot feel the world's heart beat in the ceaseless energy of living things without adoring an all-pervading Life."*

"The unity which we seek behind the diversities of the visible world cannot be physical, because out of merely phys-

*J. Allanson Picton, author of "The Mystery of Matter"; London: Macmillan & Co., 1873.

ical unity the diversity of things could not have been evolved. There must have been a primary differentiation, not involved in the laws of matter as such. Simple, naked, materialistic Atheism—that is to say, the system which would resolve all into the laws of mere matter—*is thus shown to be scientifically false;* and this from data afforded by the sciences of matter alone, without referring to those of life and mind. The ultimate unity must be spiritual, in the sense, at least, of not being material."*

"Before one can assert," says Christlieb, "that the world is without a God, one must first have become thoroughly conversant with the entire universe. One must have searched through all the systems of suns and stars, as well as through the history of all ages; he must have wandered through the whole realm of space and time, in order to be able to assert with sincerity, 'Nowhere has a trace of God been found!' He must be acquainted with every force in the whole universe; for should one escape him, that very one might be God. He must be able to count up with certainty all the causes of existence; for were there one that he did not know, that one might be God. He must be in absolute possession of all the elements of truth, which form the whole body of our knowledge; for else the one factor that he did not possess might be just the very truth that there is a God.

"In short, to be able to affirm authoritatively that no God exists, a man must be omniscient and omnipresent, that is, he himself must be God; and then, after all, there would be one. Atheism, much more than Theism, depends on faith, that is, on assumptions which cannot be proved."

A scientific philosophy of ignorance thus proves that dogmatic atheism has no basis in logic or in science.

By inductive science we are brought to the conclusion that the universe and the race of man had their beginning in time. The history of the universe is a history of the aggregation of matter. Geology tells us there was a time when man did not

*From "The Scientific Bases of Faith," by J. J. Murphy. London: 1873.

exist on our planet. How did he get there? Materialism replies that he was evolved from the forces of matter. Spiritualism says, then those forces must be spiritual, for mind must come from mind; to which Materialism retorts, that a God uncaused, and existing from eternity, is fully as incomprehensible as Matter uncaused, and existing from eternity. And to this the conclusive reply is, But you make your Matter a God, if you make it the generator of mind and consciousness.

If we use the *à priori* argument, and say that "Whatever begins to be, must have a cause," we are met by the reply, "No, this notion of causation is a mere generalization from contingent experiences, and not a necessary truth. The laws of Nature cannot account for their origin."

But the idea of cause is irrepressible, and no logic can bar it out. "It cannot be abolished," says Herbert Spencer, "except by the abolition of thought itself."

Materialism would still be confronted by the same problem, even if it were to discover a law that would explain the universe. For the law itself and the law-maker would have to be explained in their turn. Natural evolution through periods of time not to be reckoned requires an intelligent Force to account for it, just as much as would an instantaneous act of creation. Admit the facts of Spiritualism, and the Darwinian scheme affords no ground for atheistic conclusions. The argument from design, based on analogies with the works of human artificers, is not needed. We must learn to look for Divine perfection, not in the particular and fragmentary things of time, but in the universals of eternity; since here, conditioned as we are, there can be, in the very nature of things, no light without darkness, no good without evil, no truth without error, no progress without imperfection. The wise man says, "Trust and wait." The man not wise says, "Since I can see no sign that God has acted as I would have acted in his place, there can be no God!"

We have seen that spiritual and all other facts of science are tending to resolve our conception of matter into that of force. Spiritualism proclaims through its phenomena that this force must be spiritual in its origin. Only by the analogy of our own mental activity can we arrive at a conception of causative force. Even Professor Huxley admits thus much; he says: "Undoubtedly, active force is inconceivable, except as a state of consciousness, . . . except as something comparable to volition."

The domain of science is bounded by the region of second causes; and therefore the idea of a first cause, of God, can never be scientifically excluded or repressed. "If," says Professor Le Conte, "in tracing the chain of causes upward, we stop at any cause, or force, or principle, that force or principle becomes for us God, since it is an efficient agent controlling the universe."

The claim that Spiritualism is atheistic, has no authority either in philosophy or science. "In order to be something more than mere Skepticism, and to offer a consistent theory of the universe, atheism must abandon its negative form, for a positive; and it cannot do this except by merging itself in the materialistic theory." Thus it cannot logically claim Spiritualism as its ally, since in becoming positive, it repudiates the spiritual fact.

We assume that something or other unmade and without beginning has existed from all eternity; for whatever exists must have its sufficient cause either in itself or out of itself, since nothing can come from nothing, whatever Skepticism may say to the contrary.

This self-existent something, is it unorganized matter, or is it undirected force, or is it a combination of the two?

It is impossible to conceive of mind as issuing from unorganized matter; and organized matter presupposes an Organizer. Explanation of the higher by the lower, of thought by matter, must therefore be rejected as contrary to reason; and equally to be rejected is the explanation by undirected, unintelligent force.

But what of matter and force combined? Dr. Büchner has written a book to teach us that there is no matter without force, and no force without matter, and that this unity in duality can do anything. He postulates them to account for motion, and then he asks us to concede that matter, force, and motion are adequate to the production of mind and all the other phenomena of life. But if matter needs force in order to be moved, and if force needs matter in order to produce motion, it is difficult to see how in their combination they can produce the efficiency required, and emerge into an intelligent cause.

Nevertheless, if they do this, if matter and force, eternally inseparable and self-existent, are sufficient in their union to produce mind, then they are an intelligent cause—then they are God; and thus the materialistic theory must be rejected as failing to meet the demands of a scientific analysis.

When it aspires to reach the last analysis of things, and to throw light on Causation, Materialism has no advantage over the metaphysician whom it would deride. We have seen that should the hypothesis of an evolution of high organisms from inferior types be proved, it would bring us no nearer to a solution of the infinite problem of the origin of things. Nay, should Science do what Strauss wildly supposes it may yet do, achieve the creation of a man, it would still be utterly impotent to explain the origin and nature of mind and matter, and to answer the questions, Why and Whence?

The Materialism on which positive atheism would rely, tells us that the universe is the product of two factors, the atom and motion; that these two factors explain all; that as for the laws of the universe, they are simply the necessary relations between forces, the expression of the necessity of things; that hence it may be inferred how anti-scientific it is to regard the government of the universe as regulated in advance by a spirit reconciling itself to immutable laws; because if the divine will governs, the laws are superfluous; but if the laws govern, they exclude all foreign intervention. "Science," says Comte, "would now re-conduct God to the frontiers, thanking him for his provisional services."

But instead of inferring, as Materialism does, that these

immutable laws suffice to render an account of themselves, Spiritualism declares that the order which they reveal, supposes a Supreme Ordainer.*

Here are two contrary interpretations of the same fact. Which is the more reasonable one? No experimental verification can throw light on the problem; and what it is the business of the Materialism, on which atheism relies, to demonstrate, is the absolute incompatibility between the idea of an Intelligent Cause and the order of the world which maintains itself by the fixity of its laws. *This demonstration cannot be had.*

Of what use, asks the atheist, is an idle God, of whom it may be said, as of a constitutional king, "He reigns, but it is the laws which govern"? I can best answer the question in the words of the Rev. John Caird, in his Sermon on Spiritual Influence. He says: "A human mechanist may leave the machine he has constructed to work without his further personal superintendence, because when he leaves it God's laws take it up, and by their aid the materials of which the machine is made retain their solidity, the steel continues elastic, the vapor keeps its expansive power. But when God has constructed *His* machine of the universe, *He cannot so leave it, or any the minutest part of it, in its immensity and intricacy of movement, to itself;* for, if He retire, there is no second God to take care of this machine. Not from a single atom of matter can He who made it for a moment withdraw His superintendence and support. Each successive moment, all over the world, the act of creation must be repeated."

Upon what positive, demonstrable facts can Materialism maintain, at the same time with the negation of God, the thesis of the eternity of matter and its power of producing and transforming all things?†

If the universe had a commencement, this commencement,

---

*For this and several of the succeeding arguments I am indebted to "Le Matérialisme et la Science, by Emile Caro"—an excellent little treatise which merits a translation into English. In it the best thought of the philosophical Spiritualism of France seems to be summed up.

† For the substance of this argument see Emile Caro's "Le Matérialisme et la Science."

by the very conditions of the case, had an Intelligent Cause; for the laws of Nature cannot render an account of their origin.

True, one can suppose that the order of material phenomena and their laws never commenced, and it is this supposition which constitutes *dogmatic* Materialism. But what experimental verification can it claim? None whatever! And Theism replies to it by another hypothesis which neutralizes it: Theism supposes that the universe *had* a commencement, which amounts to saying that the actual order of things has *not* always existed.

How can the Materialists prove the contrary?

By the examination of the laws of Nature? But these laws can render only an account of that which *is*, not an account of what, by hypothesis, has *preceded* that which is. They may explain the actual form of the universe, not the mode of its formation, if we suppose that there was formation.

"It will not avail to reply, that if there is a question of origin to posit, all experimental explication is powerless to resolve it: you must admit that *no experience can demonstrate that there is not a question of origin to posit.*

"Atheistic Materialism would explain all things by the properties of matter, and in this it goes beyond experience and becomes a system. It indulges in mere speculation. Positive science has no other data than those afforded in the world which exists; experience can give us only that which is; no one can know experimentally that which was before that which is."

"Nay," replies Materialism, "our facts may not suffice to resolve these questions positively, but they are more than sufficient to resolve them negatively."

"But is it not to resolve these questions very positively to resolve them thus? If you maintain that *there is not even place to posit the question of a God,* do you not affirm that the world exists by itself, and is not this a solution very positive?

"Until Materialism can get out of this vicious circle which Logic traces around its fundamental conception, it cannot make one step in advance towards affording to atheism any scientific comfort or support. It may reason, after its fashion, upon the impossibility of conceiving a commencement to the system of things; to the existence of matter and its properties; but it will prove nothing *experimentally;* and, according to its own principles, that is the only way of proving anything. It will speculate, but that is very humiliating for the disdainers of all speculation; it will venture on the metaphysical, but that is the last disgrace to these adversaries of all metaphysics."

So in order to arrive at a dogmatic atheism, one must not only discard science and fall back on *à priori* assumptions, but must set aside those facts of Spiritualism which prove the priority of spirit over matter. If an atheism based on Materialism has no scientific validity, the atheism that would seek support in Spiritualism must be sanguine indeed.

"The doctrine of final causes," it is objected, "implies contrivance and therefore a limitation of the divine energy." When it is admitted that God may be *self*-limited in his manifestations on this ultimate material plane, atheism puts forth its most determined effort against the marks of design in the universe.

It tells us that Nature is blind, immoral, irrational; that she often gives birth to productions the most absurd, if we judge them as controllable by a rational will; that she allows loathsome parasites to torture the nobler organisms; that we often find her powerless to vanquish the least obstacle in her way, and reaching the contrary of that which she ought logically to reach. How can a cause which acts in a manner so mechanical and blind, so contrary to benevolence and paternal goodness, be a Will, a Reason, an Omnipotent Being?

"As for the much-vaunted design in Nature," says Professor Haeckel, "it is a reality only for those whose views of animal and vegetable life are to the last degree superficial."

All this simply amounts to saying that in an infinite number of cases we cannot comprehend the ends which Nature pursues: a conclusion that is not to be disputed. But what experimental proof can be given that these ends which evade our comprehension do not exist?

"We admit that they may be above and beyond our intelligence; but this only tells against human reason, not against divine science, of which our reason surely is not to be taken as the exact measure. The inexplicable abounds in the universe; it is everywhere, under our eyes, within reach of our hands; we meet it at every step. If the atheist would have God exist solely on condition of acting just as a man would act in God's place, we are not of those who would conceive of God thus."

We have no disposition to press the argument from design; to bring down any of the divine manifestations in Nature to an analogy with the handiwork of a human mechanician. But it should be borne in mind that *negative* facts pertaining to this question of final causes do not betray the absence of God, since, experimentally considered, they merely signify our own ignorance, the limits of our own intelligence.

"A positive fact has a wholly different value. It reveals to us an Intelligent Cause by a natural analogy which is a law of our reason. A fact like organism places finality beyond a doubt. Now if finality exists in only one case, induction would lead us to conclude that it exists elsewhere, even where we are incapable of detecting it."

To say that matter can account for these more obvious phenomena of finality, that the gases of phosphorus can culminate in consciousness, and that the vibrations of molecules can produce thought, is, as we have seen, merely to spiritualize and deify matter and not at all to dispense with spirit or with deity.

The theistic argument from design is not needed by Spiritualism; but it should be observed that the proposition which would exclude finality from our consideration has no virtue except by condition of its being absolute. This it is not, and this it can never be. It is relative to certain parts of the world, and it ceases to be applicable to other parts. "But if there is anywhere, in one single point of the world, sensible traces of finality, all leads us to believe that there are ends elsewhere, even in those places where they do not reveal themselves to our limited means of investigation."

In opposition to the Divine Personality, Spiritualism has no word of authority to offer.

Self-consciousness must be an attribute of that two-fold existence of God, at once supra-mundane and intra-mundane, which combines the theistic and the pantheistic conception of his nature. How can personality proceed from an impersonal principle? Can God create forms of existence which transcend his own?

To Strauss's objection, that the more perfect the personality the greater the limitation, Froshammer replies: "The essential elements of personality are existence, consciousness of that existence, and control over it. Distinction from and therefore limitation by others is not an essential element of personality, but an accidental sign of relative personality. An absolute personality cannot therefore be said to be impossible, for *it may find in itself the distinctions necessary for personal consciousness.* It may be said that God is super-personal. He is the supreme, the only real personality, since he is the only absolute, self-existent being. If Strauss's notion were true, then a man, brought up in ignorance of the existence of any being but himself, would not be a person!"

Atheism is a charge often too hastily brought against reverent minds, discontented with all prevailing forms of Theism, and reaching out for wider truths. Let such minds not be confounded with those which would preach atheism dogmatically, as if it had any ground of science on which to rest.

We all of us, I suppose, have our atheistic moods; moods when we venture on the thought that a beneficent, intelligent Will ought to manage the things of this world better, and help us and our friends to have a better time of it. With some this mood is persistent, as with Schopenhauer, Hartmann, Vogt, and Strauss, who cry out at the bad things of life like peevish, fractious children bewailing their stomach-aches and short allowance of taffy.

"If God," says Hartmann, "previous to the creation had been aware what he was doing, creation would have been an inexpiable crime."

"The cosmos is something which had much better not have existed," says Schopenhauer.

> "Like children crying in the night,
> Like children crying for a light,
> And with no language but a cry,"

are these philosophers in their fretful whinings. They tell us of the earthquakes, tornados, volcanic eruptions, and meaningless plagues that afflict humanity—of the malformations, excrescences, venomous reptiles and monstrous diseases; and they ask, Are all these things divine gifts?

They are truly the clouds and darkness which are about his throne; the mysteries by which he is veiled from the inquisitive understanding. But they are mere temporary negations or obscurities, and do not counterbalance the positive proofs of his eternal existence which we find in the universe, in Spiritualism, and in the soul of man.

When we hear Spiritualists joining in these outcries against God, the question occurs: "If, as you say, death is the pathway to a higher life, how do you know that all these calamities which destroy or abbreviate human life or health, and which you affect to deplore so profoundly, and to use as an argument against divine beneficence, are not meant in mercy and in love? If to die is gain, as Spiritualism teaches, why find fault with the natural causes that seem to accelerate our departure?"

No anthropomorphic argument from design is needed when the Pantheistic conception is made supplementary to the Theistic. "Analogies," says Picton, "which would turn our unspeakable worship of the Infinite One into the familiar admiration felt for the inventor of a new machine, are increasingly felt, in these times, to be two-edged weapons, with which Faith does ill to play. For only by the recognition that adaptation of means to an end, in order of time, belongs to temporal and fragmentary life—not to eternal Being—do we preserve the attitude of soul which is unassailable by the bewilderments of false analogy or materialistic despair."

Thus we feel that we are surrounded, both on the material plane of being and on the spiritual, "by an omnipresent, immutable Power, for whom nothing is too great, nothing too insignificant, but which equally regulates the orbits of worlds and the position of an atom, and in whose Divine order there is nothing common or unclean, but its fitting place is found for the lowest as well as the highest in the palpitating life of the Universe."*

The great teacher of scientific induction, Bacon, says: "So far are physical causes from drawing men off from God and Providence that, on the contrary, the philosophers employed in discovering them can find no rest but by flying to God or Providence at last."

"*At last.*" There is a significance in these words; for Bacon does not deny that science and philosophy, failing in extent and comprehensiveness, may incline to atheism. Our modern scientists leave out of their reckoning those facts of Spiritualism which Bacon knew, and which guarded him from limiting his faith in Deity to deductions from second causes.

The science that rejects the alliance which Modern Spiritualism offers is superficial and incomplete, and must continue to grope in darkness whenever it would approach those questions which relate to a future life and the divine spirituality of the cosmic principle. A reconsideration of dogmas concerning the Divine Existence may seem a rash attempt, but their relations to the phenomena of this volume are a question full of interest.

"The *heart* of man," says Picton, "recoils and always will recoil from that ghastly sense of universal death, which comes with the momentary imagination of a Godless world; but the *mind* of man is equally intolerant of obviously untenable propositions, maintained on grounds of supposed expediency."

---

* Author of "Supernatural Religion." London: Longmans, 1874.

"There is no resting-place for a religion of the reason," says Mansell, "but Pantheism or Atheism."

And yet for a religion that is not of the reason who can feel respect, and what certainty of enduring influence can be hoped for it?

As atheism must be reversed, and lost in that higher Pantheism which regards the whole universe as instinct with divine life and intelligence, so must this higher Pantheism be encircled by the still higher Theism which, while it regards God as *in* Nature, regards him at the same time as *beyond* Nature—at once the God in whom we live and move and have our being, the God of the material and spiritual universe, and the God transcendent, absolute, and infinite, the incomprehensible Unity.

How shall we approach the august problem? How reconcile these seeming contradictions?

CHAPTER XV.

In the facts and analogies of Spiritualism no congruity has thus far been found with that form of Pantheism which denies personality to God and a conscious immortality to man.

In the lower Pantheistic view, God is the universe itself; beyond and outside the world he does not exist, but only in the world; he is the soul, the reason, and the spirit of the world, and all Nature is his body; he is everything, and beside him there is nothing.

But there is a higher, an idealistic Pantheism, which makes the universe all spirit, and regards matter as a mere thought, or congeries of thoughts, so adapted to our sensations as to make us feel it real, at the same time that it is no independent entity in itself. Of these two orders of Pantheism, the one is without a real God, and the other without a real world.

In the same mind we often see the Theistic and the Pantheistic idea asserting itself almost simultaneously. Christianity is nearly as full of Pantheism as it is of Theism; for if it recognizes God as our heavenly Father, it regards him also as the one Life in which we live and move and have our being. Devotion cannot go far without running into language capable only of a Pantheistic construction.

Through our finite and fallible faculties we may not hope to comprehend God; yet Science may lead us to ever higher and more rational conceptions of his possible nature. The Copernican system has enlarged those conceptions, and Modern Spiritualism may enlarge them still more. It may help us to find truth both in the Theistic and the Pantheistic idea, and thus to reconcile what may at first seem too antagonistic to be entertained together.

In his "Principles of Mental Physiology," even Dr. Wm. B. Carpenter would seem to aim at such a reconciliation. He says: "Although if God be *outside* the Physical Universe, those extended ideas of its vastness which modern Science opens to us, remove Him further and further from us, *yet if He be embodied in it*, every such extension enlarges our notion of His being." What good Pantheist could ask more than is admitted in the words *embodied in it?* They contain the very pith of Pantheism.

Spiritualism proves that the visible mortal body is not the whole of man, and hence lifts us to the conception that the Universe, as defined by Science, is not the whole of God. Thus Pantheism, pure and simple, is lacking in that important part of the idea of God which recognizes his transcendent infinity, his independent spirituality, and his supreme personality; while Theism fails to recognize his immanence in Nature, his universality, and his multiplicity in unity. God impersonal and circumscribed by the world, and God personal and unlimited by the world, are but parts of the ineffable truth that combines the two conceptions.

"The universe," says John Scotus Erigena (810–877), "has no existence independent of God's existence; it is therefore God, but not the whole of God. He is more than the universe, yet the Divine Nature is truly and properly in all things." We have seen (Chap. XII.) that these were also the views of Giordano Bruno.

"All Nature," says William Law, (1686–1761,) "is itself a birth from God. Creation out of nothing is a fiction of modern theology. So far is Nature from being out of nothing, that it is the manifestation of that in God which before was not manifest, and as Nature is the manifestation of God, so are all creatures the manifestation of the powers of Nature. . . . Properly and strictly speaking, nothing can begin to be. The beginning of everything is nothing more than its beginning to be in a new state."

"As the spokes in the nave," says an Oriental Spiritualist, "so all worlds and souls are fastened in the One Soul."

A writer* who accepts Pantheism in its spiritual sense, attempts to show that faith in the Divine personality is not necessarily lost in the Pantheistic idea. He says: "God is neither personal nor impersonal: He is both. He is personal because our highest conception of being is a person. Only to the personal can we ascribe reason, consciousness, freedom of action. And here our idea of God emerges as that of the highest personality. But He is more than personal, and in this sense impersonal (super-personal?). Spiritual existence is spiritual, individual personality. . . . He who has grasped this great truth of the impersonality of God, and yet recognizes the Divine personality, has risen to that transcendental region where truth has its origin, and yet he has a footing on the terrene where truth is known only under the limitations of things finite, conceived through the medium of human analogies and spoken of in the language of the sensuous."

"We may deny him will, and yet he wills. He is not intelligent; he is intelligence itself. He has no designs, for the idea of infinite wisdom excludes that of design; and yet to us He is the vast Designer. He is not hoary with time, for eternity is ever young, and yet He is the Ancient of Days."

* The Rev. John Hunt. See his "Essay on Pantheism; London: 1866."

The secret things of God are past finding out, because, revise our conceptions of Him as we may, there still remains in his nature the infinite and the unfathomable. Without irreverence and with perfect humility, therefore, may the speculative faculty exercise itself in attaining to a conception in which reason and the heart's religious aspirations may draw nearer to a union.

Nature is an organism through which the Divine life is forever streaming, and imparting itself to all organic forms ; but this organism is only a temporary objective manifestation of God, and other universes may have preceded the present. Nature is subject to change, to the limitations of space and time, and to consequent imperfection. For in his manifestations on this material plane of being, God is limited by his own "self-denying energy" just as a spirit is limited by divine laws on coming within the earth-sphere. Therefore the divine life, with which the whole universe throbs, is, in a manner, automatic in its developments ; and Nature, though full of signs of intelligence, seems often to be acting blindly, and as if good and evil were indifferent to her ; an appearance which results from the self-imposed limitations by which the divine action is subjected to unyielding law in expressing itself through matter in these its ultimate evolutions. Thus God in Nature becomes Relative to God the Absolute, as existing in the highest of his three states.

"To ask," says the late J. W. Jackson,* "why God did not make a perfect creation is equivalent to asking that God in ultimates, on the plane of time and space, where he is to our perceptions necessarily conditioned by the sequences of duration and the limitations of extension, shall be identical with God in first principles as the eternal and infinite."

To attempt to authenticate this conception of God by any reference to human analogies may seem contrary to that tendency of science which would discredit as presumptuous all such comparisons. But it is not to limit Omnipotence by any

---

* An experienced mesmerist and physiologist, and an eloquent writer. Shortly before his death in London in 1872, he became fully convinced of the phenomena of Spiritualism.

human standard, to confess to that amount of anthropomorphism which is inseparable from the conviction that man, in a certain sense, bears the image of God. "Man," says St. Martin, "is a type which must have a prototype, and that prototype is God. The body of man has a necessary relation to everything visible, and his spirit is the type of everything invisible." One may believe this without irreverence, just as he may believe that the same law which moves the universe may move an atom.

In man we find unmistakably the phenomenon of double consciousness. Even Professor Huxley, in his Address, Aug. 25th, 1874, before the British Association at Belfast, describes a case in which two separate lives, a normal and abnormal one, seemed to be lived at intervals by the same individual; and Dr. Carpenter, though his experience does not take in many important facts now known to be true, admits the separate states of consciousness manifested so wonderfully in Somnambulism.* He instances, in the case of Mozart, the proofs of the automatic action of the brain, as shown in the composition of the overture to the opera of "Don Giovanni." Mozart was probably a musical medium. His aptitude is inexplicable except on the spiritual hypothesis. He himself has said of his musical ideas, "*Whence* and *how* they come, I know not, nor can I force them. Those ideas that please me I retain in my memory."

We have seen that man is described by the principal seers as a trinity of earth-body, spirit-body, and spiritual principle. The facts of somnambulism all tend to confirm this view, and

* I once kept a sensitive patient in a state of mesmeric or induced somnambulism for a whole fortnight, during which she did not once return to the state of normal consciousness. When she was at last restored to it, the occurrences of the fortnight were an entire blank to her. Not the least consciousness did she have of the interval that had elapsed. She supposed she might have been asleep an hour. The ground was heavily covered with snow, when she passed into the abnormal state; when she awoke there was no snow to be seen. What was a rose-bud on one of the bushes in her room had become a full-blown rose. These apparently sudden transformations agitated her so, that, by a strenuous effort of will, I had to throw her back into the somnambulic state in order to prepare her mind gradually for the changes she was destined to see when awake. This somnambulic state was always a higher, brighter, more rational state than her ordinary one: and when somnambulic she would speak with a sort of pity of some of the errors and misconceptions by which she was influenced when awake.

exhibit man in three states or degrees of consciousness: *first*, in his normal waking state; *secondly*, in the state represented in lucid somnambulism, where the mind is active and elevated, and the faculty of sight is vividly exercised without the aid of the physical eyes; *thirdly*, in the high state of ecstasy when the subject seems to be surrounded by spiritual realities and is anxious to quit the body. These three states of consciousness are often entirely distinct, as experienced mesmerizers are well aware. I have frequently witnessed the two higher states, and satisfied myself of their reality.

Swedenborg also teaches that there are three natures, or degrees of life, in man: the natural, the spiritual, and the celestial; and that in the celestial, men do not reason about the truth; they see it, because it is a *possession.*

A corresponding truth may be at the basis of the conception of God as a trinity in his manifestations or modes of existence; a conception of which Schelling says: "The philosophy of mythology proves that a Trinity of Divine Potentialities is the root from which have grown the religious ideas of all nations of any importance that are known to us."

We may conceive of the Supreme Being, *first*, as God in first principles, the Absolute, the incomprehensible Unity, supremely personal and conscious, because possessing all conceivable perfections in their potency and all life in its essence; the impulse of whose developments and self-limitations is an act of will; *secondly*, as God in his relations to the universe of derived spirit and mind, and self-limited according to the measure of those relations; *thirdly*, as God in ultimates, immanent or intra-mundane, and still further limited by his descent into the environments of matter and his identification with the soul of universal Nature.

Thus God, in his highest hypostasis, is the Absolute One, having within himself, in idea and in essence, all the potencies of being, whether ultimating in what we call spirit or in matter; in his intermediate hypostasis he becomes limited by relations to the world of derived spirit and mind; in his third or lowest hypostasis he is the soul, the life, and the essence of physical Nature with all her material limitations, her *seeming* inconsistencies, immoralities and cruelties; all which, however, are in harmony with his beneficent purposes, one of which is that of educating intelligent beings to comprehend and enjoy what he has in store for them; in harmony, too, with his own absolute independence of all evil, that being simply privation, negation and imperfection, without which, however, man could not be a progressive being.

In his "True Christian Religion" (33 and 47, V I.), Swedenborg says: "The common idea is, that, because what is finite does not comprehend what is infinite, finite things cannot be receptacles of the infinite. But, from those things which are said in my works concerning the creation, it is evident that God *first made his infinity finite by substances emitted from himself*, from which exists his proximate encompassing sphere, which makes the sun of the spiritual world; and that afterwards, by means of that sun, he perfected other encompassing spheres, even to the last, which consists of things quiescent; and that *thus, by means of degrees, he made the world finite more and more*. . . . The universe is a work continent of divine love, divine wisdom and uses, and thus altogether a work coherent from firsts to lasts."

If it be said that a tri-unity of being is inconceivable in God, I might reply that it is equally inconceivable in man, and yet facts and phenomena make us realize that it exists.

"The three fundamental colors, red, yellow and blue," says Christlieb, "dissolve into the unity of white light—so that this may well be called a trinity in unity. But they coalesce in such a manner that each of the three rays preserves its distinctive attribute. Red is the caloric, yellow the luminous, blue the chemical (actinic) ray. God is light; and, verily, natural light, the first of his creatures, bears the immediate impress of his triune being."

Hegel calls the idea of the trinity "the pivot of the world." According to Schelling, God is the perfect spirit in three forms, and the true idea of God is a union of naturalism and theism.

"Naturalism," he says, "seeks to conceive of God as

ground of the world (immanent), while Theism would view him as the world's cause (transcendent); the true course is to unite both determinations. God is at the same time ground and cause.

"It no way contradicts the conception of God to affirm that, so far as he reveals himself, he develops himself from himself, advancing from the imperfect to the perfect; the imperfect is in fact the perfect itself, only in a state of becoming. It is necessary that this becoming should be by stages, in order that the fullness of the perfect may appear on all sides. If there were no obscure ground, no nature, no negative principle in God, we could not speak of a consciousness of God.

"So long as the God of modern theism remains the simple essence which ought to be purely essential, but which in fact is without essence, so long as an actual twofoldness is not recognized in God, and a limiting and denying energy (a nature, a negative principle) is not placed in opposition to the extending and affirming energy in God, so long will science be entitled to make its denial of a personal God. It is universally and essentially impossible to conceive of a being with consciousness, which has not been brought into limit by some denying energy within himself—as universally and essentially impossible as to conceive of a circle without a centre.

"The fullness of God's being cannot be contained in an abstract unity, and yet his absolute personality *must have unity for its fundamental attribute. The conception of the triune God furnishes us with the sole bridge that can fill up the breach between God and the world.*"

"If we separate," says Vera, "substantially and absolutely, God and the world, we do not only impair and curtail the being of the world but that of God also. We curtail the being of the world by separating it from its principle; we curtail the being of God by admitting that the substance of the world is independent of God, and consequently by admitting two absolute substances. And the *creatio ex nihilo* could not fill up the gap, as the *creatio ex nihilo* could not affect the principles and essences of things which, under any supposition, must be coëternal with God.

"God is all things in their idea, and as a whole, and in the unity of their existence; but he is not all things individually, or in their particular and fragmentary existence. He is not what the thing is, of which he is the principle. God is the thought, the idea, the essence of the universe. The thought of God, for the very reason that it is the essence, is the Providence of each being particularly. The Providence of the plant is its *idea*, according to which it is born, it grows and dies. And so it is with everything."

The conception of God as brought into relativity by an objective universe, but at the same time existing in higher and discrete degrees of being, in the highest of which he is the absolute and perfect God, is, as I have attempted to show, not inconsistent with what we know of the nature of man. It would be no irrational speculation to hold that the divine relativity to the finite may, in its expression, vary with the character of the different earths or planets fitted for intelligent beings while passing through the discipline of a material environment; that every planet with its climates and products is adapted to the state of its rational inhabitants; that what we regard as the defects or evils of Nature as manifesting herself through our planet, are merely the emblematic reflection of our own defects or evils; and so that, as the race of man improves, the earth itself will improve.

The idea that God, as the life and intelligence of Nature, is self-circumscribed and reduced to relativity by his own "self-denying energy," leads to a view of the cosmos, in which all the objections of atheism are swallowed up. God is seen no longer as the provisional or constitutional monarch whose laws can rule the universe without his aid, his functions being merely honorary. At once ground and cause, *his* life becomes the fountain of *our* life, and all Nature is transfigured with divine possibilities; man, derived and dependent as he is, becomes a free co-worker with God; evil becomes a merely negative thing, having no real being or life; all imperfections become transitional, a necessary phase of good in the making; Humanity, with all its selfishness, its meanness, and its arrogance, becomes ennobled when looked at from the side of its possibilities rather than its limitations and perversions, and takes on more and more the Divine Expression. We are helped to judge of mankind by its martyrs and saints rather than by its tyrants and criminals. We feel that God is not aloof from us but working in us, the very soul of this divine Nature by which we live, and without the light and life of whose sun we could not exist a moment.

Nor let it be said that God's circumscription as the life and soul of Nature removes God in the Highest from sympathy with our weaknesses and our wants. To sympathize with us fully, to be Love and Providence, as well as Law and Wisdom, he must be implicitly the Nature he subordinates, besides a Power independent of it. It may be objected: God cannot be perfection, if, in his self-limitation as the substance of Nature, he is also imperfection; but to this it may be replied that the experience of imperfection may be essential to the very fullness of the Divine perfection; that in order to be the perfect he must exist in a self-subordinated state as the imperfect also.

Remember, moreover, that if God is a trinity, he is in that but the prototype of man, who, in each grade of his nature, is related to God in a corresponding hypostasis. The triunity of earth-body, spirit-body, and spiritual principle, is paralleled in the three-fold nature of God; and man, in each degree, and in all together, has God as his Providence, his spiritual Ideal, and his Infinite Father. The God of his childhood's trust and wonder is restored to him; the God of his prayers is an ever-present listener; if God is unyielding law, he is also maternal tenderness and love; if he is the life of our life, he is also the moral order of the universe; and faith is thus unchecked by science, while reason is reconciled with faith.

To many profound and to many superficial thinkers, all theistic speculation is repulsive. They would say with Hooker: "Our safest eloquence concerning Him is our silence"; or with Sir William Hamilton, "The highest reach of human science is the scientific recognition of human ignorance." But the heart and the intellect continue, nevertheless, to cry, "Oh! that I knew where I might find Him!"

As on the nature of man new and important light continues to be shed by the facts of somnambulism, thought reading, and Modern Spiritualism, may we not hope that human thought will be helped to conceptions of Deity less at variance with science, and that the atheistic objections which now oppress many sincere minds and devout hearts, will be gradually but surely lost in the dawning light?

The elements of this attempt to combine the Theistic with the Pantheistic conception may be found in all the great philosophies and theologies, not omitting those of Oriental origin. Plato distinctly teaches that the Soul of the World is a third subordinate nature, compounded of intelligence and matter.

The eminent French eclectic, Cousin, (1792–1867) in summing up his views of the Divine nature, includes much that is in harmony with the outline I have feebly sketched. He says: "The universe itself is so far from exhausting God, that many of the attributes of God are there covered with an obscurity almost impenetrable, and are discovered only in the soul of man. *God is at once substance and cause, at the summit of being, and at its humblest degree, infinite and finite together, triple, in fine; that is, at once God, Nature, and humanity.* To say that the world is God, is to admit only the world, and to deny God. However immense it may be, this world is finite, compared to God, who is infinite; and from his inexhaustible infinitude He is able to draw, without limit, new worlds, new beings, new manifestations. Invisible and present, revealed and withdrawn in himself, in the world and out of the world, communicating himself without cessation, and remaining incommunicable, He is at once the living God and the God concealed."

CHAPTER XVI.

What relation has Spiritualism to natural morality?

The mere *knowledge* of a future life may have no moral efficacy in a mind that does not see the grandeur of the possibilities involved in the fact. The knowledge must be spiritualized by meditation and by emotion before it can assume its rightful authority in shaping the moral life and constitution.

Being a demonstration of the continuous life of man through the association of a spirit-body, perfect in all its parts, with the material body, Spiritualism has manifestly as intimate a relation as any fact of our mortal existence can have, to natural morality; for it is as much related to the *present* as manhood is related to youth, or old age to manhood. It illustrates the laws that govern the relations of human life, because it explains innumerable occult facts in human history, throws a flood of light on psychological questions, and has a most direct practical bearing on our habits of thought, our affections, and our hopes. A moral science, in no wise based on spiritual facts, would be as imperfect as a science of physiology that did not recognize the brain and the nervous system.

"The essential teaching of Spiritualism," says Mr. A. R. Wallace, "is, that we are, all of us, in every act and thought, helping to build up a mental fabric which will be and constitute ourselves, more completely after the death of the body than it does now. Just as this fabric is well or ill built, so will our progress and happiness be aided or retarded."

Every mental affection we experience, as it helps to mold the spirit-body, thus leaves its impress on our inmost character; every thought we think, and every desire we feel is indelibly registered in the very constituents of our being, and becomes an integrant part of our individuality: what is once in the memory is there forever; it may be concealed from consciousness for a while, but annihilated never. Thus well-ordered thoughts and a well-ordered life issue in corresponding endowments of the spirit-body.

These facts have a most direct and unequivocal bearing on natural morality. They make us severally the authors and shapers of our own characters and destinies. They teach us that our thoughts and our deeds, good or bad, have an imperishable element which incorporates itself with our very organisms, and these become the expression of our actual interior states. We gravitate where our affections carry us.

> "Whate'er thou lovest, man, that too become thou must,
> God if thou lovest God, dust if thou lovest dust."

Spiritualism must exercise an unfailing influence for good through the affections. Let a man or a child be thoroughly convinced that the deceased mother or father he reverently loves is living a more intense life than ever, and can read his every thought and scan his every act, and such a conviction must have a restraining influence upon him, when tempted to evil; an encouragement for him, when incited to some act of self-sacrifice or generous daring. The knowledge that we think and act in the presence of a cloud of witnesses, to whom our very thoughts are as legible as our deeds, must have an influence upon us for good.

"We should live," says Seneca, "as if we were living in the sight of all men; we should think as though some one could and can gaze into our inmost breast." Spiritualism makes us realize these as conditions literally existing.

With the eclecticism which must accompany all genuine science, Spiritualism accepts and assimilates, from all codes, creeds and systems, whatever they may have of moral and religious truth. It reduces all morality to its scientific valuation, and asks for no other authority than the fact itself; regarding a revelation as in no wise true because authoritative, but authoritative only in so far as it is true; because, as Milton bravely says, "If a man believes things only because his pastor says so, or the assembly so determines, without having other reason, though his belief be true, yet the very truth he holds becomes his heresy."

And this shows why the dictation of all seers and all spirits must be resented as an insult to the understanding.

Every thought leaves its trace, every sowing has its proper harvest, and every act its fitting reward. If we look for other salvation than that whose fruit is goodness, purity, love, and spiritual growth, we are groping unprofitably. He who has these is saved already. Belief in salvation through another's merits or sufferings is merely hope in a magical impossibility.

"Here heaven is not," you say, "but yonder it shall be." To this, Spiritualism replies in the words of the elder Fichte: "Nay, what then is that which can be different yonder from what it is here? Obviously, only the objective constitution of the world as the environment of our existence."

But, by a law of our being, our objective environments in the spirit-world are the reflex of our spiritual states; and this shows how grossly those persons misrepresent Spiritualism, who object to it that it promises every one a good time in the "Summer-Land," with charming habitations and delightful scenery; as if such things could constitute a heaven, independent of the dominant affections and the ruling passions!

Morality is action according to the laws of science and of enlightened reason; and only those laws have an absolute interior authority which are in accordance with our sense of what is true, and right, and of divine validity.

Religion is faith in the moral order of the universe; it is particularly the reverent assumption, in thought and feeling, of the existence of an Intelligent Power beyond and above us, that can influence us for good, avert evil, and listen to prayer. But religion, in the high sense, is not superstition; it is not a cowardly dread of a mysterious Being who can harm or help us; it is not a greed for the satisfying things of our external life, having no correlation with the pure and generous affections; it is not a craving for any selfish and exclusive salvation; it seeks a salvation from spiritual error, impurity, and blindness. Everything which we feel and know aright is religious.

Religion, having in it an emotional element, may be lacking in a person otherwise richly endowed ; just as a sense of the beautiful in art may be lacking. And so there may be morality without religion, though there can be no rational religion without morality.

We find in spiritual science the elements of all morality and all religion ; and the task which the thinkers and moral pioneers of the race have before them is to place on a scientific basis the great deductions of an absolute morality, that shall strike with axiomatic force every healthy, unprejudiced mind, and illumine all the intricate questions in social philosophy. And as these deductions cannot have their full sanction till we believe in a divine Moral Order and an invisible world, there must be a religion broad enough to gather all humanity within its fold, and having for its simple evangel the proclamation of a heavenly Father, an immortal life, and a consequent morality.

Morality being thus based on the facts of science, the laws of the human soul, and the proofs of a divine moral order, it follows that much in conventional and social morality, that may seem authoritative to the unthinking many, becomes immoral in the sight of those who are resolved, first of all, to be loyal to what they esteem the laws of divine order inscribed in their very nature, and to be superseded by no human code.

For the class-morality founded on class-interests, on mere social fictions, or on assumed religious authority, and wholly unconfirmed by facts, spiritual science has therefore little respect. It distinguishes between what J. S. Mill refers to as *mala prohibita* and *mala in se ;* proportioning its uncompromising denunciation of the latter to its liberal charity and its reserved opinions in regard to the former.

For while the latter (*mala in se*) give evidence of intrinsic badness in feeling and character, and are wrongs which no sane person questions, the former (*mala prohibita*) may be violations of conventional order, in regard to the right of which good men may differ in opinion ; violations made imperative often by a reason known only to the individual, who all the while may be a person in every respect honorable and conscientious, and actuated by a positive regard to those higher moral sanctions, the force of which no Pharisaic clamor can make less binding on the courageous heart.

Socrates teaches that knowledge is essential to virtue; that no man is knowingly vicious. This is in accord with the whole tone of Oriental wisdom, which assumes that whoso really *sees* vices must shun them; that moral evil is from misconception, and to be cured by the pure vision of truth. So Spiritualism tells us that violations of moral purity and right leave their marks on the spirit-body just as sins against the laws of health injure the physical body; and a sane man, knowing the one fact, would be as solicitous to escape spiritual deformity as a sane man knowing that a certain diet would harm him physically would be anxious to shun it.

Thus all violations of divine law carry their penalties with them, and persistence in sin, when its dire consequences are made known, is simple insanity; but God's processes toward the whole intelligent creation being remedial and never vindictive, the insanities of men and spirits must have an end. Knowledge, in its highest sense, is, therefore, virtue, and Socrates is right. "Satan's true name is ignorance." All evil punishes itself, and thus tends to abolish itself.

And thus, in the light of Spiritualism, the moral law is not an arbitrary code, imposed by an omnipotent law-giver; rather is it a series of beneficent provisions which are simply "a formulated expression of the law of our well-being." Sin is that abuse of our moral nature which injures and retards spiritual growth. An intelligent spirit can at once read, in what we are, all that we *have* been; for our whole moral life is revealed in our physiognomy. We cannot wrong another without first wronging ourselves:

"He that wrongs his friend
Wrongs himself more, and ever bears about
A silent court of justice in his breast."

His Nemesis attends him like his shadow, becomes a part of his very nature, never to be wholly separated from him, and to be silenced only when the necessity for rebuke is superseded by the penitence that is made manifest in reparation and reform.

It was the conclusion of that saintly man and deadly foe of witches, Richard Baxter, as he advanced in life, that the good are not as good, nor the bad as bad as we are apt to suppose. "Nearer approach and fuller trial," he says, "doth make the best appear more weak and faulty than their admirers at a distance think. And I find that few are so bad as censorious professors do imagine. In some, indeed, I find that human nature is corrupted into a greater likeness to devils than I once thought any on earth had been. But even in the wicked usually there is more for grace to take advantage of, and more to testify for God and holiness, than I once believed there had been."

Spiritualism enforces upon us this divine lesson of charity. That part of a man's nature which we encounter on this normal plane of terrestrial life is not the whole of his being. The soul is three-fold in its manifestations; and consciousness is not limited by that horizon within which it seems enclosed in our common waking state.

In that high interior state manifest in lucid somnambulism, the intuitions that are ordinarily latent become often so active that the individual seems to reverse his modes of thinking on many subjects; his affections are wakened and touched, and his whole character is elevated. I have known a *somnambule* in whom this difference between the two states was very marked. In her case conventional habits of thought would seem lost in the impulses of an enthusiasm that looked on all created things as divine, and regarded nothing in its place as common or unclean. Caterpillars, insects, and even reptiles, from which she would shrink alarmed when awake, would rouse in her, when somnambulic, the tenderest sympathy and regard. She would take them in her hands without the slightest repugnance. Persons, who were objects of antipathy to her in her normal condition, would excite very different emotions in her when she was placed *en rapport* with them, and could scan them with her spiritual vision. Everywhere, even in the sinful and depraved, she would seem to detect some sanctifying ray of the divine splendor.

In his "Facts in Mesmerism" Townshend relates a similar experience. His somnambulic patient, E. A., a French youth of fifteen, was, from early associations in Paris, a thorough materialist, rejecting all belief in God and a future life. But in his state of lucid somnambulism all this was changed; nor must it be supposed that he here merely reflected the views of his mesmerizer, for there was ample evidence to the contrary.

"Utterly unsentimental in his natural state," says Townshend, "he seemed always, when somnambulic, to take pleasure in losing himself in imaginations of another world. All the hard incredulity which characterized him when awake was gone. His willfulness was become submission; his pride, humility; and, in proportion as he seemed to know more, he appeared to esteem himself less. Often would he regret the errors of his waking hours, and speak of his natural state as of an existence apart. Often would he exclaim, 'How I wish I could always see things as I do now!' There is not a person who saw him in the mesmeric state but remarked the change for the better his physiognomy underwent. His affections, also, were enlarged. Egotistical in general, and displaying but little sensibility, he, in the mesmeric state, showed all the warmth of a kind-hearted nature."

The state of lucid somnambulism must not be confounded with those imperfect developments in which some of the moral faculties seem paralyzed or perverted. Thus we hear of persons who, conscientious in their waking state, have, when somnambulic, been guilty of theft or murder. These are simply states of insanity, either produced by the obsession of malignant spirits, or by the predominance of the animal nature during the abnormal lethargy of faculties that might exercise a restraining influence.

The teachings of Spiritualism thus lead us to regard sin as spiritual disease, to be remedied only by an entire reformation of the will, the affections, and the habits; and not as that mystic irreparable offence against an Infinite Being, which only an infinite vicarious expiation can atone for and remove. On the contrary, sin is an offence against the sinner himself, and his punishment will be to realize the fact in all its hideousness; and, as memory is everlasting, so, in a certain sense, his sin and its punishment have in them an element of immortality, however purified he may become by penitence and good deeds. What more fearful punishment for the evil doer, can be imagined?

Many of the early Christian Fathers took a view of sin not very different from this. According to Origen, evil is the only thing which has the foundation of its being in itself and not in God, and which is, therefore, founded in no being, but is nothing else than an estrangement from the true Being, and has only a subjective and no objective existence at all, and is in itself nothing.

"It has been asked," says St. Thomas Aquinas, "If there is a God, whence comes evil? We should rather conclude thus: If there is evil, there is a God, for evil would have no existence without order in the good, the privation of which is evil."

Such were also the views of Spinoza, in whose system God is not a judge who inflicts punishment. The sin or crime punishes itself. Sin is privation, and privation is nothing positive, and is entitled evil in reference to our human understanding only, not to the understanding of God. This, too, is the Buddhist notion of sin, according to which every act, word, or thought has its consequence, which will appear sooner or later in the present or some future state. Reward or punishment is simply the inevitable effect of *Kam* (fate or consequence), which works out its own results.

The facts of materialization show that after he quits this terrestrial sphere man retains his triune nature; that he has still a faculty relating him to matter and to earth; a spiritual body; and an inscrutable spiritual principle.

The spirit-man, when brought within the material sphere, does not represent the spirit in the fullness of its faculties · he is under the law of limitations; in the lowest of his three states. This may explain why there is so much that is unsatisfying in the conversation of materialized or partially materialized spirits. The more they descend into the environments of matter the more do their higher faculties become closed. Thus the descriptions they give us of the spirit-world are often conflicting and confused; they mistake fantasies for reminiscences, and even their recollections of their life on earth become mixed and inaccurate.

Swedenborg tells us that "such spirits are adjoined to man as he himself is as to affection or love." He cautions us, and with reason, against the arts and deceptions practiced by the malignant and impure. I have heard of a powerful medium for physical manifestations through whom impure spirits, partially materialized, have come, and indicated their character by their acts. This shows that the repeated warnings of Swedenborg and other seers against low and unscrupulous spirits should be carefully heeded. Purity of heart and purpose and an inflexible resolve to resist all promptings to evil, constitute the only state in which the prosecution of spiritual investigations through mediumship should be ventured on. Safety is to be found, not in ignoring the subject and refusing to investigate, but in studying it under the right conditions and with a clean heart and will.

As a general rule, like attracts like; but evil spirits may try to control a rightly disposed medium, and, in order to do this, may affect a purity which is foreign to their nature. The utmost caution should be practiced in all our dealings with these still fallible and imperfect beings. We should test them very much as we would strangers in the flesh, who come to us without satisfactory credentials. The best mediums, it should be remembered, are *sensitives*, subject to impressions from both good and evil influences. That the evil sometimes prevail is not to be wondered at; and we should be prepared accordingly for fraudulent manifestations, mingled with the genuine.

In the triune principle is the key to much that may seem incomprehensible both in the microcosm of man and in the macrocosm of God. We have seen that for a spirit to manifest himself in the earth-sphere there must be conditions; there must be a conditioned medium, and the spirit himself must undoubtedly come within limitations that make him different from what he is in his *normal* state, and these limitations may be adapted to the character and state of the medium. This triune principle extends through all degrees of being till it brings the Supreme himself into relations to his created universe, and these constitute his state of limitation as expressed in Nature.

In this principle man has his assurance of an unending existence. He has been brought into being by a power beyond himself, and that power must be the universal power of Nature, of which he is a part; and the very essence and life of this Nature is the triune God himself in his self limited and relative state; and since out of God's life no life can utterly fall, or be flung "as rubbish to the void," what we call dissolution is change and progress, and there is no actual death.

Recently at a meeting of the British Association, Dr. Hooker exhibited a plant which captured and digested flies. Referring to this, a well-known secular leader, who prides himself on his outspoken atheism, remarks: "The intelligent power which planned vegetable traps to catch insects, and stew them to death, would hardly be worth worshiping." Here there is a double begging of the question: first, we are called upon to admit that there is a regular design or plan after the manner of human contrivers; and secondly, that death is a calamity to the insects, instead of being what it may be for all that we know to the contrary, namely, the means of a rise in being.

The higher Pantheism is universal life, the life of God; but to say that the universe is God is to admit the universe and to deny God. God is something more than the universe, even as man is something more than his mortal body.

Spiritualism fixes no creed, but from all creeds adopts whatever truth is reconcilable to the reason. Among the new religious sects of Germany is one bearing the name of "Confessors of the Message of Truth, Liberty and Love." Spiritualism would, I think, have little to find fault with in their creed (as far as it goes), which is as follows:

"1. We acknowledge the world to be a unity of infinite space and time, the creative energy of which we call World-Spirit. 2. We acknowledge that humanity is one of the innumerable forms in which the World-Spirit manifests himself in the series of his developments; that humanity is progressing in all ways, and that it should be every man's task to assist in this improvement with all his powers. 3. We acknowledge the indestructibility of Essence in all the phenomena of the World Spirit, and, consequently, also in men, and we therefore consider death to be only the transition into a new form of temporal existence. 4. We acknowledge that there must be a retribution for all actions, but that this is only of a temporal nature. 5. We acknowledge that all those actions are good which are in harmony with the principle of the Essence, equality of all men, and which tend to the progress of humanity; and that all actions not in accordance with this are objectionable. 6. We acknowledge the notion of God, as the idea of absolute perfection, to be a postulate of the human reason.

"The ethics deduced from this are: 1. The commands of Liberty: Be moderate, be true, be clean, be industrious, be economical, be free. 2. The commands of Justice: Offend not, ill-treat not, betray not, malign not, kill not, cheat not, steal not. 3. The commands of Love: Be courteous to all; be charitable; cultivate the good affections; be forgiving; be compassionate with the unhappy; be cheerful with the happy; assist the poor; tend the sick; protect the weak."

All that is true in this, Spiritualism would supplement and render more positive and distinct. It would teach that in the transition through death we carry our human memories and affections and all the knowledge that we have gained in the earth-life; that the departed spirit has the power and the privilege, under certain conditions, of revisiting earth, seeing those it left behind, and communicating with them, directly in their higher, or indirectly in their lower states of consciousness; that we gravitate to what we find congenial; that we mold our spirit-bodies by every thought, act and affection of the earth-life; that there is a principle in our very nature which punishes all violations of divine order, and, sooner or later, in this world or in another, works reformation without other compulsion than that of experience and knowledge;

that all the truths and all the good examples and all the religions of the past are our heritage, from which we may select and assimilate what we need for our spiritual growth; that good or bad influences may be attracted by the state of the will and the affections; that earnest prayer is no mere shouting into a void, answerless and echoless, but the expression of a true spiritual instinct, the very life-principle of religion, and having an efficacy proportioned to the right spiritual conditions under which it is exercised; that the highest wisdom is to trust rationally in God and to worship him especially by doing his will, as indicated in the laws of Nature and the human soul, and by laboring for the universal good.

CHAPTER XVII.

"Do we want a new revelation?" it is often objected; and to this some one aptly replies: "Yes; what you want is a revelation that the supreme fact of your old revelation, the fact of immortality, is an actual living truth." A knowledge of this is what Spiritualism offers. It is very near to every one of us, and yet we overlook it; for, in the words of Schiller:

> "That is the truly secret which lies ever open before us,
> And the least seen is that which the eye constantly sees."

How much of discontent and of neglect of life's grand opportunities is traceable to unbelief in a future state! There are some persons so happily constituted that they "do not need the smart of guilt to make them virtuous, nor the regret of folly to make them wise;" persons who seem as if they needed not the spur of belief to induce them to cultivate their moral and intellectual natures; who appear to inherit their morality as they do their gentle manners, and to shrink from vice as naturally as they would from vulgarity. But these are exceptional natures.

"I am always very much attached to this life," writes Alexander Humboldt to Varnhagen, "having learned from you that, according to Kant's doctrine, there is not much to boast of after our dissolution."* And yet, with a strange inconsistency, this man, as he lay on his death-bed, while the sun's rays streamed in at the window, could say: "How grand these rays! they seem to beckon Earth to Heaven!" The heart was too strong for the speculative intellect; and the great naturalist's last utterance was a realization of the idea of immortality.

William Humboldt, different in many respects from his brother Alexander, accepted the philosophy of Spinoza, and did not believe in the continuance of our individuality into another life. "I must avow it frankly," said he, "that, right or wrong, I do not hold much to the hope of another life. I would not make for myself another existence out of my human ideas, and yet it is impossible for me to make it out of any other. I regard death with absolute calmness, but without desire or enthusiasm."

How soon a man's opinions get to be his loves! A man argues in favor of annihilation till at last he gets to hope for it, to court it! Pride of opinion and other subtle forces help on the consummation. What powers of acclimation in the human soul when it can thus learn to prefer the air of the charnel-house to the breeze on the living hills bathed in God's sunshine!

Francis W. Newman, author of "Theism, Doctrinal and Practical," and many other estimable works, writes (1873), in regard to a future life, that his desire is "here very feeble;" and he thinks that "either poetical fancy, or moral speculation, or both together, originated the conception alike among barbarians and civilized men!"

---

* Although Kant in his philosophy narrows down the grounds of belief in immortality to the fact of a moral element in man, he seems, in his higher moods, to have had a vision of the truth; for he says: "Perhaps it will be proved yet that the human soul, even in this life, is, by an insoluble communion, connected with all the immaterial natures of the spirit-world, acting upon these and receiving impressions from them." I am indebted for this quotation to Dr. G. Bloede, of Brooklyn, N. Y., a most intelligent Spiritualist, whose comment on Kant's words is: "The true philosopher as well as the true poet is a seer!"

But Spiritualism shows that no explanation of the belief in immortality could be further than this from the practical truth.

David F. Strauss, author of "The Old Faith and the New," tells us that the prospect of the "eternal persistence of life" would fill him "with dismay." Innocent and interesting timidity! As if this good Mother Nature could not be trusted! As if she will not proportion our future horizons to our future capacities and needs—taking care that, as our day, our strength shall be!

Mr. Leon Case, in an extraordinary communication to the Springfield (Mass.) Republican of Oct. 30th, 1874, in which, after an eight days' examination of the phenomena through the Eddy family at Chittenden, Vt., he expresses his belief confidently in the genuineness of the manifestations, remarks: "I cannot awaken in myself a single pulse of desire for immortality, however blest." But he has naively admitted, just before: "I attribute the fact of my lacking desire there, *to my long conviction that death is the dissolution of all individuality.*" He had held the opinion, and argued for it till it became his love, and it was a serious disappointment to him to receive confirmatory and palpable evidence of a life beyond the present. Wisely does Solomon warn us: "Keep thy heart with all diligence, for out of it are the issues of life." As we think, we are. Habits of thought in a certain direction will make even ghastly death appear more lovely to us than immortal life.

Indifference to life, present or future, is always an exceptional, an artificial, a morbid state of mind. Often it may spring from the absence of those affections which play so important a part in making a reünion with beloved objects an irrepressible craving of the heart. Often it is a growth of forces and of habits, among which intellectual pride and a wish to differ from the common herd of men are prominent.

Thomas Buckle (1822–1862), eminent as a thinker and author, and very near to being a Spiritualist when he died,*

*See the London Spiritual Magazine for March, 1873.

rests the evidence of immortality mainly upon the universality of the affections; upon the yearning of every mind to care for something out of itself. For him, as for most men, the affections cry out for a future life, and he says, in words which every sound heart that knows what it is to love profoundly will be likely to respond to—"The doctrine of immortality is the doctrine of doctrines; a truth compared with which it is indifferent whether anything else be true. It is a belief which, if eradicated, would drive most of us to despair."

Spiritualism, while it founds the fact of immortality mainly on phenomenal proofs, shows that the affections and the moral nature are prescient in their yearnings, and justifies all their demands.

"If there is no life beyond the present," says Edward Laboulaye, "then is this one a lie and a mockery. Immortality is something more than a recompense; it is the fulfillment, the justification of life."

"We must be immortal," says Berthold Auerbach, "or it were a cruelty to let us men alone know that we must die. The moth does not know that he must die: he thinks the burning light is a gay and brilliant flower, and he dies in the flowery flame."

"The message with which Spiritualism purports to be charged," says Mr. St. George Stock, "is simply this—*The dead are still alive.* Thus it addresses itself to the *social affections;* and turning to the self-regarding element in human nature, it says: 'As you make yourself, so shall you be, here and hereafter. There is no magic of water, or faith, or another's righteousness to save you from the effects of your own conduct.' The belief in a future life Spiritualism professes to establish by the only method which can carry conviction, namely, by offering positive evidence."

To refuse to look into the strange and incredible is to neglect oftentimes the most precious opportunities of discovery. Hypotheses that have been jeered at as wild and monstrous by practical men have been a clew to the grandest results. It has frequently needed a large amount of credulity to persist in experiments which, in their success, have contributed largely to human welfare.

Seven years before the occurrence of the spiritual phenomena at Hydesville, I had been introduced to many cognate facts and phenomena through a *sensitive* in whom I had induced the state of mesmeric somnambulism. In her highest state of lucidity she would frequently profess to see and converse with spirits. But though I had the amplest reason to believe in her intelligence and good faith, I was not sufficiently *possessed* by the spiritual hypothesis to devote myself to following the phenomenal vein out to satisfactory results. Had I done so, I now see that I might have anticipated many of the facts, at which I have since laboriously arrived.

In 1778 Anton Mesmer made his appearance in Paris, and the phenomena by means of the mesmeric passes became known. In 1784 the Marquis de Puységur showed that a state of somnambulic clairvoyance could be induced by mesmerism; and many experimenters, both in Germany and France, caught glimpses of those further marvels which Modern Spiritualism has since made common.

From a correspondence between two French mesmerizers, Billot and Deleuze, published in 1836, it appears that they were well aware of nearly all the most extraordinary phenomena that have been repeated in our day. Billot writes that *he has both seen and felt the spirits;* he and his co-secretaries have seen and felt them, and he calls God to witness the truth of the declaration. Deleuze replies that the immortality of the soul and the possibility of communicating with spirits have been proved to him; he has not personally witnessed facts equal to those cited by Billot, but persons worthy of all confidence have made to him the like reports. He mentions the experience of a distinguished physician who has clairvoyants who "*cause material objects to present themselves.*" In regard to this, Deleuze says: "I cannot conceive how spiritual beings are able to carry material objects." Billot aptly replies, that "the question of Spiritualism is not one of opinions, but of facts: these are the things that lead to the truth." Obviously, to separate our facts from our conjectures is our duty in this investigation.

Bertrand, D'Hunin, Puységur, Séguin, and other magnetizers, who had stood on the very threshold of Spiritualism, drew back in awe and alarm from further investigation. Deleuze fears that the prosecution of inquiry may "trouble human reason and lead to dangerous consequences." "Magic is rediscovered," said Dupotet, who now (1874), at an advanced age, accepts the spiritual phenomena as the culmination of his mesmeric researches. "The magnetic forces cannot be explained," said Puységur. "We have no organs," said Morin, "for discovering spiritual beings." "The real causes of apparitions, of objects displaced, of suspensions, and of a great portion of the marvelous," said D'Hunin and Bertrand, "are inscrutable." Séguin reports that "wisdom commands him to stop on the edge of an abyss which no man can pass with impunity."

How far the *reliquiæ* of theological teachings may have influenced these affrighted investigators would be a curious subject of inquiry. Obviously they were on the verge of the great proclamation of the facts of Modern Spiritualism, but they recoiled and left the further probing of the facts to the courage of a little girl nine years old, Miss Kate Fox, of Hydesville, New York.

It would be unjust, however, did I not pause here to recall the fact that Dr. Justinus Kerner, chief physician at Weinsberg, in Germany, and who died in 1859, has left in his "Life of Frederica Hauffé, the Seeress of Prevorst," a record of indubitable spiritual phenomena occurring as early as 1826, and fully accepted by him. They include nearly all the most important that have been developed up to the present time: rappings, movements of objects, levitations, apparitions, direct speech of spirits, thought-reading and clairvoyance.

Kerner was of course ridiculed for what was looked upon as his "credulity." The editors and the *savants* decided, as usual, on these phenomena, without taking the slightest trouble to investigate them; but they found in Kerner a keen and intrepid champion of the truth, who in literary skill was their superior, and in science was not lacking. Time has vindicated his sagacity and his truthfulness.

There is a class of opponents of Spiritualism, who, having been forced to admit the phenomena, attempt to depreciate and undervalue them. Their objections are summed up in the question *Cui bono?* For what good? What is the use of it all? As if we were bound to answer the question when a fact or phenomenon of Nature is presented! As if the skeptic could not make precisely the same objection to the universe itself, and prove the nothingness of things by his *Cui bono!* He who would set facts aside with a sneer may live to find them irrepressible.

One person, styling himself a medical professor, asserts that "there is no connection whatever between the phenomena of Spiritualism and the theory of Spiritualism;" which is about as logical as it would be to say that there is no connection between our solar system and the Copernican theory. And yet platitudes like this, uttered in the loud, confident tone of a *professor*, often impose on the timid and unthinking.

The contradictory character of the communications from spirits is a stumbling-block to many. "Why do spirits talk commonplace and tell fibs?" we are asked; and the reply is: "Perhaps to show us that they carry with them their mortal traits, and that the transition to a spiritual state leaves their individuality intact."

To the just and reverent thinker the current objections to the *facts* of Spiritualism must appear as superficial as they are arrogant and rash. A fact of Nature can seem trivial only when our ignorance places it in wrong relations or overlooks its real significance. Nature does not equivocate, though she may seem to do so. The disposition to slight these phenomena, to malign or misinterpret them, is merely a proof of our impotence to read and master them.

As for those persons who admit the facts, but pronounce them diabolical, and would drive us back from investigation by the cries of "danger!" "degradation!" all such opponents transcend the domain of science and enter that of mere theology, where I cannot follow them at present. The purpose of this exposition is to deal with the facts that have led to the spiritual hypothesis, and not to discuss the question how far the spirits manifesting themselves in these days are good or evil, harmless or dangerous, moral or immoral. Surely it is something if we can prove to our modern Sadducees that spirits of any kind may exist. Even a "degraded" spirit may be a suggestive fact.

Meanwhile all advocates of the Satanic theory will do well to ponder Locke's advice to those who, in his day, would frighten him from the pursuit of truth by this cry of *devil.* "It is very becoming," he says, "that men's zeal for truth should go as far as their proofs, but not go for proofs themselves. Talking with a supposition and insinuation that truth and knowledge, nay, and religion, too, stand and fall with *their* systems, is at best but an imperious way of begging the question, and assuming to themselves, under the pretence of zeal for the cause of God, a title to infallibility."

The late Baron Guldenstubbe, a friend too early lost to Spiritualism, in his treatise "La Réalité des Esprits," remarks: "The absurd fear of demons, prevalent especially during the middle ages, is precisely the principal cause of the unfrequency of supersensual phenomena, the spirits neither wishing nor being able to manifest themselves to people who take them for unclean spectres. Surely there is nothing more fitted to alienate spirits as well as men and animals, than this invincible repugnance, this shrinking horror, this utter lack of sympathy."

"The only true remedy," says James Martineau, "for the dark infidelity and cold materialism that threaten the utter destruction of the religious life in a large portion of the people, is to give them a living faith,—true to the conscience, true to the intellect, true to the realized science of the age. The Spiritualist is professedly struggling for the realization of this object, amidst the taunts of Orthodoxy and the execrations of Fanaticism."*

Dr. Wm. B. Carpenter, in his Mental Physiology (page 627), is ready to admit all the phenomena that have come under the measuring-rod of his own experience. He can believe that a table may move from unconscious muscular pressure. But if it moves when nobody is touching it, then the spectators, who think they see it move, are simply biologized. They are "oblivious of the difference between *external* and *internal* evidence; between the testimony of our *senses* and that of our *sense*."

In other words, if we see a table rise from the floor to the ceiling, then, rather than believe our own senses and those of any number of sane witnesses, we must accept Dr. Carpenter's *à priori* assumption that there can be no such thing as a spiritual force able to move a material object, and that consequently we must be deceived.

Now which, in the light of that common *sense* to which he appeals, would be the more reasonable of these two conclusions?

I am sorry to see so erudite an Aristotelian as Mr. Thomas Davidson falling into Dr. Carpenter's word-trap for superficial thinkers, and charging Mr. A. R. Wallace with having "come to be a believer in Spiritualism *on grounds entirely illogical*"—the lack of logic being in Mr. Wallace's trusting the report of his own senses and those of a million other witnesses, rather than shaping his belief to fit Dr. Carpenter's *à priori* notion of what Nature ought not to permit!

If philosophy cannot bring more force than this against that logic of facts which makes men Spiritualists, it had better keep mute. Let it ponder what Lord Bacon says of such rash experiments before it tries to overleap stubborn facts from the spring-board of purely *à priori* assumptions.

Another class of malcontents, looking at the phenomena of

*This remark was intended for the philosophical Spiritualists, but it will apply equally well to the Spiritualists who have become such through their acquaintance with phenomenal facts.

Spiritualism from an esthetic point of view, find them "*in bad taste.*" The coarse, hard, unmannerly facts violate all their preconceptions of what the spirit-world ought to be; shock all their notions of spiritual propriety, and contradict all the theories they may have inherited or formed of spirits as refined disembodied essences, freed from material surroundings and too pure to be brought in contact with them ever again.

But Nature evidently does not consult the dilletanti in her operations. She does many things "in bad taste;" and a man, oppressed with a sense of his dignity, has to submit to many mortifying checks and natural limitations. The very processes of birth and death, alimentation and elimination, are, esthetically considered, offensive. But, as Dryden says:

"Reaching above our nature does no good,
We must sink back into our own flesh and blood."

An English clergyman of the radical school finds "much that is repulsive in the so-called revelations of Spiritualism," and is led "to hope most earnestly that it may not be true." He says: "Spiritualists appeal to a vast portion of mankind who prefer seeing to believing, who are ever hankering after signs and wonders, and whose materialistic notions of God and soul and heaven compel them to seek satisfaction in visible proofs. *We* come into the field with very different weapons. 'The weapons of *our* warfare are not carnal.' And if we cannot hold our ground with these, we refuse to adopt an inferior mode of warfare, or pander to what seems to us a morbid craving for hidden mysteries."

Hidden mysteries! So were many of the wonders of science at one time "hidden mysteries;" and the vulgar often thought that chemists and geologists were seeking after hidden and forbidden mysteries. Is Superstition now driven from the hovel to the pulpit?

But what relevancy is there in this lofty talk of "carnal weapons" and "morbid cravings"? The question is simply one of facts, not of processes of belief, nor of esthetic sympathies, nor of theological speculations, nor of "warfare" of any kind. As well might we accuse Euclid of "carnality" in proving his propositions, as charge it on Spiritualists in establishing theirs. And if, as this writer says, Spiritualists appeal to those "who prefer seeing to believing," what is this but a proof that they are profoundly sincere in their knowledge, and that they are dealing, not with hazy abstractions but with things that may be tested and verified?

As to the imputation that they "pander to what seems a morbid craving for hidden mysteries," what is this loose phrase but the easy refuge of one too apathetic, too timid, or too preöccupied to face and investigate these extraordinary phenomena? Is the geologist actuated by a "morbid craving," when he pries under slabs of sandstone and earthy layers for the evidences of his science? Or shall the marvels that have relation to the existence of an immortal soul in man, be accounted as less legitimate and important objects of study than the discovery of the fossil remains of extinct varieties of animals?

Mr. St. George Stock has well replied to this class of censors. He says: "Another *à priori* objection against Spiritualism rests on our *ideas* of a future state. But if the facts alleged are found to be facts, so much the worse for our ideas. Honest old Whately could not bear the phrase, 'I should be sorry to think.' Let truth first be established, and sentiment will soon adapt itself to it."

"Spiritualism, morally considered," says Hudson Tuttle, "is the highest scientific conception of man's relations to himself, to his fellow men, to the spiritual world, and to the divine order of things. It is the essence of philosophy. It asks nothing without giving a reason, teaches nothing without giving a cause. It urges the individual to become just and pure, because no other being in the universe will receive as great a reward for his right doing as the individual, and because every being in the universe will be better for that right doing."

CHAPTER XVIII.

One of the most common of the phenomena of Modern Spiritualism has been the appearance of hands, believed to be materialized by spirit power, and therefore called spirit-hands. Every experienced investigator has been convinced of the reality of this manifestation.

On the eleventh of January, 1876, I was present at a séance, where two spirit-hands were molded in paraffine, Mrs. Mary M. Hardy, of Boston, Mass., being the medium, and the conditions being satisfactory to those who sat near, as I did. This experiment had been several times performed in the presence of Prof. William Denton, by whom it was first suggested; and we may hope it will eventually be produced under conditions that will satisfy the most skeptical of its genuineness. Molds of spirit faces have been got through Mrs. Hardy's mediumship.

The experiment is a step in the same direction with spirit-photography, of the reality of which we have ample proofs. Some of these will be found clearly stated in Mr. Alfred R. Wallace's "Defence of Modern Spiritualism." Other and later proofs have been given by my correspondent, the Rev. William Stainton-Moses, himself a medium, a scholar, and a careful investigator, in the record of his investigatons in "Human Nature," a London publication. Mr. Beattie, William Howitt, Benjamin Coleman, M. Leymarie, M. de Veh, Prince Wittgenstein, Lady Caithness, and many others in Europe, and Prof. Gunning, Mr. Gurney, Mr. Livermore, Mr. Luther Colby, and thousands of careful investigators in America, have placed the fact of spirit-photography beyond a question.

On the 25th of December, 1875, Mr. Jay J. Hartman, a spirit-photographer at the gallery No. 100 West Fourth street, Cincinnati, stood the test of a free public investigation of his powers and of the reality of the phenomenon. Many persons had got through him unquestionable likenesses of deceased relatives and friends; still the skeptics denounced him as an impostor. But the result of this examination corroborated all the evidences we had previously had of the fact of this form of mediumship. After three unsuccessful trials, at the time fixed, and in a gallery which he had never before entered, there was a fourth trial, at which Mr. Hartman did not touch the plate or enter the dark room, and this trial was successful. Messrs. J. Slatter, C. H. Muhrman, V. Cutter, J. P. Weckman, F. T. Moreland, and T. Teeple, all of them practical photographers, and two of them claiming to be experts in detecting frauds, signed the following certificate:

"We, the undersigned, having taken part in the public investigation of 'Spirit-Photography,' given by Mr. Jay J. Hartman, hereby certify that we have closely examined and watched the manipulations of our own marked plates through all the various workings in and out of the dark room, and have been unable to discover any sign of fraud or trickery on the part of Mr. Jay J. Hartman; and we further certify that during the last sitting, when the result was obtained, Mr. Jay J. Hartman did not handle the plate nor enter the dark room at any time."

In the second edition of "Planchette" I expressed a doubt of the genuineness of the spirit-photographs got through Mr. Mumler, of Boston. My doubt was founded on words of his own, reported to me by hearers whose good faith I could not question. When taunted with trickery he had replied without resentment in language that left the impression that he was not guiltless. I am now convinced that the impression did him injustice. He knew that serious denial would be of no avail, and so he parried the chaffing of skeptics with words that were misinterpreted.

Having satisfied myself by abundant testimony that Mr. Mumler had been instrumental in producing genuine spirit-photographs, I stated the fact, and in a third edition of "Planchette" withdrew the charge of fraud. Renewed investigation has satisfied me that many genuine spirit photographs have been produced through his mediumship; and I am happy to have my opinion confirmed by Mr. Gurney, the experienced photographer of New York. In a conversation with Dr. Eugene Crowell,* Mr. Gurney said that he had full faith in the genuineness of the photographs; that he visited Mumler's gallery for the purpose of investigation; that he told Mumler the object of his visit, his name and profession; to all which Mumler replied that he was welcome to investigate the process in any way he chose. Dr. Crowell says:

"Mr. Gurney then took clean plates and examined them with the closest scrutiny, and prepared them for the camera. The camera itself he took apart, examining the interior, the object-glass, etc., and when all was prepared for taking the picture—a friend of Mr. Gurney's being in the chair—Mr. Mumler placed his hand upon the camera, the lens was uncovered, and in a minute or two the photograph was taken. Upon proving the negative a spirit-form was visible upon the plate beside the likeness of the sitter. The process was repeated with like results; Mr. Gurney managing everything from beginning to end; Mr Mumler not touching an article, excepting when he placed his hand upon the camera at the moment of taking the picture.

"Mr. Gurney sometime afterward, *providing himself with plates and chemicals of his own*, visited Boston again, and calling at Mr. Mumler's rooms again, went through the process, using only his own materials, with similar results. He spent some hours in scrutinizing everything about the room, and everything pertaining to the process, and he was perfectly satisfied there was no deception.

"I then inquired if he—Mr. Gurney—could produce similar pictures. He replied: 'Yes, nearly similar; but it would require some days to effect the purpose, while Mumler produces them in three minutes.'"

Dr. Crowell testifies in the most explicit manner to the facts of materialization. He says:

"Innumerable are the proofs that have been furnished of the identity of my spirit friends. Sometimes, when requested, they have given their names, and at others have unexpectedly announced them. Many have presented themselves to me visibly at Moravia, and at Dr. Slade's, some of them while visible conversing with me; *and two of them I have seen apart from any medium.* I have in hundreds of instances been touched by spirits; have been lovingly patted by their hands, and have felt and heard the rustling of their robes. Many times I have heard music from material instruments, produced by spirit touches, and once have heard it as clearly and distinctly when no material instrument was in the room."

* Author of "The Identity of Primitive Christianity and Modern Spiritualism," perhaps the most thorough exposition of the subject that has yet been made. Dr. Crowell is entitled to the gratitude of all those who prize truth above authority.

Whilst I am bringing this volume to a conclusion, the testimony in regard to the materialization phenomena crowds on me so fast, and from so many trustworthy parties, that I should be embarrassed in my choice did I deem that further facts were needed. Col. Olcott has prosecuted his investigations at Chittenden, Vt., in the most thorough manner, testing the Eddy phenomena in various ways, and satisfying himself fully that they are genuine. In this he is supported by numerous competent witnesses, whose names are published in the New York Graphic. Mr. Max Lenzberg, of Hartford, Conn., in a letter to the Daily Times of that city, gives an account of his and his family's experiences at Chittenden. He describes the battery test applied to Honto, the Indian spirit-maiden, by Dr. Beard, a skeptic. The full power of the battery was let on, and Honto received it without flinching. No mortal could have stood it.

Mr. Lenzberg states that the spirit-form of his wife's brother, Abraham, who died seventeen years ago in Texas, appeared on the stage at Chittenden in his shirt-sleeves; and he adds:

"My wife recognized him at once, and said to him, 'Let me introduce you to my husband.' I spoke to him in German; he answered, 'Ja, ich bin es; ich freuse mich sehr'—('Yes, it is I; I am much delighted.') It was a very distinct apparition; there could be no mistake as to the reality of the figure, and my wife said there was none as to identity.

"Another night he came again, and spoke to us in the peculiar idiom of that German dialect which belongs to Westphalia; I detected the idiomatic peculiarity and recognized the words as those unmistakably of a person from that region where my wife came from; the word '*morgen*' especially—the German for '*morning*,' when he was saying 'to-morrow morning'—was beyond any mistake as to the part of Germany the speaker had lived in."

Mr. Lenzberg further saw the apparition of a little daughter he had lost from earth when she was less than a year old. She was led in by the spirit of his wife's mother, and "appeared as a child of two years, but preserved her own look." He says:

"I went to the railing and spoke to her close by—'Oh, my darling angel Sophie, I can see you!' She smiled, and danced to show her joy at the recognition. My daughter Lena had also come to the railing, and said, 'Do you see me? do you know me?' and the little child, laughing, rapped yes on the railing with her fingers. Her mother sat as if spell-bound; she recognized her child."

Mrs. H. P. Blavatsky, a Russian lady, resident at 124 East Sixteenth street, New York City, having seen in the newspapers a letter from Dr. George M. Beard, who had given less than two days to the investigation of the Eddy phenomena, declaring that the brothers are "frauds who cannot do even good trickery," generously replied to the attack by stating her own most conclusive experiences in a letter to the public, dated October 27th, 1874. She says:

"I remained fourteen days at the Eddys'. In that short period of time I saw and recognized fully out of one hundred and nineteen apparitions seven spirits. I admit that I was the only one to recognize them, the rest of the audience not having been with me in my numerous travels throughout the East, but their various dresses and costumes were plainly seen and closely examined by all.

"The first was a Georgian boy, dressed in the historical Caucasian attire. I recognized and questioned him in Georgian upon circumstances known only to myself. I was understood and answered. Requested by me in his mother tongue (upon the whispered suggestion of Colonel Olcott) to play the 'Lezguinka,' a Circassian dance, he did so immediately upon the guitar.

"*Second*—A little old man appears. He is dressed as Persian merchants generally are. His dress is perfect as a national costume. Everything is in its right place, down to the 'babouches' that are off his feet, he stepping out in his stockings. He speaks his name in a loud whisper. It is 'Hassan Aga,' an old man whom I and my family have known for twenty years at Tiflis. He says, half in Georgian and half in Persian, that he has got a 'big secret to tell me,' and comes at three different times, vainly seeking to finish his sentence.

"*Third*—A man of gigantic stature emerges forth, dressed in the picturesque attire of the warriors of Kurdistan. He does not speak, but bows in the Oriental fashion, and lifts up his spear ornamented with bright-colored feathers, shaking it in token of welcome. I recognize him immediately as Saffar Ali Bek, a young chief of a tribe of Kurds, who used to accompany me in my trips around Ararat in Amenia on horseback, and who on one occasion saved my life. More, he bends to the ground as though picking up a handful of mould and scattering it around, presses his hand to his bosom—a gesture familiar only to the tribes of the Kurdistan.

"*Fourth*—A Circassian comes out. I can imagine myself at Tiflis, so perfect is his costume of 'nouker' (a man who either runs before or behind one on horseback). This one speaks. More, he corrects his name, which I pronounced wrong on recognizing him, and when I repeat it he bows, smiling, and says in the purest guttural Tartar, which sounds so familiar to my ear, 'Tchoch yachtchi' (all right), and goes away.

"*Fifth*—An old woman appears with a Russian headgear. She comes out and addresses me in Russian, calling me by an endearing term that she used in my childhood. I recognize an old servant of my family, a nurse of my sister.

"*Sixth*—A large, powerful negro next appears on the platform. His head is ornamented with a wonderful coiffure, something like horns wound about with white and gold. His looks are familiar to me, but I do not at first recollect where I have seen him. Very soon he begins to make some vivacious gestures, and his mimicry helps me to recognize him at a glance. It is a conjurer from Central Africa. He grins and disappears.

"*Seventh and last*—A large, gray-haired gentleman comes out attired in the conventional suit of black. The Russian decoration of St. Ann hangs suspended by a large red moire ribbon with two black stripes—a ribbon, as every Russian will know, belonging to said decoration. This ribbon is worn around his neck. I feel faint, for I think of recognizing my father. But the latter was a great deal taller. In my excitement I address him in English, and ask him: 'Are you my father?' He shakes his head in the negative, and answers as plainly as any mortal man can speak, and in Russian, 'No; I am your uncle.' The word 'diadia' has been heard and remembered by all the audience. It means 'uncle.'"

Among the materialized spirit-forms that appear at Chittenden is that of the mother of the mediums. Of her appearance Col. Olcott says:

"I know the full value of words, and I mean to say unequivocally that a woman—a breathing, walking, palpable woman, as palpable as any other woman in the room, recognized not only by her sons and daughters, but also by neighbors present, as Mrs. Zephaniah Eddy, deceased December 29th, 1872—on the evening of October 2d, 1874, walked out of a cabinet where there was only one mortal, and where, under ascertained circumstances, only this one man could have been at the time, *and spoke to me personally in audible voice!* And nineteen other persons saw her at the same time and heard her discourse."

Mr. Leon Case, a lawyer of Hartford, Conn., of whose experiences at Chittenden I have already spoken, gives the following description of the same apparition:

"One night there came upon the platform, stepping vigorously forth, a woman of apparently middle age. At once Mr. and Mrs. Brown (an Eddy) and Horatio exclaimed, 'Mother!' and others present hailed her as 'Mrs. Eddy.' She was dressed in white skirt with dark colored sack, etc. She appeared very character-full. Her face was not very distinct to my eyes, save in profile, but it was to others. She bowed and answered her children's salutation pleasantly but rather curtly, as if she had something else on her mind, and raising her hands and slightly throwing back her head she proceeded to utter, in full, strong voice, one of the most cogent, earnest and beautiful prayers I ever heard, addressed to 'Father of my Spirit'—which words, and no other individual appellation, she repeated three or four times during the prayer, and then withdrew behind the veil, but quickly turned around, so quickly that the clumsy veil had not had time to fairly fall into place behind her, came out, and posing herself like an accustomed platform speaker addressed us in a voice too loud to be in good taste before a limited audience, but evidently at much expense of will force. Her gesticulation was vigorous and appropriate. Her remarks related to the 'new life' principally, and she said some things tenderly of her children—their present works, etc. I think she might have been heard distinctly throughout a common size country meeting-house. Her language was well chosen, indeed elegant, and without grammatical error—save one—the misuse of the verb 'lays' for 'lies;' as 'lays along your path.' I was struck with the singularly forceful character and pertinence of the utterances of this woman; because she was the mother of that brood of illiterate 'mediums,' of whom I had heard so much, not having suspected that she possessed the graces she manifested."

Mr. Case tells us that on one occasion Col. Olcott weighed the Indian spirit, Honto, on one of Fairbanks's platform scales. She was found to weigh eighty-eight pounds. She went behind the veil, reäppeared, and was weighed again, this time weighing fifty-eight pounds. At another time she was found to weigh sixty-five pounds. Her bulk at these several weighings was apparently unchanged. Honto is five feet three inches in height, according to measures which Col. Olcott placed on either side of the closet door, and which all could distinctly see. William Eddy, the medium, is five feet nine and a half inches high, and weighs one hundred and seventy-nine pounds.

A highly intelligent investigator, Mrs. A. A. Andrews, of Springfield, Mass., from whose account of her experiences at Dr. Slade's I have already quoted (Chapter III), has, at my request, kindly supplied the following description of what she saw at Chittenden, through the Eddys, during the autumn of 1874:

"During the five evenings that I was present at the séances, I saw a great number of materialized forms. Santum, an Indian chief, six feet and three inches tall, five or six inches taller than the medium, of fine proportions, and dressed in full national costume, presented himself; also the Indian girl Honto, graceful, lithe, and with that peculiar ease of motion which we see in savages whose muscles have never been fettered by an unnatural dress. She made her appearance every evening, walking rapidly, with noiseless steps, across the platform, and often drawing from the floor, the bare walls, or from the person of a gentleman or a lady called up from the circle to sit or stand upon the platform, large shawls of different colors and textures, which shawls she threw over the railing enclosing the platform, or held up, in her outstretched hands, so that all might see them, and afterwards threw into the cabinet, lifting the curtain hung before it for this purpose. I also saw her give a lock of her long black hair to a gentleman who had lately come on from Philadelphia to witness the manifestations. On one occasion she took a pipe from a gentleman present, lighted it with a match, and smoked for some minutes with much apparent relish.

"This form often dances with a lady (Mrs. Cleveland), who is a neighbor of the Eddys, and who told me that in taking hold of the arm of the spirit it had sometimes seemed to crush up in her fingers, it not being fully materialized.

"The first evening that I was present I complained of the darkness of the room, saying that I could not see the spirits distinctly. The next night the spirit of an old woman, calling herself the 'Witch of the Mountains,' said, in a distinct voice, 'One of the ladies here complained last time that she could not see distinctly the faces of the spirits; if she will come up to the platform she may see me, and take hold of my hair.' I went up, as desired, looked into her face, which was utterly unlike that of the medium, though pronounced and rather coarse in feature, and having that peculiar pallor so often observable in materialized forms. She raised one hand, and drawing out a lock of gray hair from under a kerchief which partially covered her head, held it out to me. I took hold of it and pulled it, assuring myself that it grew upon the scalp. It was harsh, dry and coarse, like that of one much exposed to the weather, and whose hair has not been taken care of. This old woman often spoke with us for ten or fifteen minutes at a time, alluding to her past life, and giving good moral advice.

"On one evening she brought with her from the cabinet a slight twig or wand, which I at first took to be the shaft of a small arrow. As she seated herself upon a chair placed for her upon the platform, she drew this wand back and forth through her hands, talking to us meanwhile as usual. I observed that, as she handled it, it gradually increased in size until it became, after a few minutes, a stout staff upon which she leaned in rising from her seat, and in returning to the cabinet.

"One of the female spirits, I think the one they called 'Grandmother Eaton,' spoke painfully of the trials endured in the earth-life. I failed to catch all her words, but, while thus speaking, she opened her dress upon the breast, and, as if from within it, there arose fluctuating flames, reminding me of some Catholic pictures which one sees of Jesus where the heart is represented as burning with flame. It was to me a most weird and painfully thrilling sight, made more so by the dreary voice and sad words which were uttered at the time.

"I saw the mother of Mr. Pritchard of Albany, or a spirit-form which he declared to be that of his mother, put her arms about his neck and embrace him ; I also heard her talk with him for some time in a low voice. This recognition of forms and faces goes to prove that there can be no deception, since strangers, going there unbelieving, could hardly be deceived in such a matter. The dress, little peculiar ways and modes of expression, the calling of sons and daughters in the circle by pet names, were spoken of by several as proving to them beyond a doubt the identity of those claiming to be relatives. I saw some six or eight spirit forms that were recognized by persons in the circle who came there quite skeptical, and left convinced of the genuineness of the manifestations by this recognition of friends and relatives.

"I was entirely convinced, before leaving Chittenden, that the Eddy brothers were honest as mediums, and indeed utterly incapable of such a fraud as their manifestations would be if not genuine. Such a deception would require great skill, indeed a most remarkable talent, the possession of a theatrical wardrobe, and the aid of confederates, none of which, as any one staying a week in the house can satisfy himself, do these mediums have. They are simple and ignorant, their mediumship having interfered sadly with their education, and their house is bare of all means and appliances needful for the production of artificial phenomena of this kind. Having remained only five days with them, I cannot give an adequate idea of the wonderful manifestations to be witnessed, both during the light and dark circles, in this old farm-house; but I saw enough to feel assured that Col. Olcott's very interesting record of the phenomena, as published in the New York Graphic, is unexaggerated and every way reliable."

Accounts of new mediums for the materialization phenomena reach me from many quarters as I draw this work to a conclusion.* Skeptics in regard to the manifestations

---

* Among others I have received through Dr. Henry S. Chase of St. Louis a remarkable account, from the pen of the Rev. Isaac Kelso of Alton, Ill., of materializations through Mr. Mott of Memphis, Tenn., and of independent spirit slate-writing through his daughter, three years old. One of the best authenticated proofs of spirit identity I have ever met with is one given by Mr. Kelso in a letter to the St. Louis Democrat of Nov. 16th, 18 4. The parties and facts are known to Dr. Chase, and vouched for in his letter to me. (See page 33 of this volume.)

At one of Mr. Mott's séances, Oct. 25th, 1874, the apparition of a man of forty, wearing spectacles, called for a young lady present, Miss Kate Dwire of Canton, Ill. She started forward, exclaimed "'Tis my father!" grew agitated, and stopped, confessing she was afraid; at which the apparition wept, and being asked why, said, "Oh! it hurts me to think my own dear daughter is afraid of me." Miss D. then went up, and talked with the spirit several minutes, but was greatly overcome. A white-robed female apparition rushed with open arms toward Mr. Kelso, touched him, and said she was his mother. A flash of lightning illumined the room, making her snowy garments glisten and her features glow. The recognition was not wholly satisfactory. The lightning seemed to weaken the materialization. As the form staggered backward it sank to the floor like a melting snow-drift, became a cloud of white vapor, and thus floated back into the cabinet. Mr. Kelso got a letter from his two sisters, written by some occult power under test conditions on a clean slate, the medium being Essie Mott, three years old and ignorant even of the alphabet. The writing was good and correct, the communication "thrilling." Was it the child's "psychic force" that did it all?

abound not only among the opponents of Spiritualism, but among Spiritualists themselves, and stories of fraud and imposture are rife. I have endeavored to confine myself to narrations of those phenomena of the reality of which abundant confirmatory proof has been offered in spite of all opposition and dispute.

Referring to the "badgering and tormenting of mediums, the nailing them to the floor, or sewing them up in sacks, or binding their hands, feet, neck and limbs tightly with cords, in order to keep them from cheating," Thos. R. Hazard remarks:

"It seems to me that enough has been conceded by spiritual mediums in the way of permitting investigators of the phenomena to prescribe conditions under which our spirit friends shall manifest their presence. It has been tried long enough to prove by its results that the gospel of Spiritualism, like that practiced and preached by Jesus of Nazareth, is not adapted to minds so full of conceit and fancied knowledge that there is not room for anything new to enter them. As a class, the most learned in the sciences and what is called divinity are the furthest off from what relates to spiritual truths than all others. The most stolidly ignorant are in advance of such, for, as the thoughtful Helvetius wisely says, 'Ignorance is the middle point between true and false learning. The ignorant man is as much above the falsely learned as he is below him of real science;' and again, 'He who is falsely learned and has lost his reason when he thought to improve it, has purchased his stupidity at too dear a rate ever to renounce it.' Exactly so; and this is just the ground that most of the *learned* (so-called) in the sciences, divinity and medicine occupy in our day. Investigators from classes who have devoted years to studies conducted on a backward track from truth, and acquired imperfect, not to say false notions of what relates to the spiritual side of man, scorn to surrender the scholastic theories they have imbibed at so great cost of time, money and labor to the dictation of unlettered mediums, whether inspired by devil or angel. Jesus showed his great wisdom in wasting no time on such as these, for the simple reason that he knew it would be of no avail. 'Whosoever (said he) shall not receive the kingdom of God as a little child shall in no wise enter therein.'"

That there are frauds and self-delusions in Spiritualism every careful investigator knows; but that there is a residuum of proved facts of the most wonderful kind, explicable by no theory of deception and deserving the attention of all earnest thinkers, is equally true. These facts can no longer be evaded or slighted by those who dare to face the truth however it may reverse their opinions.

The Springfield (Mass.) Republican, of Oct. 30th, 1874, publishes a long account of the Eddy phenomena, and characterizes them as "the most mysterious facts that have been thus far recorded in the history of Spiritualism." But while thus accepting the phenomena as proven, it concludes as follows:

"The information the apparitions vouchsafe is as valueless as all such information has been. One of them lectures vaguely, one improvises songs, one dances and weaves spiritual cloth for other 'spirits' not so capable as herself, one merely nods and smiles. None of them have told us yet about the new life; we are no wiser than of old. The manifestations in the Eddy homestead, thus far, remarkable as they are, have simply added a deeper mystery to the strange thing called Spiritualism. We know it is not all imposture, we know it is not all illusion; where and what the truth is, we yet wait to see."

To all which the sufficient reply is simple enough: *In the nature of things what fact could any spirit possibly communicate to be compared in magnitude with the* PROOF PALPABLE *of its own existence?*

The wonderful fact of a future life is, at the present time, either practically ignored, or but faintly entertained, or else ridiculed and rejected by more than three-fourths of the people of Christendom; an atheistic Science lifts its voice and proclaims annihilation as the only consistent creed for a *savant;* the prayer even of believers is, "Help thou my unbelief!" and now, when spirits come and reveal themselves palpably to our senses, and claim recognition, and get it, and declare to us that death has not destroyed them, or changed their affections, the stupendous demonstration, instead of being welcomed with exultation, is met with the complaint, "None of them have told us yet about the new life; we are no wiser than of old!"

"No wiser?" Does the fact itself leave us actually no wiser? Can any one who laments the loved one gone before, and longs for a reünion, say that the information which the apparitions vouchsafe is "valueless"? Valueless? And the information they vouchsafe is, that the departed still live?

Hear the testimony of one who has seen and heard and

touched. I have already (page 121) related my own interview with the Rev. Mr. Pope, who went with his wife to see the manifestations at Moravia, N. Y. He writes to Dr. Crowell, Feb. 28th, 1873: "We went there almost totally unbelieving as to the possibility of seeing our spirit-friends, but our doubts and unbelief were soon swept away. We went there oppressed with a great sorrow; we saw those we mourned, as alive from the dead; we looked into their faces as in other days; we received messages from their spirit lips; we felt their celestial hands touching us, and we went away sorrowless, our hearts singing for joy. All things now seem changed; the world wears a brighter aspect; and I tell people I am one of the happiest men on earth. I always believed and preached that the departed are alive, and near us, *but believing and seeing are widely different things*, and I thank God for the ocular demonstration, and for the joy it gives."

It is not quite correct to say that spirits tell us nothing "about the new life." Their accounts of it are as various as their characters. As the objective environments of a spirit are supposed to correspond with his moral and mental state, it is quite consistent that the descriptions of their "new life" by these revenants should differ greatly.

It is a question, moreover, whether it would not require the development of a new sense in ourselves before we could fully comprehend the descriptions we might get of life in the spirit-world. Even if we got something *new*—some truthful and extraordinary account of the "new life"—what would it amount to unless we had the faculty of accepting the truth when it was offered, and appreciating it accordingly?

We are told that through Spiritualism "we are no wiser than of old." Truly, that depends. A mere fact adds nothing to our wisdom until the fact is accepted for what it is worth. All the information which the highest archangel could impart in regard to the "new life" would profit us nothing unless there were the proper conditions of mind and heart, or the opening of a latent sense, for its reception.

Spirits and seers, ancient and modern, have given full and

various descriptions of the "new life"; descriptions which may be true, false, or mixed; but obviously they are nothing to us until we have the data and the faculties for testing their accuracy. Mrs. A. A. Andrews says she has seen autograph letters, enough to fill a volume, written by spirits, under strictest test conditions, upon paper untouched by the medium, and containing descriptions of daily life in the other world, which gave as vivid a conception of existence there as it seems possible for those still in the flesh to form.

To attempt to throw discredit on the significance of spirit materializations simply because something *new*, beyond the amazing fact itself, is not added, is obviously unwise. In ourselves, and not in the fact, must the requisite condition be presented before anything new in regard to the future life can enter our minds. A mere assertion takes no root in an unreceptive understanding.

Suppose that a true account of the occupations in spirit-life of Plato, Shakspeare or Columbus were written out and published: what impression would it make unless we had been prepared, by thought, sympathy and prescience, to recognize the verisimilitude of the description?

The objection, therefore, that spirits "tell us nothing about the new life," does not hold; they tell us a good deal, but what they tell us is valueless indeed so long as we are unqualified to form an opinion of its truth. The prophecies of Cassandra were none the less true because they were not believed.

As for the objection, so often raised, "Why do not spirits forewarn us of many accidents, public or private, which their premonitions might avert?" the Spiritualist is not bound to give any other reply than this: "I do not know." Any person who will take the trouble to investigate may learn that, in many individual cases, premonitions *are* given, and calamities *are* averted by spirit interposition. Why this is not done oftener, or in a manner to impress the public at large more forcibly, is a matter on which we may speculate but cannot speak with confidence.

Objections may be multiplied, but they cannot invalidate the one great fact which must suffice. Proofs palpable, given in the reäppearance, in temporarily materialized forms, of deceased persons, are now so numerous and so fully attested, that no incredulity or opposition can impair their force. The phenomena are admitted by all who have qualified themselves by patient and unprejudiced investigation to pronounce an opinion.

Since the phenomena of Modern Spiritualism cannot be explained by known natural laws, and *seem* frequently to occur in violation of those laws, "there remain only for their explanation either the magic forces of the mediums, or of foreign spirits." Such, as I learn from Dr. Bloede, is the conclusion of Dr. Maximilian Perty, Professor of Natural Science at the University at Berne, Switzerland, author of "The Mystical Phenomena of Human Nature;" who further admits that there are many undeniable facts which can hardly or not at all be explained by the forces of a medium or his surroundings, and must be attributed to spiritual beings.

Thus to the spiritual theory all persevering investigators are brought at last, sooner or later, according to the extent and thoroughness of their experiences and studies. To the proofs mental and supersensual we have now added the proof palpable of immortality; and the result of our examination is that no theory, other than the spiritual, is ample enough to include all the facts, and to offer for them a rational solution.

THE END.

ALPHABETICAL INDEX.

www.ingramcontent.com/pod-product-compliance
Lightning Source LLC
LaVergne TN
LVHW050520100826
845148LV00002B/398